Abiel Silver

The Holy Word in Its Own Defence

Abiel Silver

The Holy Word in Its Own Defence

ISBN/EAN: 9783337290351

Printed in Europe, USA, Canada, Australia, Japan

Cover: Foto ©Lupo / pixelio.de

More available books at **www.hansebooks.com**

THE

HOLY WORD

IN ITS OWN DEFENCE:

ADDRESSED TO

BISHOP COLENSO

AND

ALL OTHER EARNEST SEEKERS AFTER TRUTH.

BY

REV. ABIEL SILVER,

OF NEW YORK,

AUTHOR OF "LECTURES ON THE SYMBOLIC CHARACTER OF THE
SACRED SCRIPTURES."

"Then opened He their understandings that they might understand the Scriptures."—LUKE xxiv, 45.
"The entrance of Thy Word giveth light."—PSALM cxix, 130.

NEW YORK:
D. APPLETON AND COMPANY,
443 & 445 BROADWAY.
LONDON: 16 LITTLE BRITAIN.
1863.

PREFACE.

REGARDING the Sacred Scriptures as the Holy Word of the Great Jehovah, and believing that the Words which God speaks unto us, " *they are Spirit and they are Life* " to human souls, given for their regeneration and salvation; and that they are the Foundation and Embodiment of all true Laws and Rules of Life, for the establishment and preservation of order, peace, and happiness, in heaven and on earth; that they were dictated to the writers by Infinite Wisdom, and designed to be understood, loved and practised by men, and are therefore free from all contradictions and discrepancies, and expressed in the best possible form for meeting the vast variety of wants, states, and conditions of human beings, for all time and for eternity; religiously believing this, we feel it to be the highest privilege and duty of man to acknowledge them, revere them, study them, love them, and obey them; to defend and sustain them, under every circumstance or event, whereby the opinions or writings of men may tend to throw doubts into the public mind, as to their entire truthfulness and perspicuity when their real meaning is seen; and to ever strive, as we value the salvation of men, to bring before the world their pure and heavenly light, until every doubt of their Divine Excellence and Perfection shall pass away before the increasing glory of that Spiritual Light which gradually reveals, to the opening intellect and obedient heart, their perfect symmetry and beauty; that thereby, the promised day may be hastened, when the "Watchmen shall see eye to eye," and when "there shall be no more saying, every man to his neighbor, Know ye the LORD; for all shall know Him from the least unto the greatest."

Under these settled views and convictions, we read the work entitled, "THE PENTATEUCH AND BOOK OF JOSHUA, CRITICALLY EXAMINED, *by the Right Rev.* JOHN WILLIAM COLENSO, D.D., *Bishop of Natal. New York:* D. APPLETON & Co., 1863;" and we rose from the perusal, laden with the impression that we should offer to the public what we have written in this Book. Not, however, as an answer, in detail, to all the particular objections of the Bishop, but a General Answer, covering all the ground, not only of "Part First," but also of "Part Second," of the work above mentioned, and, indeed, of all other works which such objectors may publish. But though we cover the entire ground, yet it will be readily seen, that a work of this size can be but a mere opening of the Great Subject of all subjects, with such references, illustrations of Scripture, and arguments, based upon First and Eternal Principles, as are self-evident and irrefutable, and which we hope may throw such light upon the subject, from the Holy Word, and the Works of God, as may arrest the progress of Infidelity, by turning the thoughts of many, through the Analogy of the Divine Language, into a spiritually rational, religious channel; and which may also serve as a suggestion to abler pens, to improve the present opportunity to give, to inquiring minds, the rational and illuminating views of God and His Word, and of the Way of Life, which the wants of the present age of commotion so much demand, and which the merciful Lord, by the Spiritual Light of the Word, has so amply provided.

In this work we lay no claim to originality, either in the harmony of the System, the Doctrines we present, or in the Science of Correspondences. The diction and manner of treating the subject, only are ours. All the principles and views rest in, and can be rationally sustained by, the Word and Works of the Most High God. Our entire argument, therefore, is, *Thus saith God's Word*, and, *Thus say God's Works*.

We have confined ourselves chiefly to God's Word and Works, without note or comment upon the views of others. This is because there is no other source of knowledge, and because to this Court we must finally appeal to determine the truth or falsity of anything contained in the countless volumes which have been written upon the Holy Word. And our desire and aim have been to defend the Sacred Scriptures, or rather to let them defend themselves, against the skeptical influence which the objections that Dr. Colenso and his Reviewers are raising to the literal narrative, and then leaving it in the dark, may have upon the public mind. This we have hoped to do by showing that the contradictions and discrepancies which appear upon the surface of the letter of the Word, *are not errors which have crept into the work through any carelessness, ignorance, or unfaithfulness of the hands through which It has passed;* but that He who gave us the Holy Word, made it, in the original tongues, perfect, and has carefully preserved it; and that, when understood, it will be found to be free from all errors.

It is not a matter of surprise, that Dr. Colenso, in his sincere searching of the Scriptures and desire for the truth, for the salvation of the souls of men, should, in the honest convictions of his heart, be troubled at the obstacles which appear in the way of their truthfulness. And we respect his noble frankness in declaring to the world his convictions, while he still retains a profound reverence for the Book. Standing where the Doctor does, and looking with the eyes with which he sees, he is right in his conulsions that the "Mosaic narrative . . . cannot be regarded as *historically true,*" so far as regards all the natural events mentioned. But we hope to convince the sincere and faithful reader of the following pages, and from the Word itself, that It is a *true history* of *mental things,* or of the creation and actions of minds; that there is, running through the entire Word, a history of higher things than those of time and matter, describing the thoughts and feelings of the souls of men and the consequences of their character under all states and circumstances, whether in this world or the next; and also revealing to us a knowledge of our God, of our souls, and of our duty; and that, in order to give to man this knowledge of spiritual things, natural things are used as symbols; and that thus it is that we may rationally *look through nature up to nature's God*, and know that the "Invisible things of Him from the creation of the world are clearly seen, being understood by the things that are made, even His eternal power and Godhead." (Rom. i, 20.) Not that there is not generally a true, literal sense in the Word, by the influence of which many souls are saved. But notwithstanding we have, in most of the Divine Word, an account of things which have taken place in this natural world, and the plain commandments given which all may understand, yet there is given, at the same time, a correct narrative of Spiritual or mental things, which may be seen and understood, by the sure law of Analogy which shows the relation between natural and spiritual things, revealing a Spiritual Sense within the literal. And our only hope of use, in preparing this work is, that Light from the Holy Word Itself, showing Its Symbolic Character, may tend to sustain Its Divine Authenticity, and elevate It in the public estimation; and, at least, to convince some wayward and doubting souls of the true Nature and Character of God and His Word, and thus to bring them to the Divine Fountain, that they may drink of Its Spirit and Its Life, and be saved. For if there are any things of more importance than others for man to know and to lay to heart, they are a true knowledge of his God, of himself, and of his duties and destiny as revealed in God's Word. "Forever, O LORD, Thy Word is settled in heaven. The entrance of Thy Words giveth Light; it giveth understanding unto the simple." (Ps. cxix, 89, 130.)

CONTENTS.

10 CONTENTS.

CHAPTER I.

God has given His Word to Man to teach him,—First, what God is: Second, what Man is: Third, how Man loses God's image and becomes a devil: Fourth, how he obtains that image and becomes an angel; and, Fifth, the consequences of being either an angel or a devil. Every sentence of the Holy Word involves something of these things.

As words are signs of ideas, so they point in the Word to two kinds of ideas,—natural and spiritual. Natural ideas relate to things of the body, and of this world: spiritual ideas, to things of the mind, and of the spiritual world. We must have some natural thing, that we know something about, as a symbol of the quality of a certain principle of the mind, and through which we can look, by correspondence, or we cannot entertain the true spiritual idea of that mental principle. We are living here in a world of externals, with all internal things discreetly above the natural senses and all natural thoughts. Every spiritual idea must be embraced through a natural thought, by analogy. Every spiritual idea must have a natural idea as a body through which it may be seen.

Now, the words of the Lord are used to express both natural and spiritual ideas. But men generally see in them only the natural ideas. All natural things may, by correspondence, be called words of God, whether spoken by the mouth or not; whether named in a book, or seen in the fields of nature. All things of nature speak; and they speak both natural and spiritual things. The natural ideas are often seen by men, the spiritual but seldom. A beautiful landscape suggests thousands of thoughts upon natural qualities. But the spiritual ideas are not seen, without some knowledge of the analogy between the quality and use of the natural things, and the life which infills them; and also of the relation between that life and the human mind. For the forms, qualities, and uses of natural things, always express, by analogy, spiritual principles, or qualities of the human mind. It is for this express purpose, that the things of nature are so much made use of in the Holy Word.

But the analogy stops not here, but reaches into artificial things. Everything of art or labor suggests the natural ideas of the mind that formed it. And, if it be an artificial work, directed by the Lord, and recorded in His Word, like the Ark of the Covenant or like the Temple, it suggests spiritual ideas through natural ideas. Thus everything a man does is expressive of the thoughts and feelings which bring it forth; and, when recorded in the Holy Word, it denotes spiritual ideas and principles. Therefore, all histories recorded in the Holy Word contain, within them, histories of things which take place in human minds.

In every part of the Holy Word, there must be a spiritual signification. And mankind ought to know this from the plain literal teachings of the Lord. For He expressly says He speaks to them in parables : and that, " Without a parable spake He not unto them." By this we learn that the plain literal events, recorded in the Word, even where they occurred precisely as stated, are all parables ; that is, they all contain a hidden meaning higher than the literal sense.

Now, a literal event of which we read in the Word, may have occurred as recorded, or it may not. It is a parable in either case ; and conveys true spiritual instruction by correspondence. And so a command may be intended to be obeyed naturally, or it may not. If it simply says, " Thou shalt not kill, steal, or lie," the literal sense is, Thou shalt not do it in outward act of the body. But the spiritual sense is, that thou shalt not do it in will, intention, thought, or desire. And both of these senses should be understood and obeyed.

So, when the Lord says that unless we eat His flesh and drink His blood we have no life in us, there are also two senses ; but both of these senses cannot be obeyed. This scripture only teaches that we must appropriate to our souls the goods and truths of the Word, to which the flesh and blood correspond. The words ' flesh and blood ' give the natural ideas, through which we reach the spiritual. We can have no idea or thought of goodness and truth as abstract principles, until, by correspondence, we can see them as real spiritual substances that can be appropriated to our souls.

Thus, all Holy Scripture is applicable to human life, and is profitable for doctrine and instruction in righteousness. And, when we come to parts of the Word, which seem to us to present no practical instruction, and are mysterious, we should set it down, as a matter of course, that its essential meaning and use to us are in the internal sense. And, in looking for the spiritual sense, we must always look into the human mind. We must not lose sight of the fact, that the spiritual sense of the Word is *mental*—completely and *in toto* mental. And that, in looking through the literal sense, we look into the world of mind. Then, when we come to a passage of Scripture from the letter of which we cannot draw any instruction of practical use, we must remember that the Almighty God has spoken it: and though the literal sense, which is in man's language, appear unimportant, yet the spiritual sense, which is in God's language, must contain matter of the highest importance and benefit to man.

Then let us approach its illustration with that reverence due to the Word of the Most High God, feeling that it is addressed to each of us individually; and that, to find its highest use to us, we must look through the letter into our own minds; remembering that every circumstance or thing mentioned in the Word corresponds to some principle or movement in the human soul, or in God. For we see no possibility of any person's having true ideas of the Lord, either in this world or the other, but from the Holy Word. We regard the Word of God as the only true medium between our Heavenly Father and man, whereby we can know the Lord, because He is the Word. It is therefore the only light by which the understanding can form any correct thoughts of Him. For the Word of God is the Light and Life of heaven; therefore, without it the angels could neither see nor speak. And while God is the very Life of the natural universe, and all things, more or less, speak His Word either in direct or in inverted accents, yet it is seen there only in appearances, and fallen man could never know his God without a revealed, written, or spoken Word, from the Lord Himself.

But it is asked if angels cannot teach man divine truths. Good angels must know the Word, and must use their efforts to infuse the spirit of that Word into man, by inclining him to open his heart to the Lord, and His Word, for that Spirit. But they surely would not under-take to teach man divine things, except from the Word. For they must know well their own weakness, and their entire dependence upon that Word for all true thoughts and right feelings. Therefore, could we now meet them .face to face, and ask them for divine wisdom and instruction, they would doubtless direct us to the written Word, and to the power of the Lord Jesus Christ therein given. For they would of course say, as did father Abraham to the spirit of the rich man who wanted a messenger sent back to this world to warn his brethren to prepare for heaven, " They have Moses and the prophets; let them hear them." And it is a solemn truth, that if men hear not Moses and the prophets, neither will they be per-suaded, though one should rise from the dead. The rea-son is, the Holy Word is a nearer and better medium of life to man than any angel can possibly be. For it is infinite in varieties, and is adapted to every possible state and condition of man, either in this world or the other. Its Spirit and Life are infinite, rational, affectionate, and powerful, knowing and feeling for the wants of all, and how best to reach them. Through the Word, the Lord has an immediate connection with men, much stronger than He can have through angels. For, as the Lord's words are spirit and life, so, when men drink them into their souls from that Fountain, the truths come more pure and refreshing than through any human mediums.

Now, without truth from the Word, men cannot, in any way, converse with each other rationally about the Lord, nor express any proper thoughts or ideas concerning Him. And, at this age, it requires the *spiritual* truths of the Word to remove the clouds, which the traditions of men have thrown around the plain literal sense. This spiritual truth opens the Prophecies, so that we can look understandingly back, and see the true process of their fulfilment. And, by the Law of Analogy, we can also look forward and behold something of the order in which they are to be spiritually fulfilled. The Lord has not yet come the first time, to those who receive not the literal truths of the gospel; nor has He come the second time, to those who receive not the spiritual truths. And we cannot better introduce the reader to the confidence we feel in the spiritual sense of the Word, and to the high ground which the Word Itself will take, in Its Own defence, in the following chapters, than by a quotation from our "Lectures on the Symbolic Character of the Sacred Scriptures," just published by D. Appleton & Co., New York.

"All truths are eternal verities. They are ever and unchangeably the same. About them, when seen, men do not differ. It is about falsehoods, and where truths are not seen, that the intellectual world is contending.

"The doctrines of the Word, when seen in the light of correspondence, become themselves the indisputable evidence of their own truth: for correspondence is a language. It may well be denominated *the* language; for it is the sure language of Jehovah. It is, therefore, a living language. It is the only language that has spirit and life. It is a universal language: the language in which not only the Holy Word, but universal nature, with her ten thousand tongues, is speaking to us. Does any one doubt the existence of such a language? Let him learn to read it. No one who has ever learned it has any such doubts. Does he say no one ever has learned it? How does he know that? Thousands of persons, entitled to respect, say they have studied it, and find it to be a most sure and certain language. Where, then, rests the weight of evidence? Who is the best judge of a book, he that has read it, or he that has not?

"By this science, the Sacred Scripture is convincingly proved to be the Word of the Infinite Jehovah. All its parts thereby blend into harmony. The darkest and most obscure passages are opened and explained, and the simplest portions are filled with profound wisdom. Every passage is, indeed, seen to be "Profitable for doctrine, for reproof, for correction, and for instruction in righteousness," according to the apostle's declaration. But, without this science, has any one found it to be so? If the Bible was given by God to man to teach him something, was it not intended to be understood? Has God endowed man with reason, addressed him as a reasonable being, said to him, " Come now, and let us reason together," given him His Word as a rule of life, to show him what he must do and what he must not; and, at the same time, interspersed throughout that Word thousands of things which he can never understand, and which are of no use to him? Not so. Infinite Wisdom has not so indefinitely expressed Himself that He cannot be understood.

"The difficulty is with man. He, by a false and evil life, has lost the pure Language of Analogy in which God speaks. But, by the Divine Mercy of the Lord, that language is again restored. That sublime Key to the inexhaustible Treasury of intellectual Wealth, contained in the Word and Works of· God, is now mercifully made known. The great Seminary of scientific wisdom has become accessible to man. For this divine Key not only unlocks God's Book of Revelation, but also, at the same time, His Book of Nature. And as we are thereby conducted within the veil of the letter of the Word, and permitted to feast upon the pure bread and water of life, and to admire the glory and beauty of that divine Sanctuary, so we have, also, a passport within the veil of universal Nature, where we find enthroned pure spiritual Philosophy, expounding the invisible relations which unite heaven and earth; elucidating those otherwise incomprehensible affinities which exist between life and matter, God and Nature, the mind and the brain, the soul and the body. In passing this veil we enter the School of all schools, look up to the Teacher of all teachers, and study the Science of all sciences. The books we read are the Books of all books—the book of Nature and the book of Revelation. They are both published by the same Author illustrate the same principles, and lead to the same conclusions. Both books are necessary to the proper study of either. All the objects in nature are so many true indices, pointing to the history of their creation and the cause of their existence; and referring us for information to the written Word, to which they are the Grand Concordance. At such a seminary, with such books, and such a Teacher, we may obtain heavenly wisdom and feast on angels' food.

" But, it is asked, what is the strongest and most conclusive evidence which we have to offer in proof of the truth and certainty of this new science? We answer that no evidence can be sufficiently clear and full to satisfy a mind that will not look at it, or that has no taste nor desire for things beyond the gift of this world. But, if even such a person were entirely unacquainted with the Chinese language, and should remove to China, and there learn to speak and write that language, so as to read their books and understand them, and should find that they contained a rational and consecutive chain of ideas and history of events, he would certainly be convinced that they had a language, and that he had learned it. It is precisely so with the language of analogy. It must be examined, and learned, and tested by reading analogical language before it can be understood.

"Now, let that same man come to the Sacred Scriptures, and look at the first eleven chapters of Genesis, the twenty-fourth chapter of Matthew, the tenth of Ezekiel, and the twenty-first of Revelation, and he will be as much at a loss to know their true meaning, as he was that of the Chinese language, when he went to that country. But let him learn the language of analogy, until his heart is warmed by the spirit of the Holy Word, and he can see a beautiful and consistent course of useful instruction, pervading the entire chapters mentioned; and, not only them, but also the whole Word, making it a new Book, most clear and instructive; and he will then be much more strongly convinced of the indisputable verity of this language, than he was, or could possibly be, of that of the Chinese.

"Now, we can say to such persons, that many are the human minds, of different nations of the earth, who are becoming thus convinced. Will not God's Holy Word, then, yet become known, as it is, and be universally received, loved, and regarded? Will it not become the great law of the land, and restore universal 'Peace on earth and good will toward men'? It most surely will. That glorious shout of the angels, at the birth of our Lord, was not made in vain—'Behold, I bring you good tidings of great joy, which shall be unto *all* people.' "

Those who desire to investigate the doctrines of the Word and the science of correspondences presented in the following pages, may find the *rationale* of them, clearly and satisfactorily shown, in the voluminous works of EMANUEL SWEDENBORG, referred to in chapter xviii of this book. But we have made no quotations from those works, desiring rather to reach the public mind with facts and arguments drawn exclusively from the Word and works of God; to which the prejudices of men cannot reasonably object.

CHAPTER II.

"In the beginning was the Word, and the Word was with God, and the Word was God."—JOHN I, 1.

WHAT is the Word of God? This is the great question before us. The answer to this question is the answer to all Dr. Colenso's objections. Now, as the Word is declared in the text to be God, and as the Lord declares that the Words which He speaks to us, "they are spirit and they are life," and as "God is a Spirit" (John iv, 24), the first question before us is, What is God? Indeed, all true knowledge of God, His Word, or His works, must take its rise in a true idea of God Himself. For, according to the ideas men have of the qualities and character of the God they revere and love and worship, must be the character of their religion, and of their views of the theology of the Holy Word. Therefore, if we would successfully study God's Word and Works, we must commence with the study of God. But here we are asked, "Who, by searching, can find out God?" We are not to find Him out by our own wisdom. We are to humbly seek and receive Him as He has revealed Himself in His Word. There, we

are commanded to become like Him. This can be done
only as we gain a knowledge and love of Him.

Now, His entire Word treats of Him. The Law and
the Prophets constantly declare Him, and He is emphatically manifested in the Lord Jesus Christ, who says, " I
and my Father are one." And the Word teaches that
God is Infinite, Omniscient, and Omnipresent ; Unchangeable and Eternal ; the Creator and Sustainer of the universe. And the question at once arises, Can a finite mind
have a rational thought of such a Being ? We answer,
Yes. Not an Infinite thought, but a rational one, in its
degree. Now the first approach toward a real thought
of God is an idea of spiritual substance, which is mental,
and entirely discrete and distinct from matter, and which
cannot be reached by the senses of the natural body. If
we do not entertain this idea of spiritual substance, we
have no distinct thought of anything above gross matter ;
therefore no distinct thought of God, angel, spirit, or even
of man ; for the material body is not the man, but the
tabernacle of clay in which he lives.

Having an idea of spiritual substance, the next step
toward a true idea of the Lord is a proper thought of the
quality of His substance ; for we may know that we can
have no real knowledge of anything but by its *qualities*.
We have now before us an infinite, almighty, spiritual
substance. What are its qualities ? The Holy Word tells
us that the Lord is Life, Love, Wisdom, Goodness, Truth,
Righteousness ; that He is Our Righteousness ; that He
giveth life, wisdom, goodness, truth, and righteousness to
the people.

Having proceeded thus far, are we not now ready to
define Him, from His own testimony, to be Substantial
and Almighty Love and Wisdom, or Goodness and

Truth? What other, so high, ideas of excellence can enter the human mind? The thought can grasp at nothing else so high as Infinite and Almighty Goodness and Truth. But we are now asked if these are not mere attributes of a great Being and entirely passive in themselves, operating only when exercised by the will and understanding of that great Being? But why ask this question now? Has the interrogator so soon lost sight of mental substance? Let us ask him what other substance than Goodness and Truth can constitute the great Jehovah? Will he bring it forward within the reach of our thoughts? What other substance can be omnipresent? Goodness and Truth are not passive or dead principles. The life of Goodness is Love, and the life of Truth is Wisdom. Love and Wisdom are Goodness and Truth in action. What can give forth more Love than Infinite Goodness, or more Wisdom than Infinite Truth? What human mind without goodness has any genuine love, or without truth has any real wisdom? And where does he get these things? What else could God give to our wills that would make us so merciful and happy as would His goodness; or to our understandings that would make us so honest and just as would His truth?

But here we are told that, when the Lord regenerates a man, He makes him a good and true man, and that then He will be merciful and just. But does not the Lord, in this work, take away from him something evil and false, and give him something good and true? Is it man's own righteousness or the Lord's that dwells in him, that is kind and just, and does the good works? It is a mistaken philosophy which would teach that all the elements of the man are innate in the infant, and that all that is necessary is properly to call out and develop those principles. For, if so, why is one developed a merciful man and another a murderer, both springing from the same Divine Source? Man's mind is developed by what he appropriates of the goods and truths, or evils and falsities which are offered it. As well might the natural body of an infant be developed without natural food, as the mind without spiritual food. Therefore, the Lord says, "Behold, I stand at the door, and knock: if any man hear my voice and open the door, I will come in to him, and will sup with him, and he with Me." (Rev. iii, 20.) What is this reciprocal supping but the receiving of goodness and truth from the Lord, and returning them to Him in love and obedience? What other divine food is there for them to use? The Lord says, *He* will come in and sup with them. Does not some substance come in? It may be replied that it is His Spirit. Very well. Is not His Spirit something substantial and powerful? The Lord says, He is Life; and that He giveth life to the world. Now, if this life is not substance, He does not give the world anything. For no substance is nothing. Here, then, we have a substantial Heavenly Father, with qualities we can think of and love, and Who feeds our souls with His goodness and truth.

And as He has substance, so also He must have form. But, what can be the form of that Substance which is Infinite and Omnipresent? Of this, no finite mind can fully conceive; for Infinity is not limited by time or space. And an idea of form without an idea of boundary is above the reach of our natural thought. And yet we see that, in order to bring the reality of the Mighty God rationally within the sphere of human thought, He must be presented to the understanding in a form. For no form is no substance, which is equivalent to no God. And though the form, as presented to man's finite mind, must necessarily be finite, and thus not full, yet we have reason to believe that the Lord has so adapted His Word to our capacities as to give us, in a degree, a true, though faint and limited idea of the Divine Form. Now, God is represented in the Word as having the organs of the human body, and man is said to be created in His image. And, inasmuch as "God [in His love, wisdom, and power] was manifest in the flesh;" and it is written that the Lord, "being in the *form* of God, thought it not robbery to be equal with God" (Phil. ii, 6), we may rationally conclude that, in looking at the form of God as human, we are, to say the least, looking *toward* the Great Infinite Form; and that thus, having before the thoughts a great and glorious Human Form, with His face shining as the Sun, and His raiment white as the light, we have the best idea the finite mind can have of the Infinite Form of the Lord. Indeed, what other form than human could we give Him? it being the most perfect form that has entered our thoughts. We have now before us a distinct idea of God, suited to our states and capacities. We can think of Him as a Heavenly Father in substantial form, Infinitely good and true, whom we can love and worship as the Author of every blessing.

We have thus found the Word which was in the beginning with God, and which was God. This Word is the Truth, for God speaks nothing else. It was "in the beginning with God," for God is Goodness, and Goodness speaks It. It "was God," because It was His Wisdom. This Word is the great Source of all being, because "All things were made by Him, and without Him was not anything made that was made." This Word is the Divine Wisdom, because "God, by Wisdom, made the

2

world." This Word contains the Divine Love, because "In Him was Life," and Love is Life. This "Life was the Light of men," because Light is Truth, and Love or Life speaks it. This Word was the Lord, because "the Word was made flesh, and dwelt among" men, and they "beheld his glory." This Word had Divine Powers, because, "as many as believed on Him, to them gave He power to become the sons of God." He is "the only Wise God our Saviour," because He has "all power in heaven and on earth," is the "Alpha and the Omega, the Beginning and the Ending, the First and the Last." In Him was the Father, because He says, "The Father that is within Me, He doeth the works." The Father—the Love Element—is the spring of action, and the Truth or Word executes—"God, by Wisdom, made the world." This Father and Son, or Love and the Word, are inseparably one Being, because He says, "I and my Father are One." "He that hath seen Me, hath seen the Father." "Why sayest thou, Show us the Father? Believest thou not that I am in the Father, and the Father in Me?" He possessed the Holy Spirit, because "He breathed upon His disciples and said, Receive ye the Holy Ghost." Well, then, could the Apostle say, "In Him dwelleth all the fulness of the Godhead Bodily."

Here, then, we have the Triune God—the Father, Son, and Holy Spirit—presented in the Love, Wisdom, and Power of the Lord. A regenerated man is in His image and likeness, and is a recipient of the three Elements. They constitute the Living Influx from the Divine Mind into the human, without which we could have no true thoughts, good feelings, or right actions. To study the Holy Word and understand its elements and doctrines, we must never lose sight of the Trine of First Principles.

It is only in this one grand'idea that we can have a rational thought of God. And we should bear in mind that we can have no distinct idea of anything, unless that idea contains a true thought of its qualities. And the qualities of the Divine Trinity of First Principles—Love, Wisdom, and Power, or Goodness, Truth, and Force—are the standard by which we are to test the relative quality of every spiritual thing, of every variety of feelings, thoughts, and actions. Indeed, we see nothing spiritually and clearly right, unless our thought reaches to God's qualities, and rests in a rational view of His Nature and Character. And in preparing the mind for the Spiritual sense of the Word, we cannot dwell too much upon this point, nor become too firmly settled in this divine idea of the *Oneness* of this Trine. We need to see that the Elements are one Substance and inseparable, though perfectly distinct; that, without the Father, or Love Principle, God would have no feelings; without the Son, or Truth Principle, He would have no Knowledge; and without the Holy Spirit, or Force Principle, He would have no power. They are as essential to each other as are the will, the understanding, and the energy of the mind. And their distinct Trinity in Unity is well symbolized in the burning lamp; the heat denoting the Father; the light, the Son; and the burning, the Holy Spirit. Take away the heat, and the light and burning cease; take away the light, and the heat and burning cease; take away the burning, and the heat and light cease. Thus, each Element in the Trine is necessary to the existence of the other two. And had we a lamp too bright and intense for our eyes, so that we could bear neither its heat, its light, nor its force; and should a ground glass be put around it, adapting its rays to our

vision, that glass would faintly symbolize the assumed
nature, bringing the Lord down into our sphere of life,
and thus adapting His Goodness, His Truth, and His
Spirit to our states and wants. Here, then, we have One
Infinite, Divine Being, with one Will, one Understanding,
and one Energy. Thus "the Lord our God is one Lord."
And well may the first law of God to man be, " Thou
shalt have no other gods before Me." And when we
rationally see that one Infinite Mind is All; that It wills
all that Infinite Love can will, knows all that Infinite
Wisdom can know, and does all that Infinite Power can
do, and that nothing can be added to this Infinite Mind;
that this One Mind is spiritual Substance, possessing
three distinct Essentials, one of which is Infinite Goodness, making God infinitely Merciful; that another Essential is Infinite Truth, making Him Infinitely Wise and
Just, and that the other is Infinite Power, making Him
Almighty; and that this Love constitutes the Will, this
Wisdom, the Understanding, and this Power, the Force of
God; that this Love embraces every possible variety of
goodness, mercy, affection, and indeed every shade of
principle belonging to the department of the Will,
enabling Him to reach every state of the human heart;
and that this Divine Wisdom constitutes every variety of
the Element of Truth, Justice, Judgment, everything
belonging to the department of the Understanding, thus
enabling Him to reach every principle of human thought;
and that this Divine Power includes everything whatever
belonging to God's Energy and Might, enabling Him to
reach and control all the forces of the universe; so that
these three great Essentials—Love, Wisdom, and Power
—embrace the whole vast Being of Jehovah Himself, and
all His sphere of operations;—I say when men see this,

they will behold the eternal Trinity of the " One Only
Living and True God." And, what more can there be ?
One fills all space; where could another be located ?
And here we find that the Jehovah of the Old Testament
is the Lord Jesus Christ of the New Testament. In His
Love we have the Father; in His Wisdom, the Son ; and
in His Power, the Holy Spirit. And we see most emphatically the truth of the words of the Lord in Isaiah
xliii, 11 : " I, even I, am Jehovah; and beside Me there
is no Saviour." " I am Jehovah thy God, the Holy One
of Israel, thy Saviour " (xliii, 3). " I am Jehovah, . . .
and there is no God else beside Me; a just God and a
Saviour; there is none beside Me. Look unto Me, and
be ye saved, all the ends of the earth ; for I am God, and
there is none else." (Isa. xlv, 5, 21, 22.) " I am Jehovah thy God, . . . and thou shalt know no God but Me ;
for there is no Saviour beside Me." (Hosea xiii, 4.)
Now, this view of the Trinity rationally answers all that
is said, in the Word, of the Father, Son, and Holy Spirit.
We can see that the Love or Goodness Element is the
Father of the thoughts and actions—the begetting principle ; we never act till we desire to. Thus the Word or
Truth Element may be called the Son of God the Father ;
for the Goodness of God can give birth to the Truth, just
as a tender father speaks it for the instruction of his children. Thus the Word, or Truth, that was in the beginning with God and was God, came a Light into the
world, being spoken from the Lord's Love or the Father
within. And the Holy Ghost is declared to be the
" Spirit of Truth," the Power of God. Again, this same
God is " He that appeared unto the prophets." But,
what appeared ? Not the material body. Let the
prophets themselves answer many times over. " The

Word of the Lord came unto me;" and it came, "saying." What was this *Word* but God's Truth or Son? and, what spake it but Love or the Father? Again, it is the Son of God that is declared to be "the Judge of all the earth;" it is He that is coming to "judge the world," and yet the Lord Himself, as a person, says, "I judge no man," "my Word judges you;" and again it is written (John v, 22), "The Father judgeth no man, but hath committed all judgment unto the Son;" still, the Son says, "He that hath rejected me, and received not my Words, hath One that judgeth him; the Word that I have spoken, the same shall judge him at the last day." (John xii, 48.) Now, we may all know that God Himself is the Judge. But God, being Love, must judge by His Word—His Truth—His Son; and therefore His Son is called the Judge; and thus it is that the "Father hath committed all judgment unto the Son."

Again, the Son is called the *Mediator* between man and the Father; and this has been considered a sure evidence of two separate and distinct Beings. But when we look at the Father as Divine Goodness, we can readily see that His Word of Truth is the only Mediatorial Principle between us and that Goodness; for in order to come to God the Father, we must become good, break off from sin by righteousness, and come up into a better state of heart. Now, nothing but the Truth, which the Father gives, can serve as a "Mediator to bring us to God." The Truth directs the way. It is the Intermediate Principle between Wickedness and Righteousness. Without the Truth we could have no idea of Goodness, nor could we know our evils. The truth is the Teacher, the Schoolmaster, the Mediator, to bring us to Goodness—our Heavenly Father.

But the Son is also said to be the *Intercessor* with the Father; and He is represented as standing at the right hand of God, and pleading with Him to have mercy upon sinful men. And the thought that the Son is at the right hand of the Father, making intercession for us, presents the strongest idea in the letter of Scripture indicative of two persons, because it seems to express two minds; but as it nowhere says in the Word that God consists of more persons than one, but, on the contrary, positively declares that He is but *One;* that the LORD our God is *one* Lord; that Jehovah is the only Saviour and Redeemer; that the Father and the Son are one God, so that the Son with the "Father that dwelleth in" Him could say, "I am the Alpha and Omega, the Beginning and the End, the First and the Last;" and as sound reason and true philosophy, as well as Scripture, bear testimony to the truth of One Divine Mind, and to the impossibility of two Infinite Wills, Understandings, and Powers, we must of course seek for the truth in some other view of the intercession of the Son at the right hand of the Father, than that of two persons or minds holding intercourse. And, by analogy, we shall find the true view very plain. For hands, when mentioned in the Word, denote power. And as God the Father is the Love Element, and God the Son is the Truth Element, we readily see that the Son is really the Right Hand of the Father, or the Power of Love. For Love can do nothing without Wisdom, the Spirit of Truth being the Holy Ghost, the Power of God. Thus it is said that God's "Right Hand and His Holy Arm hath gotten Him the victory." The Lord, as the Word, is therefore the Right Hand of the Father—the Power of God unto Salvation.

What, then, is the Intercession? Spiritually viewed,

it is the same as Mediation. It is an intermediate act. Now, it is man that is interceded with, man that is propitiated or appeased, not the Unchangeable God. And Truth is the only principle that can act upon man's understanding and will, and excite to nobler action. But the truth of this view of intercession may be seen in the popular idea of the intercession of the Son with the Father, if men will look at God the Father as the Love of God, and at God the Son as the Truth of God, and at God the Holy Ghost as the Power of God, and all in one person. For illustration: personify a man as God—his will or love as the Father, his understanding or truth as the Son, and his energy or power as the Holy Spirit. This man casts his eye upon the water, and he sees a boat capsize with a child. Now, it is the understanding—the truth or Son element of his mind—that sees the accident. But no sooner is it seen than the will—the Love, the Father element—is moved to compassion. Thus the Son intercedes with the Father, and the Father and the Son immediately rush to the rescue. This energy of the two Elements denotes the Holy Spirit. The Son Principle first sees the accident, because the understanding is more external than the will, or Truth than Love: Love is the centre, Truth the circumference. The Son Element of God is therefore between the Father and mankind, and is the Interceding or Mediatorial Principle.

But while we are seeking a knowledge of the Divine Being in the quality of His Elements as taught in His Word, we should not lose sight of the fact that these Elements are *Divine Substance in Form*, and that all Truths in the Complex are the Lord as the Word, who declares that He is THE TRUTH, and that this Complex of all

Truths is in Infinite Human Form, and is the Divine Humanity of the Lord Jesus Christ, being the Great Jehovah, in His merciful approach to mankind for their salvation.

2*

CHAPTER III.

"The serpent beguiled me, and I did eat."—GEN. III, 13.

HAVING, in the preceding chapter, taken the first step toward preparing the mind for a proper examination and understanding of the Sacred Scriptures, by seeking a true view of the qualities of the Divine Author; and having thereby, from His own Word, and the use of the reason with which He has endowed us for this purpose, found a rational premise in the admission that all His principles and qualities, in their divine harmony, must be contained in the Infinite Love, Wisdom, and Power of one Almighty, Substantial, and Unchangeable Being, who declares Himself to be Goodness and Truth, Spirit and Life; and yet, as there are many things contained in the Bible which seem to be of a different character, making the Word appear inconsistent, mysterious, and contradictory, and therefore, as though these parts of it must have sprung from some other source; representing even God Himself as sometimes angry, wrathful, and revengeful, and as unstable or repentant; it therefore becomes necessary, in order to be well prepared to examine understand-

ingly into the true character and teachings of this Divine
Book, that we next obtain a rational view of what those
opposite principles and characters are, and whence they
originated. And this investigation will lead to a true
understanding of what man is, and what part he plays in
the drama of life; what his depravity is, and how he
received it. For, until these questions are rationally settled, there must, after all that has been said of the Lord,
either be a cloud of darkness still overshadowing the
beauty and loveliness of the Divine Character, or else a
spirit of skepticism will be excited against the Truth and
Divine Authenticity of the Scriptures.

Now, in keeping the Great Divine Essentials or First
Principles always before us, as the *Starting Point* and
Grand Test, by which the character and quality of everything else are to be tried, and its origin known; and in
looking up to those Principles for Light, and resting
upon them as the "Rock of Ages," God Himself becomes, in our mind, the Teacher and Judge: and thus,
not by our own wisdom, but in the Lord's, we may, in
our present investigation, obtain true ideas of the nature
and origin of evil, and of the elements and powers of
man; and thence of the reason why the Bible, in many
places, appears so wonderfully strange and hard to be understood. And having once obtained this desirable knowledge, the way will be fairly opened for a successful investigation into the Spirit and Life of the Word, and for
coming thereby to a true understanding of the Sacred
Scriptures, and of the cause of their apparent Mysteries,
Contradictions, and Discrepancies.

Beginning then with the view we have taken of our
Heavenly Father, as the Great First Cause, the Creator
of all things, Infinitely Merciful and True, the question

which has so much perplexed the religious world comes up at once fully before us, asking boldly and peremptorily, *What and Whence are Evils and Falsities, Discords and Contentions?* And falling back upon the true qualities of God for answer, the decision is made at once and decisively that, whatever may have been their origin, such things cannot be the expressions of Goodness and Truth—that God does not give forth evils and falsities. But here an interrogator meets us with the Words of God, saying, " Shall there be evil in a city, and the LORD hath, not done it?" (Amos iii, 6.) "I form the light, and create darkness: I make peace, and create evil: I the LORD do all these things." (Isa. xlv, 7.) To this we might answer that "A good tree bringeth not forth corrupt fruit." (Luke vi, 43.) But to all such questions or objections to what we are saying in this chapter, as may arise in the mind of the reader, coming from the letter of the Word, we here simply remark that we are not now explaining the Word, but are trying, by the True Light of God's own Qualities, *which Light is the Word, in its Spirit,* to prepare our minds to understand the nature and character of the Divine language, so as to see the true meaning of all such expressions of the Word, and of all its apparent contradictions. And we would further remark, that the letter of the Bible seems to give a great variety of characters to God, and some of them quite contradictory, though His true character beams out conspicuously through the whole, and that there is a good reason why the Word was so written, and that when we clearly understand the object of this chapter—the origin of evil—we shall be better prepared to enter upon the investigation of the Word in these peculiarities. Therefore, all inquiries after truth, in this chapter, will be answered by reasoning in the light of First Principles; and to such answers, properly made, no rational objection can be raised. Now, what we want clearly to understand is the difference between good and evil, truth and falsity, and their origin. Some have attributed all evil to a great diabolical power or being, standing up in opposition to the Lord. But whence has any creature power, but from God? He has all power in heaven and on earth. But is God then changeable; sometimes kind and sometimes unkind? He is Unchangeable Love, and His mercy endureth for ever. How, then, shall we solve the dark problem? Is there no such thing as evil or wrong? Some have falsely said so; but who can look around our world, and behold the murders, thefts, deceits, and crimes of every hue, and come to any such conclusions?

Yet many at this day, for the want of a true knowledge of the origin and nature of evil, are coolly declaring that evil is only a state of imperfection; that, God alone being perfect, all other things are necessarily imperfect, because finite, and that from this imperfection is all evil; but that God is constantly improving the creation, and will eventually do away with all evil and misery. But what are the grounds of this conclusion? Is Infinite Wisdom becoming wiser by experience? Is the sun more bright, the rainbow more beautiful, the diamond more brilliant now than formerly? Does the bee make sweeter honey or more perfect cells; or do the birds sing more sweetly? Now, if the lower orders of things do not improve by age or generations, we cannot from thence conclude that man does. Let us then examine man himself, and see if he is constantly making progress in good-ness. We know that we are progressing in certain kinds of science and knowledge. But are we naturally, from infancy to age, growing wiser, better, more honest, pure, and lovely? All experience teaches to the contrary. If we look into our hearts we know better. And if our natural propensities do not incline us upward, but downward, what becomes of the law of progress in moral excellence? Strange progress upward that, of the man who commences life an innocent, confiding infant, passes through a less artless but sportive childhood, becomes a licentious and deceitful youth, an adulterous and revengeful man, and ends his career on a murderer's gallows. But, say the advocates of moral progress, this is all the fault of society, not of the man. *He* was all well enough, and would have come out all right under other circumstances. But what compose society but individuals? And if *they* are all right, why is not society right also? This taking the blame off from individuals and putting it on to society is strange reasoning. Besides, if individual members of society may go downward, so may society.

There is no philosophy, however ingenious, that can rationally do away with the *fall of man.* The fact of man's degeneracy from the laws of order stands enstamped upon the whole face and conduct of the race. Besides, Infinite Goodness and Truth cannot be chargeable with the evils, falsities, and miseries of mankind. For God would have all men to be saved; "not willing that any should perish, but that all should come to repentance." He would have them saved now, saved always, saved everywhere, from all sin and suffering. And He and His laws are in effort to do this always, to everybody. Evil, therefore, springs not from God nor from His laws.

Whence, then, is evil? It is from man. What is evil? It is a disposition to violate the laws of life, and it is also the sufferings consequent upon such violation. There are two kinds, or rather two degrees of life—natural and spiritual. The violation of the natural laws brings physical evils; and the violation of the spiritual laws, spiritual evils. Thus all evils spring from the violation of these laws.

But can man oppose the laws of Him who made him, and sustains him, and gives him all the powers he has to feel, think, and act? If man could not do this he could not steal, nor lie, nor murder; for such acts cannot be according to the laws of goodness, and Goodness or God forbids them. If man has no power to break the laws of God, he has no power to keep them. And what would be the use of laws, either of God or man, for the government of creatures who are ever impelled onward by a force which they can neither resist nor avert? Who, that has examined his own heart, does not know that he is not this blind machine?

But how could man originate evil? He could not *originate* evil. Evil is not an original thing. It is the perversion of good. But how could man pervert the laws of his being, when he has no power but from God? He did not pervert the laws of his being: he acted from those laws. Did the laws of his being, then, make him transgress? No: the laws of his being made him free: but it does not follow that because he was free he was obliged to transgress. Here is the grand point which men lose sight of. What would man be without freedom? Would he be anything? He certainly would not be a man; for men can make laws, and obey them or disobey them. He can reason, deliberate, and choose. Freedom is the grand characteristic of his nature. Without it man could not reason. Without freedom there could be no right, no wrong, no responsibility, no love, no happiness, no heaven. What a glorious boon is freedom! It gives us the privilege of becoming good and true, lovely and happy. It is true, it gives us the liberty of being disorderly and miserable; for true freedom could do no less than this.

But how could man, through the exercise of his freedom, violate the laws of life, unless there had been given him a disposition to violate them? On the contrary, how could God give to man a disposition contrary to His own laws? for His laws are an expression of His own will. All the propensities which God could give to man must be orderly, pure, and heavenly.

But here we are asked if we are not to understand, by the teachings of the Bible, that there is a being called *the devil*, who is the great leader of men into sin, the tempter to all transgression, the common "Adversary" of souls, who was once an angel of heaven, and was cast out for his wickedness? To answer this, let us fall back upon First Principles, and see what they will create. We read that in the creation of all things at "the beginning," everything was good. There was no devil created, no hell. There was a serpent created which "was more subtle than any beast of the field which the LORD God had made;" but still he was "*very* good." And yet this is declared to be the identical serpent which tempted Eve. The doctrine of fallen angels has been drawn almost exclusively from the twelfth chapter of Revelation, the result of the war between Michael and the dragon. But this whole chapter is a beautiful allegory, containing useful instruction to be understood by the spiritual sense of the Word, explained in the following chapters of this book.

It seems very strange that men should ever have supposed that the dragon, with seven heads and ten horns, who was cast out of heaven more than four thousand years after the fall took place, should be the serpent which tempted Eve, when the whole Apocalypse is a prophecy of things which were to take place after the work was written. John expressly declares the matter stated to be things that " must shortly come to pass."

The first passage of Scripture that looks toward the idea of a fallen angel was written more than three thousand years after the account of the fall, and says, " How art thou fallen from heaven, O Lucifer, son of the morning! how art thou cut down to the ground. . . . For thou hast said in thine heart, I will ascend into heaven ; I will be like the Most High : yet thou shalt be brought down to hell." (Isa. xiv, 12, 13, 14, 15.) But we here see that he had never been in heaven, and that he fell because he aspired to be equal to God. He fell only from his *anticipated* or *imaginary* heaven. Indeed, he fell as Adam fell, in asking to be as God, and as all men fall who become " wise in their own eyes."

The next passage that may be thought to favor the doctrine of fallen angels is in Luke, where " the seventy returned again with joy, saying, Lord, even the devils are subject unto us through thy name. And He said unto them, *I beheld Satan as lightning fall from heaven* " (x, 17, 18). But the Lord then explains by saying, " Behold, I give unto you power to tread on serpents and scorpions, and over all the power of the enemy:" thus teaching them that the power of Satan, or of *false light*, falls from the imaginary heaven of men's minds as they tread upon, or keep down, the serpents and scorpions of the wicked heart.

The next and last passage touching the subject is that

of Paul to the Corinthians : " Satan himself is transformed into an angel of light." (2 Cor. xi, 14.) This is the only passage in the Bible where the devil is called an angel, and here it is said to be by transformation, and is not his real character.

We have now mentioned all that the Bible says, in the literal sense, upon the subject of fallen angels, or of the origin of evil ; and it fails to produce the least evidence that an angel of the heavenly abode ever fell and became a devil on the earth.

Milton's PARADISE LOST, and not the Word of God, is what has impressed men with the idea of the devil as a fallen angel. The lively imagination of Milton has painted the picture in glowing colors ; and it leaves a deep impression on the minds of religious people who love to read it. But had Milton had the spiritual sense of the Scriptures, he would have painted a very different picture. And in the subsequent part of this book we shall give the true spiritual view of the fall. We can here only treat of it in the light of natural deductions drawn from First Principles.

What, then, are we to understand by the phrase, " *the devil* "? The most correct brief definition that can be given to that phrase is, *the love of evil*. The fall of man gradually engendered the love of self; and as this love increased, the love of God diminished, till man loved himself supremely. This self-love led him into covetousness, deceit, theft, murder, and all crimes, for the sake of self, which filled him with the *love of evil*, or with *the devil*. This love of evil, therefore, did not exist before the fall ; consequently there was no devil. How could there be a love of evil, when there was no evil to love and no desire to love it ? Evil and the love of evil are, therefore, in their essence, inseparable, and came into existence to-gether. They are perverted states and principles of the human heart.

Now it is certain this devil is not of God's creating. A good tree cannot bring forth evil fruit. And surely there cannot be a self-existent, uncreated Devil, for such a being would be Infinite, and we should then have two Infinites, a good one and a bad one (which is most absurd and impossible), neither of whom could conquer the other ; whereas the Saviour did conquer death, hell, and the devil ; and offers men the power, in His Holy Spirit, to do the same.

The devil, then, is *the love of evil in the complex.* Every person whose ruling love is the love of evil is a devil. Thus the Lord called Judas a devil. Now the head of " that old serpent the devil " is, *the love of self.* This love of self is the serpent's head which the Lord came to bruise, as will hereafter be seen from the spirit-ual sense.

Evil, then, is not an original thing : it is a perversion of good, a depraved love and its consequences, brought about by habit and cultivation, through the abuse of the good principles given us. God implanted no desire for evil, no taste or relish for it, in the human heart. Indeed, He could not, for it is contrary to His nature. He could not give what He did not possess Himself.

God gave to man three things to be kept inviolate as his own. These three things are what distinguish him from the brutes, unite him with his God, and thereby give him perpetual existence, and make him capable of becoming either an angel or an evil spirit. These three things constitute what may be called man's *selfhood ;* for they give him individuality and elevate him above machinery. These three important endowments are *Freedom, Rationality*, and *Desire for knowledge*—reason to determine, freedom to act, and curiosity to know. Without these endowments, man could never be elevated above the beasts that perish. With them, he is a free, rational, and progressive being. These three endowments, as given by God, are all right. And though, from the very nature of these endowments, man may abuse them and become depraved, yet they are positive necessities of his being. And the possibility of abusing them and falling into evil exists in the possibility of using them and rising into heavenly knowledge and happiness. In the freedom and ability to do right are necessarily involved the freedom and ability to do wrong. But no man, in the exercise of the freedom which God has given him, is obliged to do what he knows to be wrong. In the truth, by which he sees the wrong, God gives him the power to resist the temptation and do right, if he will look to the Lord and make the effort which he is free to do. Thus everything necessary for man's salvation is carefully provided by the Lord.

Man was not obliged to fall. God did not desire him to fall, for He commanded him not to eat of the knowledge of evil; or, in other words, not to know evil and make it his good, by practising it, and thus appropriating it to his affections. God told him that if he did eat of it he would surely die. The forbidden fruit was the same that is now forbidden in the Decalogue.

Nor did man intend to fall. He could not have had any such desire at first, for it would have been evil. Therefore, the fall must have been imperceptibly slow at first. Man, in the exercise of his curiosity to know new things, gradually overreached the true line of virtue and justice, in such slight degrees as not to be aware that he was really diverging from the course of truth and righteousness. He was young and ambitious, with everything to learn, and a desire to know everything: with no historic paths or beaten tracks of life before him; no symbols of vice to warn him of his danger, nor examples of depravity to show him his faults. Thus he went on, gradually falling from the love of good to the love of evil.

This fall may be illustrated in many ways. A man, ignorant of the quality of the poppy, while examining, tasting, and testing its medicinal properties, and its influence upon the human system, may gradually obtain, by habit, an artificial relish for it which God did not give him, and, following up the growing demands of a disordered appetite, he eventually destroys his physical existence by it: and so of antimony and alcohol. Thus, without any relish implanted in his nature for these poisons, he by habit obtains a love for what is destructive of physical order and happiness. Precisely so could the people of the primeval age, without any inherent tendencies to evil, obtain a love for that which is destructive of spiritual order and happiness. For illustration: the inebriate is out of alcohol: the voracious appetite loudly demands it. The love of self and self-gratification—the very head of the serpent—is determined to have it at any cost. But the circumstances are such that it cannot be obtained without stealing it. The better judgment sees the injustice of the theft; but the serpent's demands are imperious, and the judgment finally yields; and the Divine command is broken—the soul has eaten of the forbidden fruit. And the next time it will be broken more easily. Thus he yields to the bite of the serpent, whose tooth he had poisoned by his own indulgence, in permitting it to run wild when he might have controlled it.

Thus the love of evil, brought on by gradually vitiating the orderly demands of mind and body, is that old serpent the Devil, who " as a roaring lion walketh about, seeking whom he may devour." And is not this the great enemy of mankind? What evil or crime was ever committed that this devil did not do? Look at the wretch in human form, with this devil in the midst of his depraved and morbid appetites of soul and body! What else have we so much to fear? His hand is pollution to everything he touches.

These serpents of the human heart are the evils to which the Saviour alludes when He says He will give His disciples " power to tread on serpents and scorpions, and over all the power of the enemy." They had no more power over the snakes of the earth than other people. But over the serpent of the mind they had power from the Lord. Paul to the Corinthians says, ' I fear, lest, . . . as the serpent beguiled Eve through his subtlety, so your minds should be corrupted from 'the simplicity that is in Christ." Here Paul is afraid that the minds of his disciples will be corrupted *as* the serpent beguiled Eve, or *in the same way* that she was beguiled. This is proof positive that Paul did not suppose that any natural serpent tempted Eve. For it cannot be believed that Paul was afraid that the snakes of this earth would lead his disciples into sin. No: it was their sinful desires to gratify the wayward demands of the heart, that Paul was afraid of.

Thus, immediately after the fall, the Saviour was promised to bruise the serpent's head, or the love of self. This work was the great object of His mission. It is nowhere recorded that He killed a snake. When He came in the flesh the kingdom of Satan, or of the serpent, ruled on earth. Christ came to destroy the works of the devil in the human heart, and establish His own kingdom there. When the serpent rules, the whole mind is in disorder. When Christ rules, all is happiness and peace.

CHAPTER IV.

ACTION AND REACTION: OR, GOOD AND ITS REWARDS; EVIL AND
ITS CONSEQUENCES.

THE Lord, in His Word, says to us, "Judge not, that ye
be not judged. For with what judgment ye judge, ye shall
be judged: and with what measure ye mete, it shall be
measured to you again." (Matt. vii, 1, 2.) He says,
" give, and it shall be given unto you :" that according
to what we sow we shall reap: that " the soul that sin
neth,' it shall die:" that " the righteousness of the
righteous shall be upon him, and the wickedness of the
wicked shall be upon him." (Ezek. xviii, 20.)

The spirit and life of these passages bring before us an
eternal law, which is as reliable. and certain, in spiritual
things, as that of *action and reaction* is, in natural things.
We know that the earth bears as hard against the man
who stands upon it, as he does against the earth, and by
this means he can walk. And this is but a natural illustration of a higher law which appertains to spiritual things
with equal certainty. And while this law, in the natural
plane, pervades the universe of matter ; and no machinery
could move, and nothing could exist without it ; so, in the
spiritual plane, it pervades the universe of mind, and

nothing could move, or exist, without it. And a proper understanding of this law will throw much light into our minds, from the Holy Word, and enable us the more readily to understand the divine teaching and the laws of our spiritual existence.

Now, it is a sure law of our being that whatsoever we do to another, spiritually, that is, as to our will and design toward him, whether it be intended for his good or his evil, must, as a matter of course, affect us for good or for evil. We must receive back upon our souls an impression of the same quality and force as that we intended to give. And if men truly saw and felt the consequences of breaking this law, as sensibly as they do that of the physical law, by the pain they feel when they burn their fingers, they would be very careful how they desire, or perform, anything but good to others. And when this great law, for the regulation of all minds, is properly felt and acknowledged, by the human race, the world will come into order.

It would seem that it ought to have been thus felt and acknowledged ere this; for it is, in reality, the basis of all law, civil and religious. And, in the ignorant ages of the world, God suffered the law of receiving according to what we give, to be carried out in ultimates, in physical retaliations, to the very letter. Thus, the command to the Jews was, "Life for life, eye for eye, tooth for tooth, hand for hand, foot for foot, burning for burning, wound for wound, plague for plague, stripe for stripe." And these laws were rigidly observed and enforced. Whatsoever a man did to another was done to him in return. This law was carried into all the departments of life, civil and religious. If a witness testified falsely against a man, the command was, "Ye shall do unto him as he sought to do unto his

3

brother." If the false testimony would have convicted the brother of a crime deserving death, then the witness was to be put to death.

The Jews had a great variety of these retaliatory laws. Why did God give such laws? Because they sprang from the great principle that whatsoever measure men mete to others, spiritually, or as to will or intention, must be measured to them again—must come upon their souls. The Jewish law was, therefore, an exemplification, in the letter, of the truth of a spiritual law. God desired thus emphatically to teach it, in His Holy Word, and to that people as best for their good; and, also, that future ages of the world might thereby learn to see, and regard it in the spirit. But in the New Testament the law, in the letter, is not enforced.

We may now will to our enemies physical punishments, and inflict them, without being obliged, by the civil law, to receive the same corporal sufferings. But if we do not inflict it on them for their soul's good, or for the good of mankind, and do it, not in a spirit of kindness, but with a revengeful spirit, to torment them, our own soul must reap its bitter reward.

Now, although the law is a spiritual law, and is therefore positive and sure, yet the Jews were so low that they could see it only in the letter, and to reach their states it was recorded in the letter. And, to persons in their sensual and depraved condition, it was a wholesome law, even in the letter, and served rather to elevate than to lower them. For the prompt and sure execution of the penalty impressed them with a sense of the vileness of the crime; and restrained them from a thousand wicked indulgences, and held them in the fear of God's power, and in respect to His Law.

Now, the law of the New Testament, commanding us to do unto others as we would that they should do unto us, and assuring us that the measure we mete to others will be measured to us again, is only another form of the retaliatory law of the Jews. The spiritual import of both is the same : one is suited to one dispensation, and the other to another.

But, as people see that the law, under the Christian dispensation, is not carried out, in the letter : that men do not receive, upon their bodies, the measure they mete to others ; many have settled down in the belief that the law means nothing ; or, at most, its penalty is a very doubtful matter, and but little to be feared. Such minds can only be reached by a conscious certainty of the spiritual sense, through a rational view of the law itself. But men will yet see that the law, whereby the souls of men, in their intentions and purposes, must receive back the measure they mete to others, is as certain as that God liveth.

Upon this eternal law rest the safety of the spiritual world and the order and harmony of the universe. It is the golden rule of the Gospel, the spirit of the whole Divine code, the essence of the two great commandments, and the foundation of all wholesome, civil laws.

And there is no mitigating or averting it in the least. Nor is there any possibility of transferring the penalty from one person to another ; for it comes as the legitimate effect of a cause ; not solely, as a command of-God. It would come if God had not said so. The written laws of God are only expressions of Eternal Principles which exist in the very nature of things. The Written Law does not bring the penalty ; nor does God. It is the violation of the Law. Man, by violating the Law of love to God and the neighbor, brings upon his own soul the same measure he metes. And upon his soul, and no other, can it possibly fall. " The soul that sinneth IT shall die."

Now, what is this death? It is the loss of some love of right: and the death extends just to the degree of the loss. For the love of right, or love of good, is life: the loss of it is death. What is the effect of this death? Unhappiness. What occasions the unhappiness? It is the want of harmony with the laws of happiness, or of love to God and the neighbor. What inflicts this misery? The condition of the sinner. Does God or His Law con·· demn him? No: " this is the condemnation, that light has come into the world, and men loved darkness rather than light, because their deeds were evil." Does God want him to remain dead? No: He invites him back in the tenderest manner; and pleads with him, and entreats him to return, with all the compassion of a Father for a child. He assures him that " when the wicked man turneth away from his wickedness . . . and doeth that which is lawful and right, he shall save his soul alive." (Ezek. xviii, 27.) Is the Law opposed to his coming? No: it is given on purpose to show him the way back. " The Law of the LORD is perfect, converting the soul. (Ps. xix, 7.) He has placed himself in opposition to the Law; but the Law is still his friend, ready to receive him with open arms. What then are God's desires toward the sinner? That he should be happy. " Have I any pleasure at all that the wicked should die? saith the Lord God; and not that he should return from his ways, and live? " (Ezek. xviii, 23.) What will give man that happiness? A return to harmony with the Law. What obstacle is there in the way of his return? None but the sinner's own indispostion. " Whosoever will, let him take the water of life freely." Is he free to

return ? Yes ; and has the power constantly extended to
him to do so. " Turn ye, turn ye, for why will ye die."
How is this return to be made ? By repenting of his feelings of opposition to the Law ; faith in the Lord and in
the truth which shows him his evils and the way back ; and
faithful and prayerful obedience to that truth till he loves
the Law, and God, and his neighbor. Then he is happy.

But, here we are told that we are at variance with the
doctrine, that Christ suffered the penalty of the sins of
men in their stead. We answer that we have not written
this book in any spirit of religious controversy, but simply
to speak the irrefutable teachings of the Holy Word in all
that we say ; and we now speak understandingly when we
say that Christ, in His coming, changed no Divine Law :
that He came not to destroy the Law, but to fulfil ; and
that there is nothing in the Holy Word that teaches that
God ever affixed any penalty to sin that could not be remitted by the sinner's breaking off from it by righteousness ; nor is it anywhere taught that the Saviour suffered
the penalty of man's sins, or even that God forgives them.
But, on the contrary, it is decidedly and universally taught
that men must suffer the penalty of their sins. Thus it is
written in Jer. xiv, 14, " I will recompense them according to their deeds ; " in Luke xxiii, 41, " We receive
the reward of our deeds ; " in Rom. ii, 6-11, " God will
render to every man according to his deeds," " for there
is no respect of persons with God ; " in Ps. lxii, 12,
" Thou renderest to every man according to his works ;
and in Rev. xx, 12, 13, concerning the final judgment,
when the books of men's lives were opened, it is declared
that " the dead were judged out of those things that were
written in the books, according to their works."

The fact is, we have grown up from childhood under

the idea that forgiveness of sins is the relinquishment
of punishment.   And it is hard for men to see that
the removal of evil dispositions is the only remission
of sins.

There is much said, in the Word, about the forgiveness
of sins, but the penalty is another thing. Sins are the
evils of the will. Their action brings forward the penalty ; these evil loves or sins may be remitted, by the Lord,
through faith and repentance, and the resisting of temptations, till we obtain good loves. And when these sins or
evils are removed, the penalty is gone. The sin, or evil
in the soul, is the cause of the penalty or unhappiness,
and therefore the penalty must stand against a man till
the cause is removed. God neither inflicts nor remits the
penalties of transgression. They are the sure effects of
man's sins. He remits the sins when men repent of them
and forsake them.

Then, as God does not forgive the penalty of man's
sins, but the transgressor bears it, the Lord could not
suffer it. But, we should not, on this account, undervalue
the great work of Redemption. We owe everything to
the Lord for what He then did for us. We were sinners
in a lost and most miserable and hopeless condition. And
the Merciful Lord wanted to save us. The event, therefore, is just as important to us, as though He had actually
suffered the penalty of our sins. It provides a rational
and consistent way for our salvation : and all was done
gratuitously and in pure mercy, for us. It is therefore
recorded that He *died for us*. But, what died ? Every
propensity of His nature that could be tempted—every
tendency toward self-love. He crucified them in His assumed nature, that He might be able to reach us and dis-
pose us, in His Spirit, to crucify them in our nature.

It is also said that *by His stripes we are healed.* That is, by His stripes He was made perfect; and His Spirit was thereby brought to our aid, so that we might be healed of our sins, by following Him. We are taught that He was made perfect through suffering. And in Luke, it is written, " Ought not Christ to have suffered these things and to enter into His glory."

Again we are taught that *He became sin for us ;* and that *He bore our sins.* That is, He assumed our sinful nature, and thus bore our sins, or the sins of the world, in their tendencies, but not in actuality. He never sinned. And He would now aid us to bear our sins as He did without sinning ; and also to resist them in His spirit, and thus to follow Him in the regeneration.

Again, *He was a Propitiation for our sins.* Now, a propitiation is a reconciliation. He took our fallen and unreconciled nature, and propitiated, atoned, or reconciled it to the Divine nature. And He became that propitiation *for* our sins, or *because* we had sins, and He wanted us to become propitiated, or reconciled to God, through His spirit, by forsaking those sins.

Now, it has been supposed that the acts of the Lord, here mentioned, had reference to the *penalty* of man's sins ; but that is a mistake. It does not say that He died for the penalty of our sins ; or that He bore the penalty ; or that the penalty is removed by His stripes ; or that He was a propitiation for the penalty. Indeed the penalty is nowhere alluded to in the whole Scripture, but as something that the sinner himself must bear.

Much is said of what Christ has done for the sins of the world, and for the forgiveness and remission of these sins. But the forgiveness of the penalty is in no instance alluded to, but plainly denied. " The righteousness of the righteous shall be upon him, and the wickedness of the wicked shall be upon him."

It has been supposed, by some, that the Lord has changed this great law of receiving according to the measure we mete, because He says in Matthew, " Ye have heard that it hath been said, an eye for an eye, and a tooth for a tooth ; but I say unto you that ye resist not evil." But what rational mind cannot see that an Infinite Law cannot be changed ? God's laws are the expressions of His own immutable Will and Wisdom.

By the words above, from the Sermon on the Mount, we may readily see that the punishment for sin never comes from God. God, and angels, and all good men are kind toward the good and the bad. Evil intentions bring upon the soul its own disordered state, and consequently its unhappiness ; and when carried out they often bring the corporal punishments of the civil law upon man.

Now we repeat, that the law by which we receive back the measure we mete to others, is as essential to our spiritual being, as is the law of action and reaction to our natural being. Indeed, we see no other way that evil could be restrained, or the order of the spiritual universe preserved. It is therefore a great blessing that we suffer the penalty of the violated Law. Take away the penalty of the civil law, and how soon the world would go to destruction. Take away the pain we feel at the violation of the physical law, and children would cut off their fingers, and put out their eyes, and be crushed to pieces by carelessness. It is the great law for the preservation of physical life ; and the spiritual law of receiving according to what we give, would be equally preservative, if it were as well understood and felt.

How promptly does the rope walker watch and obey

the mechanical law of action and reaction, that his whole weight may act against the rope ; lest he suffer the consequences of the violated law by the reaction of the solid earth, by a concussion.

Now man is made rational and free that he may obey, or disobey, this great Law, either in its mental or physical operations. We know the consequences of breaking the law, physically. Would to God we were as sensible of what would follow the spiritual violation ; that of love to God and the neighbor. Then would man turn from his evil way and live.

We brace ourselves against the wind, making our reaction just equal to the force, that we be not blown away. So, we may spiritually resist the current of temptation which besets us, that we be not swept away by a torrent of vice. " The Stone which the builders rejected, the same is become the head of the corner : this is the Lord's doing, and it is marvellous in our eyes : and whosoever shall fall on this Stone shall be broken : but on whomsoever It shall fall, It will grind him to powder." (Matt. xxi, 42, 44.)

3*

CHAPTER V.

In order to prepare the mind to receive the ideas expressed in the next chapter, upon GOD AND CREATION, or Cause and Effect, we here interpose a few thoughts on the Law of Influent Life, as a supplement to Chapter III, and an introduction to Chapter VI.

If the premises, as to the Divine qualities, laid down in the second chapter, be true, the conclusions to which we have arrived in the third and fourth chapters, as to the nature and character of man, and of evil and its origin, as well as the law of Action and Reaction, must also be true. For the premises being true, this sequence must follow. Any argument, therefore, that may be offered against the view we have taken of the fall, or against anything we may say in this book, will be made against the First and Eternal Principles laid down for our guidance in the first chapter. For on them we rest, and from them and what they teach, we shall draw all our conclusions as to what is right or wrong, good or evil.

Now, we are taught by those principles that the Lord is THE LIFE (John xi, 25); that He is THE FOUNTAIN OF LIFE (Ps. xxxvi, 9); and that He *giveth Life to the World*

(John vi, 33) ; that He *giveth Life to all* (Acts xvii, 25) ; that this Life is spiritual and eternal substance ; and that even the words that He speaks are this very life. (John vi, 63.)

From all this we see that Life is not a *created thing ;* but something given to all men and things by the Lord. God breathes into men the breath of life. Nothing, therefore, can exist but in connection with the Lord, by the constant, unbroken stream of influent life. This life, in its Essence, being Love and Wisdom, the human will and understanding are the only receptacles of it, which can affectionately feel, and rationally understand this connection. Men can know something of God, and can love Him. Other things receive the life, but know nothing about it. This Divine Life, then, ever flows into and vitalizes the entire universe, and is consequently the motive force of all action.

It is a mistaken philosophy which supposes that the Creator gave to the universe, at its creation, certain laws ; such as motion, gravitation, heat, light, life, germination, growth, and reproduction ; and that these laws were made innate, and were given to the universe as its own ; and that having been put in motion, all things must continue to move on till the Hand that created them shall see fit to stop them. For the laws, in reality, belong not to nature. Strictly speaking, nature has no laws. God's thoughts are the only laws, and His feelings are the only impulses which move this vast domain. Should He cease to think and feel, all would stop ; yea, all would cease to be. Nature itself cannot think, feel, nor act. The Divine Love, Wisdom, and Power are its life, laws, and energies. Nature without these is but a dead body. Nor has it life enough to move onward a single step further without the influx of more.   The creative and propelling powers are the same.

This creative force is the spring of all conception and birth—whether spiritual or natural; whether human, animal, vegetable, or mineral.   It forms the gem, opens the bud, expands the flower, and ripens the fruit.   It is the fountain of all heat, and the source of all light.   But, it is asked, Does not the sun give heat and light, germination and growth to the things of earth?   We answer, No: the sun has no power to do anything.   It is a mere instrument through which the Lord operates in this lower sphere.   The heat and light of the sun are but the ultimates or effects of God's Love and Wisdom.   This Love and Wisdom are in every ray of light which the sun gives forth.   Should God's Love and Wisdom cease to flow into the sun, it would not only cease to shine, but it would cease to be.   The sun, therefore, has no heat but from God's Love, and no light but from His Wisdom.   And yet the heat of the sun is not Love, nor is its light Wisdom.   They are but the effects or correspondences of Love and Wisdom.   Thus the natural universe of things is the effect of God's Love, Wisdom, and Power, as the great First Cause; and the Cause is ever giving life to the effect.   This must be so: for *God is Life*, and He *giveth Life to the world*, and *to all things*, and the Words which He speaks are this life; for His Words must contain His Love and Wisdom.

The operation of this Divine Influx into all things, is the great law of Creative Life.   By its outgoing influence the universe was created, and all was pronounced *good*.   And when that work was finished, to the extent that man was created, and all was *very good*, everything was under this Divine Law of Love and Wisdom, and the

Divine Law was in everything: "I in thee and thou in me," saith the Lord. Man was an image of his Maker and the world was an image of man, and all was in perfect harmony from the dust of the earth up to the great Jehovah. The divine, outflowing Love was the life of all; and the Divine Wisdom was the Law in which everything moved, at the Infinite impulse of the Divine Love. Not an impure thought to beloud the understanding, nor an unkind feeling to disturb the bosom of happy humanity. The heavens declared the glory of God, and the firmament showed His handiwork. Sun and moon praised Him. All stars and light praised Him: fruitful trees and all cedars; beasts and all cattle; worms and feathered fowl. Everything that had breath praised the Lord. Nature was one universal harp, with every string in concord. The balmy breath of heaven swept its ten thousand strings in perfect harmony. It was prepared, in all its sweetness and beauty, for man's delight, edification, and development.

Under these blessed auspices, man was introduced into being, in the infancy of his days, as the highest and tenderest object of the Divine care. All was made for man. Here he was in the bright sunshine of youth, with a soul in perfect concord with the golden harp of nature; with the beautiful earth spread out at his feet, and the shining heavens rolling above him. Thus we first find man in the garden of paradise, with a mind just opening for the reception of knowledge: God the Teacher, man the pupil, and the universe his text-books; and every page told the truth. Not an object before him, in the vast creation, but which was lovely, and spake to him in accents of wisdom and kindness, from the Fountain of his being. And his soul responded in emotions of good will. One universal law of light and life pervaded the scene; and there was no evil in existence. God was the source of all Power, and all *that* Power ever went forth from Him in the Laws of Wisdom and Love; and all was harmony.

Could that harmony be disturbed? It could: and man was the only being in existence that could do it. All other created things but acted out, by intuition, the perfect uses of their existence. They had no will nor wisdom of their own. They were made for this world only, and answered the full purpose of their being.

But man was designed for a higher sphere of life. He was now only in the germ of his manhood; possessing an innumerable variety of undeveloped principles and faculties. Everything in the universe corresponded to those principles. Each object denoted something which God possessed in its fulness and man in the germ. And it was only in the proper development of these principles of man's nature, that he could obtain true knowledge. But in their orderly development, he would obtain knowledge of everything—of God, of the universe, and of himself.

Now, it is because man possessed in himself, from the Lord, the elements of the universe in embryo, that he was capable of scientifically investigating nature, and her laws of action. Man could learn nothing of lower things if he did not, from the Lord, possess some elements of them in himself. All knowledge whatever that man can possibly obtain, is only an insight into human nature and its relations, making man thereby acquainted with God and His works.

The reason an animal cannot be taught science is, he is but a fragment of something, and that fragment is all that he ever can be. A certain animal corresponds to a principle in man's affections. To that particular character he is limited; having no variety of principles whereby he can compare, distinguish, and reason. But man can learn anything, not Infinite, because he is the embodiment and combination of the elements of all finite things; for man was made in the image and likeness of his God, and therefore must contain, in a limited degree, the capacity to receive something of all the Divine Elements contained in nature. Eternity, therefore, cannot fully satisfy this capacity.

Nor can these elements or possibilities of the human mind be developed from any powers or principles which man possesses in himself. All power is in God, and the Life of all the Elements of being is in Him. No created thing can be developed beyond its capacities, and everything is developed by influx from God.

The elementary capacities for obtaining all science and knowledge are in man, as the elementary capacities for the development of the tree are in the acorn. But, as the tree cannot be developed from the acorn without the heat and light of the sun, so neither can man be developed without the Love and Wisdom of God. But there is a great difference in the mode in which the heat and light of the sun are brought to bear upon the acorn, in the development of the tree; and that in which the Love and Wisdom of God are brought to bear upon the human mind, in the development of man. And a full knowledge of this difference shows the origin of all discord.

Now, there is something in the acorn besides matter. There is life there, with all the tendencies to produce trunk, branches, leaves, blossoms, and fruit. So there is life in man at his birth, with tendencies to produce a human soul in full manhood. Both the tree and the man are to be developed by means of influent life from the Lord. But the tree is entirely passive in its development, while man is active in the formation of his mind. Indeed, none of the lower orders of things have any free agency in their formation. They are obliged to be formed just as they are. Nor can they change in the least the order or character of their development. But man has an agency in establishing the character and quality of his mind. He is not obliged to cultivate his mind at all. Indeed, he must work hard, in order properly to develop his faculties. And he can change the order and character of the growth of his mind. He can cultivate either a kind or an unkind disposition.

The reason why animals cannot change the order and character of their development is, that there can be no separation between their thoughts and their feelings; they being, in their fragmentary condition, neither free nor rational. Their thought is an intuitive act of the mind flowing from instinctive feeling, by means of influent life. Therefore, the thought is but an outward expression or action of the feeling, and cannot be separated from it. There can, therefore, be no hypocrisy in an animal.

The reason man can change the order and character of the development of his mind is, that he can separate his thoughts from his feelings. He can think one thing and desire another. He can, therefore, say what he knows to be false. Thus man can do what no other creature can do, nor even God himself. Man can lie. No other creature can bear false witness. If an animal be angry, he manifests it the moment the anger rises. But man can approach you with a smile in his face, malice in his heart, and the concealed dagger in his hand to plunge into your bosom.

Now, here is a quality not in harmony with God or His laws. Indeed, it is the very essence of hell, and is the means of all discord and misery. It nowhere existed when God pronounced all things good. Man, therefore, must have introduced it into the world. It could not spring from God; for God is love. It could not come from His laws, for they condemn it. Man, by habit, corrupted his own affections and thoughts, and thus introduced sin and death into the world.

But, why did not God make man so that he could not fall? Because that would be making him so that he would not be a man. God desired to make man, not a machine. All that God does is right: man only does wrong.

CHAPTER VI.

A glance at the movement of Creative Life, by Efflux and Influx, producing Action and Reaction, and establishing the Divine Law of Analogy between Spiritual and Natural or Mental and Physical Things.

THE first principle in existence is Life—Life Infinite, Self-existent, Substantial, and Eternal—Life that can neither be increased nor diminished, but which is constantly manifesting Itself in new creations and varieties of forms and qualities, with given powers, and means of perpetual multiplication and extension. This Life is therefore the Centre, the Source, and the Father of everything; ever sustaining and giving life to all It creates. And though It is Infinite, and therefore above man's comprehension, yet we obtain the first rational approach toward It in thought by contemplating It as consisting of three inseparable, essential Elements—Infinite Love or Will, Infinite Wisdom or Understanding, and Infinite Power or Energy. This Life, therefore, is Divine Substance—The Great Jehovah Himself—the Infinite and Eternal Cause of the created universe, as the finite effect. This effect is ever connected with the Cause, is sustained by It, and is constantly filled with life from It.

As this Divine Life flows out from the Creative Centre, It produces and sustains all things in their order, from highest to lowest and from lowest to highest, creating in Its descent all the various spheres of action in regular succession. Through these spheres, into the final ultimate or mineral kingdom, upon which all other things rest, the Divine Elements are ever descending and operating for new creations. For, in the material plane, all power can be exercised in the forces of action and reaction. Matter is, therefore, the field of action for all creative life. Without it, the effluent Life from God would be unproductive for the want of a created substance or base to evolve Itself in and act upon, for the creation of new and higher forms of being. All the angels of heaven, therefore, must have commenced their existence in this ultimate plane of being, and have ascended from these low beginnings up the scale of life, forming the various heavens, and must be still approximating the perfection of their Heavenly Father by the higher elements of life He is ever imparting to them adapted to their advancing states, for their more full and perfect development. Thus the angel whom John was about to worship on Patmos said, " See thou do it not : for I am thy fellow-servant, and of thy brethren the prophets : " and though in heaven, yet their life must ever rest and act upon the ultimates in which their existence commenced. For every human being is a recipient and medium of life from God, and that life stops not in its descent until it reaches the ultimate of all existences—the great work-house of creation. Every variety of life, therefore, is represented in the material world. Therefore the Lord says, " The heaven is my throne, and the earth is my footstool." (Isa. lxvi, 1.)

This life, being spiritual substance, is discretely distinct from matter, yet matter manifests it and is filled with it, as the human body is filled with a living soul. Thus there are two universes—the spiritual and the material, or the universe of mind and the universe of matter. The spiritual or mental world consists of God, the angels and spirits, and the souls of men, and the elements of life in all their variety of forms and qualities. The material world embraces the bodies of men and all other matter of the universe. The spiritual world is the world of causes, and the material world is the world of effects. And as there can be no effect without its cause, so there can be nothing in the world of matter which does not distinctly represent something in the world of mind. And it represents it by the perfect Divine Law of analogy. This law is the relation which must exist between a cause and its effect. Therefore, between the world of Mind and the world of Matter this law of analogy universally prevails; so that spiritual things are to be understood by analogy, through natural things. Thus when *light* is mentioned in the Word it means, by analogy, *truth*. This analogy is not like a common figure of speech. It is a higher law than can exist between one natural thing and another. It is the union of inner things with outer, or higher things with lower. Indeed, it is the great law by which the spiritual and natural worlds exist. For as an effect cannot exist without a cause, so neither can a cause exist without an effect.

Therefore the entire created universe is a constantly renewed and sustained result from and by the Lord. It is not God, but is the effect of God. God is the Cause; and He fills the universe with life. It is because the effect is related to the cause that He can fill it with life.

This relation is the law of analogy, and it is the means which holds the universe together and to its Creator.

Now the great end or object of the Creator, in giving existence to the universe, must have been the production of His own image and likeness in created intelligences, whom He could forever bless and make happy by His own goodness and truth, whereby they could know Him and love Him, and thus be filled with heavenly life and joy. This we may see from the universal law wherein everything is in the effort to produce its kind—to bring forth its own likeness. The imparting of *that* law to all His creatures emphatically bespeaks its existence in God.

Now a man, in true order, is in the image and likeness of God; but any other created thing, below man, is only an image of some principle in God or in man.

The order of the outward creation of the world was from lower things to higher: first minerals, then vegetables, then animals, and finally man; thus orderly and gradually approximating, by higher and purer organizations, the real Divine Image, until God finally crowned the creation with man as the sum total and embodiment of all things below him: for when all but man was created, and everything was in readiness to produce him, the vast varieties of things scattered throughout the universe were but humanity in fragments. Everything was an image of some principle which was to be in man; and it took them all combined to make man. Man could not exist until these things were created; for upon them his body must subsist, and through them his mind must be educated. And when all these materials were brought harmoniously together in man, and all was pronounced good, the vast universe represented man, and man represented his Maker.

Who cannot see that the things which God creates must, as they come from Him, be in their degree like Him, so far as finite things can be like the Infinite? His Love desires their creation, His Wisdom devises the mode, and His Power executes it; and they come forth, not out of nothing, but from Himself, and He gives them their life and existence. The withdrawal of His Love from any created objects would at that instant cut off the stream of life, and they would cease to be. It requires the same power to sustain as it does to create. Preservation is perpetual creation.

From this ground we see that, during the whole process of the creation, God was making man; that He is the Infinite Man, the Eternal Creator of His own image; and that all things that He creates must, as they come from His hands, be in their degree expressions of something of Himself. But He does not add to Himself. He makes nothing Infinite. Infinity is all. Everything is involved in it.

The highest individual image of God is the wisest and purest man or angel. But even that image is being constantly improved by the further reception of goods and truths for its ever-expanding mind and increasing wants. And the affectionate union of various wise and good minds into a society, imparting to each other what the Lord gives them, is a higher and more full image than an individual. And this image will be forever improving by the advancement of each of its parts, and by the continual accumulation of more individuals. For no two men are alike, and no two receive alike from the Lord. Each individual added to the society is a new medium of life to the general body, having something to give which the society did not before receive, and thus supplying a deficiency in the general image, and adding to the life and happiness of all. But the perfection of the Divine Original can never be reached, though forever approximated. For Infinity can never exhaust itself by giving forth new finite expressions of its parts in created intelligences, filling them with life.

Now in the process of creation, when all things were in readiness for the production of man; when the vast variety of human principles lay scattered throughout the mineral, vegetable, and animal kingdoms in living forms; when all nature was a beautiful page of mental symbols in physical robes, with no created rational being on earth to read the expressive characters, and love and worship the Author; then it is that we behold Man making his appearance—Man, the sum total of creation—the connecting link between God above him and nature below him, and thus the crowning act of the creation.

And as man was made above all other things in the scale of creation, by being endowed with rationality and freedom; and, at the same time, embracing within himself all the various qualities of life which animated the natural world; therefore life had, thereafter, to be supplied to natural things, through the medium of man. For the order of influent life from God must ever be through higher things into lower.

As this stream of life passes through the thoughts and feelings of man, he imparts to it his qualities: consequently, as man fell the various creatures and things below man partook of his depravity. Thus they became changed and modified, according to the various vicissitudes and changes of man's states and qualities. Nature became corrupted through man's vileness. The earth brought forth thorns and thistles; the wild beasts became quarrelsome and ferocious; and poisonous serpents and reptiles, hawks and owls, moles and bats annoyed the human race. And the labor necessary to cultivate the earth, subdue the thorns and thistles, and guard against and control the wild beasts and serpents, in order to sustain and secure man's physical life, perfectly represents the mental labor necessary to subdue and control the evils and falsities of the soul, for the proper sustenance and security of spiritual life.

But here an objection may be raised on the ground that carnivorous animals, reptiles, fishes, and insects, existed and preyed upon each other before man was upon the earth. But it does not follow from this that there was anything like anger or malice in them—anything that disposed them to fight for the sake of fighting. They had appetites that demanded food, and they could satisfy those appetites without feelings of revenge, or any spirit but what flowed from the innocent demands of nature. The fishes could prey upon each other, and the birds upon the insects, as a means of subsistence and general good, without disorder. Fishes and insects seem to be multiplied for this purpose. And did not the fishes prey upon each other, the exuberance of their progeny would fill the waters and produce general destruction. The things of nature must subsist upon what nature brings forth, as a matter of course; and all are for the service and subsistence of man. The question is, whether there was anything infectious or malignant in nature—venom in the serpent's tooth, or poison in the mineral or vegetable kingdom; or thorns and thistles, blight and mildew destroying the good fruits, or warlike and quarrelsome propensities in the animals. And God's very Nature forbids us to believe it possible. And His Word seems clearly to teach that these things are the consequences of the "Fall."

As this stream of instructive or creative life leaves the Heavenly Father, it is, of course, pure. And, coming from the Divine Mind, it must be goodness and truth in Divine Feelings and Thoughts. Therefore, its first reception must be into angelic minds nearest the Lord—into wills and understandings of the first order. And the Lord, from His Infinite prescience, must mercifully adapt this instruction to their finite capacities. These celestial angels, in imparting these elements of mental life, this food for souls, to the thoughts and feelings of their pupils, must, in order to adapt it to their states, impart to it something of the quality of their own affections. And these new recipients must, by their qualities, attemper the mental stream to the minds next below them. And thus the stream must flow on and spread around each sphere or state of life, imparting to it something of its own peculiarity of thought and feeling as it gives the mental food to the neighbor ; each one receiving it according to his state, until, from the general sphere of humanity on earth and the particular sphere of each individual, it flows on down into the irrational though animate creation, below man ; carrying with it, into the animals, all man's various qualities of temper, disposition, and propensity, both good and bad. From thence it flows down into the inanimate creation, through the vegetable into the mineral kingdom. Here it reaches the basis of all creative action—the common ground for the beginning of the creation of all organic life.

Now, does any one, in reading this chapter, doubt the truth of this law and order of creation ? Let him read understandingly the preceding chapters, and he will come to the conclusion that, the first chapter being true, the second must be true also, and that the truth of the third

4

and fourth follows as a matter of course; and then he will see that the truth of this chapter is a necessary sequence of the whole; that they all stand in their order, upon the eternal laws of God, as read in Revelation and Nature; that there is no breaking the chain of argument; that we must adopt the whole or none. If the premises laid down in the first chapter be false, then we are afloat upon the broad ocean of uncertainty, amid all its shoals and whirlpools, without a compass or chart. No pure Heavenly Father, and no Divine Revelation, that can enter the rational faculty and commend themselves to the human heart. O God of Light and Life, save us from this wreck. "Open Thou mine eyes, that I may behold wondrous things out of thy law." (Ps. cxix, 18.)

CHAPTER VII.

THIS science not only shows the relation between the literal and spiritual senses of the Word, but also between the body and the soul of man. By means of it, we look through the literal sense of Scripture, in all its mysteries, and obtain a rational knowledge of the spiritual sense ; and then, by means of this knowledge, we gain a clear understanding of the design and use of the literal sense ; and, thus, a confirmation of the truth of the Word is established. So, also, we may look, by correspondence and the light of the Word, up through our physical system, to our spiritual being, and obtain a rational knowledge of the soul, and then, by means of this knowledge, we may gain a clear understanding of the design and use of the material body, and how to treat it.

In seeking this view of the spiritual sense of the Word, our efforts will be much facilitated, by keeping in mind the *fact*, that we are seeking, solely, a knowledge of God and of man, for the purposes of human salvation ; that the Word is given for no other purpose. It is, therefore, filled with Divine thoughts and feelings, and with symbols of human thoughts and feelings, all clothed in human language, and adapted, by correspondences, to the understandings of men.

These Divine thoughts and feelings are elements of life for our souls, designed for our understandings and wills. They come, in practical lessons of Divine Wisdom, for the improvement of the mind, and the action of the body, always presenting, first and foremost, as the standard of all excellence, the qualities of the Great Jehovah, that we may know good from evil, truth from falsity, and see where we stand, and, the Way of Life.

In all this we look above the bodies of men and their acts, to the souls and their intentions : we look, by correspondences, through the things of this world and their history, to the thoughts and feelings, the elements and actions of the mind and their history ; and thence, down to our outward duties ; so that all Sacred Scripture becomes profitable for doctrine, reproof, correction and instruction in righteousness.

But most men have been so long looking down to matter and natural things, instead of up to mind and spiritual things, that they do not know themselves. The soul of man is the great enigma of the age. Of its substance, quality, life, and destiny, the natural man has no rational thought. But an intense and growing anxiety is being felt on the subject, and will continue to increase until the problem is solved. The only key to its solution, for men in this world, is the science of correspondences : and the only Light which presents it is the spiritual sense of the Word. And, when we find this light, it is the Lord coming to judgment. If we open our hearts to receive Him, He will show us what and where we are, and whither we are tending.

But in this feverish and sensual age concerning spiritual things, most inquirers, unfortunately, are not looking to the Word for a knowledge of the soul and its destiny; the darkness of the literal sense, without the spiritual, has turned them away from it. And thousands are exceedingly active in searching for light amid the selfish, unsettled opinions of frail, finite beings, through crude and contradictory manifestations, made to their natural senses; they relying upon their own sagacity to distinguish truth from falsity. But, when wayward humanity shall have fully run its wild and fruitless career after spiritual knowledge, amid the trash of human weakness and presumption, it will come to the Holy Word, in its spirit and life.

And that career must be short; for it is enveloped in mystery. And the present age of free thought, and progressive intelligence, cannot long be satisfied with darkness, while the very spirit which moves man demands a reason for everything it is asked to believe. And this demand extends throughout every department of science and knowledge.

Religion, therefore, is called up, before the chair of universal Intelligence, to answer for her faith and doings. And, even the Holy Word itself, is brought upon the stand to give testimony to the intelligibleness of its teachings. And according to the answers they give, before this tribunal, they stand or fall in the public estimation. It is only as they give clear and cogent reasons for every principle they teach, that they can live in generations which are to come.

And though most of the minds who are seeking spiritual knowledge are so natural that spiritual things are not readily seen, yet, mystery is ceasing to satisfy them;

and they are demanding a reason, suited to their natural judgment. And, as doubts and darkness rest upon all their experiments, as well as upon the meaning of the Word, therefore, universal skepticism stares them in the face.

All this but increases the anxiety for a rational view of the nature and laws of man's spiritual being; and many minds are becoming ripe for the reception of anything that will give them the desired light. The Word, in the letter—as well as everything else—has failed to do it for them. And strong and honest minds are eager for wisdom. They feel themselves afloat upon the ocean of uncertainty, without a pilot. Left to wander in the mazes of helpless unbelief:—a mental world without a God! A universe without a sun!

But this is the very preparation of mind necessary for the reception of true light. Let all such come, by the science of correspondences, to the Holy Word, for its spiritual light, and the demands of their reason and their heart will be satisfied. Let us, then, ever approach it, with a prayerful desire to be taught of the Lord.

And first, in order to establish well in our mind the complete distinction between spiritual and natural substances, or between mind and matter, and their correspondences, we will commence with ourselves. We will look into our own spiritual or mental world, and see what we are, besides the material body, and what the correspondence is between our material and mental beings, and how far, and for what purpose, matter belongs to us. For we must look into our own minds to understand the Word; and the organs of the body are often brought up to illustrate things of the soul. And, as we learn to see the value of the soul above that of the body, we shall fix a similar value to the spiritual history of the Word above that of the letter.

Now, strictly speaking, we are substantial spiritual beings, not material. We have each an organized spiritual body, of full human form, filling every part of the material body, and which was created and formed with it, and within it. This spiritual body is composed of spiritual and eternal substances and is, therefore, indestructible; while the material body is subjected to the constant changes common to all matter; never remaining the same body even from one day to another; but is constantly being worn out, and wasted by time and action, and supplied with food, until it is finally put off by age, sickness, or violence; leaving the spiritual body complete and unharmed by what we call death.

Thus Paul says, "There *is* a natural body and there IS a spiritual body;" not that there *will* be a spiritual body made of the natural. He definitely teaches that we have them both, while we live in the world, when he says, "For we know that if our *earthly* house of this tabernacle were dissolved, we *have* a building of God, an house not made with hands eternal in the heavens." Here we learn that we have, not only an earthly house or material body made with hands, or fed with hands from infancy, and which will dissolve, but also a building of God, or spiritual body, not made with hands, but by the Lord; and that, at the dissolution of the earthly house, we shall retain the spiritual body and have it forever. In confirmation of this, Paul says, again, "We, that are in this tabernacle do groan, being burdened; not for that we would be unclothed." Here he considers the material body mere clothing. But Paul has been much misunderstood. When he says, "We shall all be changed, in the twinkling of an eye," he does not mean, by " *We*," the natural bodies, but the souls that dwell in them ; and that these souls will be changed, only, to a higher mode of existence, at the putting off of the material body. For the word " *We*," when he says " *We* shall all be changed," means precisely what it does when he says, " *We* that are in this tabernacle do groan, being burdened."

And, that men go into the spiritual world, at the death of the body, with the spiritual bodies, we know by the appearance of the angel whom John on Patmos was going to worship, but who said, " See thou do it not, for I am of thy brethren the prophets ; " and by the appearance of Moses and Elias, at the transfiguration of the Lord, whom Peter, James, and John, saw and talked with. They had left their material bodies in this world ; and yet, they were men, with bodies.

Now, the separation of the spiritual body from the natural, at death, is " *The resurrection from the dead.*" Therefore, Paul says, " But some man will say, How are the dead raised up ? and with what body do they come ? Thou fool, that which thou sowest is not quickened except it die : and that which thou sowest, thou sowest not that body that shall be." Thus, as the green blade in its life comes up from the wheat that is sown, leaving the kernel to " return to the dust as it was," so the living, spiritual body rises from the material body ; leaving the latter to decompose. True, Paul says, " This corruptible must put on incorruption, and this mortal must put on immortality ; " but when he says, " put on," he does not mean " changed into ; " for he expressly says that " flesh and blood cannot inherit the kingdom of God ; neither doth corruption inherit incorruption." He simply means by that, we put off the corruptible and mortal, and live in

⹃ne incorruptible and immortal. And the Lord teaches the same resurrection, in Mark, when He says, "And as touching the dead, that they rise : have ye not read in the book of Moses, how in the bush God spake unto him, saying, I am the God of Abraham, and the God of Isaac, and the God of Jacob? He is not the God of the dead, but the God of the living." Thus teaching that their resurrection had already taken place.

Here we see that the soul or the spiritual body, with the life, is the man. The material body is merely its representative ; and there is a perfect correspondence between the natural body and the spiritual body ; the same as there is between the literal and the spiritual senses of the Word. And though these material bodies are not our real selves, but only the clothing we wear in this world, yet we cannot, here, approach one another sensibly except through the medium of this clothing. So we cannot approach the spiritual light of the Word, with our spiritual being, except through the medium of our natural senses, by reading or hearing the literal sense of the Word, which is the body of the spiritual sense, and which, by correspondence, enables us to understand it.

It is true the literal sense of the Word has life ; but it is of, and from, the spiritual sense. So the material body of a man has life, but it is of, and from, the spiritual body, which receives it from the Lord. Thus we feel one another's hands, when we clasp them ; but the life and sensation are all in, and from, the spiritual hands which infill them. It is not the natural eye which sees, nor the natural ear that hears. They are mere instruments by which the soul has communion with the material world. And so with all the organs of the body.

God and men, then, are spiritual beings, of spiritual

4*

substance; all their thoughts and feelings belong to the spiritual world. Consequently, God's Word is a spiritual book, coming from a spiritual Fountain. It treats of spiritual things; of the Great Jehovah, and of angels, and men's souls; of heaven and hell, of good spirits and bad ones. None of these things are material. And yet, they are mentioned as being substance with form: God, angels, and spirits, having heads and bodies, with all their organs. And the natural man might suppose they referred to material things, when it is the soul's welfare that God especially regards, and every word He speaks is to souls, and for their benefit. True, He is not unmindful of men's bodies, and He abundantly provides for them. But it is all for the sake of the soul.

And the bodies of men, and natural things, are always made use of, in the Word, to teach us the states and conditions of our souls. Therefore, when the Word speaks of man's being sick or diseased; naked or clothed; hungry or thirsty; lame or halt; deaf or dumb; blind or seeing; dead or alive; circumcised or baptized; or in any other condition, we must look, by correspondence, to the state of the soul; for that is the essential teaching. The language may refer to the condition of the body also, or it may not. Every miracle, lesson, and act of the Lord, when in the flesh, toward the sick and afflicted, had, besides the effect on their bodies, an effect also on their minds, inspiring them with faith and trust in the Lord, and with a yielding up to His Will; and He often told them their faith saved them. Not that they were healed, simply, because they thought they should be, but because they yielded themselves entirely up to the current of the Divine Life, and were ready to act with the Divine Impulse, which gave a new influx, and healthy action to the physical system, and crowded off the disease by a universal law : for the life of the natural body is through the spiritual body. The personal sphere of the Lord was very strong, and it often had a powerful influence upon those who humbly gave themselves up to it and acted with it. But all these cures were effected, because there was a correspondence between the state of the soul and that of the body ; and the soul was first moved. True, persons were sometimes healed when the Lord was not personally present, as in the case of the centurion's servant, but he knew his master had gone for the Lord, and the Omnipresent God could, nevertheless, reach him ; he being in a state to receive His Spirit. And all these lessons are instructions to us for the healing of our spiritual diseases, by His spiritual coming.

Now, because the natural body is not the man, but only the tabernacle of clay in which he lives ; and because it has no senses of its own, but only the senses of the spiritual body, which act through it, therefore, men are often spoken of, in the Word, as being lame, sick, halt, blind, deaf, dumb, dead, buried, asleep, or in darkness, when their natural bodies are not so. It is the soul, in such cases, that is diseased ; it is the organs of the spiritual body that are out of order. Man is lame in his spiritual walk, sick with sin, halt in his duty, blind to the truth, deaf to the commandments, dumb in prayer, dead in trespasses, buried in depravity, asleep as to his religion, and in the darkness of error. So he is mentioned as hungering and thirsting when his body has enough to eat and drink.

And if our hand or foot offend, we are commanded to cut it off ; and, if the eye offend, to pluck it out, because it is better to enter into life halt or maimed, or with one eye, rather than having two hands, feet, or eyes, to be cast

into hell. This, in the letter alone, is very strange teaching. Who, without correspondences, regards it, or knows
what it means ? Is he who loses an eye of the material
body to have but one eye to his spiritual body ? By such
reasoning, the destitution of the natural body would
destroy the soul also, and that would be the end of us.
The hand or arm, always, in the Word, denotes power.
Hence it is written, " His right hand and His holy arm
hath gotten Him the victory." Thy " hand shall lift me
up." " O God lift up thine hand."

For our hand to offend is to use the power which God
gives us in violating His laws, thus making it a wicked
hand or power. To cut it off, is to cease to use the vile
hand ; to cast it from us is to resist the propensity to do
wrong, till we lose the desire. The foot, from its position, in the dust, denotes the lowest and most external
principle of the mind. For the foot to offend is to indulge
in low external acts of vice. To cut the vile foot off is to
give up the evil indulgence ; to cast it from us is to resist
the temptation, in the Spirit of the Lord, till we loathe
the evil. Hence the Lord washed the disciples' feet to
teach them to help one another to keep the natural man
clean. And He said to Peter, " He that is washed need-
eth not save to wash his feet, but is clean every whit.'
Thus showing that corruptions enter through the sinful
acts of the external man. And that, when once clean,
there was no danger, if they kept the feet or external man
clean, or guarded well the grovelling avenues to sin.

The eye denotes the understanding. For the eye to
offend is to practise deception, and embrace falsities as
truths. To pluck this false eye out is to cease to deceive,
and to stop trying to reason from fallacies. To cast it
from us is to resist every false thought, and seek for light

from the Word, and declare it till we love the truth and hate the lie.

And, as to its being better to enter into life halt or maimed, or with one eye, rather than having two hands, feet, or eyes, to be cast into hell fire ; this means that it is better to be good and happy here, and hereafter, in simple truth and virtue, though we cannot know everything and have all power, rather than, by being wise in our own eyes, esteeming ourselves great and worthy of great dominion, while we still remain in the love of self, to thus cast ourselves into the fires of envy, jealousy, and malice, and all their attendant miseries.

The selfish man would think himself spiritually maimed, if his overbearing powers were curtailed. He would think himself halt, if his feet were restrained from their wonted paths of vice. He would think himself half blind, if not allowed to reason falsely and deceive his neighbors. And the Lord teaches him, by this scripture, that it is better to try to become good and happy, in what he imagines would be a cramped and mutilated condition, rather than be miserable in the full possession and indulgence of all his selfish powers and wants.

Besides, we may see that we cannot enter heaven with two eyes, or rather, two opposing understandings, one dealing in falsities and the other in truths ; we cannot go there double-minded, serving two masters ; we must have an eye single to the Lord or the Truth. Nor can we go there with two hands, or opposing powers of mind, one exercised in things evil, and the other in things good. Nor with two feet, or opposing external principles, one practising virtues and the other indulging in vices. We can go there only in singleness of heart, mind, and action ; led and governed by the Lord.

Thus we may see that the science of correspondences is the key to our own spiritual being, and to the spiritual sense of the Word, which shows us what we really are, and for what we are designed. And the pursuance of the investigation will show us the wonderful relation we bear to all the Divine teachings, and their peculiar applicability to the human race under all circumstances. "Great are Thy tender mercies, O Lord: quicken me according to Thy judgments." "Behold, Thou desirest truth in the inward parts: and in the hidden part Thou shalt make me to know wisdom."

CHAPTER VIII.

As Man is a recipient of life from the Lord, and that life is substantial Goodness and Truth, received into the will and understanding, giving quality and character to his feelings and thoughts, we may readily see that, before the " fall," while that will and understanding were un-adulterated, and man affectionately and rationally re-ceived the Divine Elements, he would heartily respond to every new impulse and direction which his opening in-tellect and growing desires received from the stream of life, which was ever meeting all his progressive, intellec-tual wants. For, though he had the elements of a self-hood given him as his own, consisting of *freedom, ra-tionality* and *desire for knowledge*, whereby he could be elevated above the beasts, be connected with his God, and progress forever ; yet, as he had not abused that self-hood, it, of course, would act in perfect unison with the Divine Love and Wisdom ; and therefore, as far as his faculties were developed, he would see things in the true light, and act with the Lord. In this primeval condition, while seeing and feeling from the Lord's Wisdom and Love, man would act in the divine current, and do everything he did, almost as intuitively as the bird builds its nest. But still, in consequence of his self-hood, it would seem to him as though his life were his own, and from himself, and that he acted entirely from his own powers. And thus it seems to all men.

But after man had depraved his will and understanding, and thence had perverted the stream of life, by turning it into selfish and disorderly channels, and sending it out to deceive and rob his neighbors, instead of to bless them, his ability to see correctly, by intuition, was gone, and he was without any Divine Guide. He could now see, feel, and act only from his own selfish states. Nor can we see how it is possible, under such circumstances, for the Lord to change those states for the better, or arrest man's downward progress, without giving him a written Revelation, or outward Law, for the direction and government of his feelings, thoughts, and actions. For, though man still had power to act, from the stream of life given him, through his internal mind, though that stream was perverted; yet he now needed a Divine Law for the external mind, as a rule of action, in which were also the elements of life; a law which the external understanding could see to be right, and which offered to the mind new powers and influences, as well as new duties; and which explained to him the true principles of the life which he had perverted; a law which would teach him how to repent and return to true order; a law wherein man could meet the Divine Sphere of the commandments as a ground of reaction, whereby his corrupt affections and thoughts could be seen, weighed, and examined by the light of truth; and thus he be placed in a position of equilibrium, in which, if he pleased, he could take hold of the offered power of the Law, and resist his evil and false inclinations, and return to true order, life, and happiness. For, unless man's external mind could meet elements of life in goods and truths from without, the internal forces would drive him along blindly in the perverted current of life from within, without his having either powers of reasoning or of choice; leaving him a mere machine.

True, there is life from without, filling the universe. Its effects would meet his senses in all the things of nature. And between the influences from within, and those from without, he could freely think and act. And when the things of nature were not before his senses, he could use the knowledge he had of them in his memory, as a ground of mental action. But as nature would present to him such a confused picture, and as his fallen nature would incline his heart to the evils and temptations which he there saw, he would be sure to run wild without a Divine Law. But when the truths of the Word are given man in a written Law, he has both the sphere of nature and of the Word as a basis of action, and he is then free to do right or wrong. For whatever may be the character of any religious impressions he may have from within, he can now reason and decide upon them either from the truths of the Word, or from the things of the memory or of nature.

Moreover, whenever, in the present state of mankind, sudden impressions are made upon our mind, we cannot always tell whether they are made from within or from without, whether by the means of the Holy Spirit or of angels, or evil spirits. But no impressions concerning the doctrines or duties of life, the character of God and His Word, or the destiny of man, should be sanctioned, unless they stand the test of the Holy Word. For that Word is the only safe interpreter of the character of all spiritual influences or impressions.

We have, therefore, rational grounds for concluding that the means which the Lord makes use of, through the written Word, for man's salvation, are absolutely necessary, and that men can be reached and saved only by those means. Indeed, it looks like an axiom, that what Infinite Wisdom does, is infinitely right and necessary, and that, therefore, no other course would be right or successful.

From these premises we may see the reason why, since the "fall," the Merciful Father has always had a written Law for the good of mankind: and just to the extent that *that* Law has been respected and obeyed, the people have been civil, orderly, and virtuous. The reason is, they have had in this Law a Divine and powerful plane of spiritual force for their internally received elements of life to act against, and be directed by, so as to give the freedom of man the power of choice, and without which those elements must have gone out from fallen man in wild disorder. For, having flowed into a perverted and depraved sphere, they must go out with the character of that sphere, the same as pure light, flowing through a discolored lens, carries along the color, and is also changed in its course and influence. And as God is dealing with free and rational beings, and works by means, we see not how any powers from within can ever change fallen man without the written Law. Are we cited to wonderful instances of influence of the Spirit upon men, and to the *still small voice:* it must be remembered that those men all had some knowledge of the Divine Law; some education of what was right and what was wrong, as a ground of reaction, whereby the Spirit could return upon the con-science and perform its work of repentance upon a free mind. Are we told that the Spirit sometimes moves, to some extent, the heathen heart which has never known the Divine Law? There are no tribes of men, however low, that have not, by tradition, some knowledge of what is right and just—some rule founded, to some extent, on the Divine Law, and which has, at some time, been given by God, in language, for the guidance of men. We can come to no other rational conclusion from the facts before us.

Now, because the revealed Word is necessary to all success in virtue and true knowledge, we may see the reason of the entire failure of all the various experiments of men, for the elevation of society by their efforts to gain a knowledge of spiritual things, and to build up a religion from internal influences, and loose impressions and suggestions of principles more in agreement with their own depraved desires, and which they consider superior to, and at variance with, the Bible. They therefore lay the Sacred Scriptures aside as erroneous. Thus they aim a blow at the very root of all that is virtuous and heavenly in families and societies; the bitter rewards of which many are reaping; while some are beginning to see that their only hope of purity and peace is a faithful return to the Holy Word, and its saving influences; seeing that man can have no other standard than this, to show him what is true or false, right or wrong; no other ground to judge of the character and source of his spiritual influences or internal impressions.

Some have thought that the works of God, in nature, can teach these things. But as fallen man cannot draw true ideas of the nature and character of God and His laws from internal feelings and influences alone, so neither can he do it with the aid of the works of God. He may examine the things of nature, and also the human family on earth, as closely as he pleases, but he can draw from them no true ideas of God, nor of His qualities, nor of man's origin and destiny, without the revealed Word. No matter how strong the man's intellect, nor how active and powerful his reasoning faculties, nor how extensive his other education, if he is ignorant of the Sacred Scriptures, he can draw from the world and its inhabitants none but blind and erroneous ideas of the Being who brought them into existence. What, he asks, mean the tempests and convulsions, the blights and mildews of nature; the raving madness of her animals and wild beasts, the poisonous venom of her reptiles, and the deceit, murder, and vengeance of her people? Is this the work of an Infinitely Wise and Good Being? Thus he reasons, until he gives up all thought of a Divine Being, and rests entirely on nature, as the all in all.

Thus nothing short of a revealed written Word can give fallen man any ideas of God; and that must reveal to us His true qualities, or we shall still be in darkness. What, but a perfect blank, does the idea of life amount to, if we do not know that it is love and real substance? How long the learned have puzzled themselves over the idea of life, and left the subject as dark as they found it for the want of knowing that it *was something!* But when we think of it as Love, we have something tangible in our mind; something that we can *feel* to be true.

In these reflections, we may be assured that we can see nothing in its true light, unless our thought reaches back to God and rests on First Principles. Without the great truth that Love and Wisdom are substance, centered in God and flowing into man, enabling him to feel, think, and act, men have supposed that thought and feeling originate in the brain of the material body. And seeing not that life is received substance, all has been dark. And when they look at nature, and behold her teeming with life in many varieties, having no idea of the origin, substance, and quality of that life, the same darkness hangs over nature. And when, by the aid of natural science, they geologically search nature for the first manifestations of this life, and find it in the mineral kingdom, in the most feeble expressions of effort to produce vegetables, it seems to act entirely from the rock as its author. They next see it in higher and stronger forms in the vegetables, still stronger in the animals, and highest and strongest of all in man. But the higher things seem dependent upon the lower for life and existence, and all upon the cold mineral. Thus nature appears as everything —the mother of all. But all is total darkness. They see not how lower things can produce the higher; the cold, dead mineral giving forth the beautiful vegetable, with delicate texture and velvet flowers; and the inanimate vegetable giving forth the living creatures with their five senses of animal life; and man above all with his sublime powers of mind resting upon these inferior things for origin and sustenance. Alas! what darkness! But this is the best that nature alone can do. Without a revealed Word from God, man could know nothing higher than matter. But with the Holy Word before him, man can turn his thoughts from nature up to nature's God, and by a right knowledge of Him, in the substance and qualities of the Trine, a flood of light pours into his mind. He sees the stream of Love, Wisdom, and Power from his God flowing down through higher things into lower, until it reaches the mineral kingdom as a basis of reaction, and returning, produces the successive orders of creation, till it is given back to God in the true love, wisdom, and power of human souls. This Trine of Principles is the key of knowledge. All knowledge is of and from God. It is He that breaks the seals and opens the Book; and all by this key to a knowledge of His own qualities. From these qualities we are to judge of the qualities of everything, seeing them more feebly or more fully expressed in some things than in others; and either in direct or in inverted order.

Thus we have, in the revealed Word, the elements of spiritual life; and from that Word they must be applied to our souls. And as they are principles of truth and goodness for the understandings and wills of men, therefore they must be understood and loved in order to belong to the mind. Thus they are principles that men can offer, one to another, through their thoughts, feelings, words, and actions. But we do not lose a truth if another receives it from us and lives it. It is an endless principle. It may be in thousands of minds at the same time, uniting them all together and to the Lord, if they love it. The reason why the order of the reception of goods and truth from the Word is through higher minds into lower, may be readily seen from the fact that no mind can know a truth until he is taught it, nor can it be his till he loves it, nor can he love it till he has practised it. And he cannot be taught it without a teacher. Those who have the truth must teach it to those who have it not. And when we reflect upon the fact that these Divine Elements are for the nourishment and growth of the souls of men, we are ready to ask ourselves, how mind can grow without something for the understanding to receive, and the will to embrace—something to supply the inquiring wants of the reasoning faculties and the desires of the heart?

and also what has made the mind of the man greater than
that of the infant, unless it be what he has received; and
what has made the difference between the good man and
the bad one, except the goodness and truth with which
one has been fed, and the evils and falsities which have
fed the other? And seeing clearly this plain law of mental growth by means of the revealed Word, the argument
for the necessity of the Word comes home with great
force, particularly when we consider the fact that these
goods and truths, or elements of life, in order to be rationally received and affectionately embraced so as to expand
the intellect and nourish the heart, have to be given us in
laws or rules of action, which the mind can understand,
see the use of, and must practise, before it can really
know their value, love them, and appropriate them to the
soul. Thus God gives His goodness and truth for our souls
in commandments and rules, for the government of our
feelings, thoughts, and actions. These Words, he says,
are spirit and life; and that if we would enter into life,
we must keep the commandments. And we enter into
life, or become living, when the life of the commandments
enters into us.

Now, when men see that they were made to act, and
that the goods and truths of the Word are rules of
action, as well as elements of life, and cannot be appropriated to the mind but by practising them, and that God
is the Fountain of Truth, they will then see that man
never could have had them without being taught them
from God in language. Hence the absolute necessity of
the written Word. It was, therefore, generally spoken
in an audible voice, in the ears of most of the prophets,
and heard and recorded by them verbatim, as given by
the Lord. Thus they say many times over, "the Word

of the Lord came unto me, saying." So the voice of the Lord was heard by Adam in the garden. True, some of the prophets, and more especially Ezekiel and John, saw some future events in visions. This is because the thoughts of the Lord, who knows all things, can so flow into a human mind that is humble, confiding, and open to receive them, as to show that mind, for the time being, future things, when God desires it. Thus John saw and recorded the things mentioned in the Apocalypse, and Ezekiel saw a certain state of the "House of Israel," or Jewish Church, in his vision of dry bones. (Ezek. xxxvii, 1–14.)

Before the "fall," God taught men from His Book of Nature, by the Law of Analogy. Therein was a Divine Speech, a living language, as will be shown in the following chapters. And God therein taught man, intuitively, the great principles and laws of life ; or man, by the Divine Truth, saw them in their true light. But, during the long process of the fall, man, by his depravity, lost the ability to read the laws of life in the Book of Nature. Indeed, Nature herself became changed, and had apparently a confused and uncertain speech; the Divine Law of Analogy became above man's reach; his spirituality was gone; and God gave him, through Moses, the written Law in man's own language, containing natural goodness and truth, suited to man's state, but filled also with spiritual goodness and truth to be seen by analogy. And since then, no people on the earth have been without some truths, however dim, drawn from this written Law, and handed down through all time. For no fallen soul can exist without something from the Lord, as a rule of action, that would either elevate it or check its evils, if it would regard it; and which it is free to do or not; and the Lord, from His very qualities, must come to all men with blessings adapted to their states; so that those of very little light, who regard it, will be better off in the next life than those of much light, who disregard it.

The laws of true life were given, in the commandments, on Mount Sinai; and were spread out and adapted to men's various states throughout the Word. They contain truths spiritual, and truths natural, and even celestial. They are adapted to the whole mind, internal and external, suited to men and angels, to earth and heaven, and even to hell. They reach men in every state and condition of existence. Without them, no thought of mental being, no thought of a rational soul, no thought of a future life, no thought of anything higher than matter, could have ever again entered even the imagination of man, after he had fallen into mere naturalism. And though man is the Lord's rational, intelligent being, made to know His God, and to love Him, and exist forever— made to learn and rationally to understand spiritual things; yet these things, nothing short of the Most High God could teach. And the instruction had to be given to man, in signs of ideas that he could understand. It, therefore, had to be given in a written language, common to the race; a language more than internally spoken to his consciousness; it had to be addressed to his outward senses, in audible phrases, which he could speak and hear spoken, understand, and obey.

And this Truth of the written Word has now become the common medium of spiritual instruction and life to mankind. And all persons, either in this world or the other, who teach truths concerning the nature of God or of man, of regeneration or degeneration, of heaven or of hell, must obtain those truths, either directly or by tradition, from this Holy Word.

5

Herein God has given His Divine Truths a practical form, in words suited to all the various states and conditions of men, angels, and spirits, from the highest to the lowest. These truths are expressed in the best possible form, because given by the Lord Himself. This Holy Word, therefore, is *The Mediator* between the otherwise unapproachable Jehovah and man. Even in the personal presence of Jesus Christ, or God manifest, this Holy Word was the Great Mediator. He spoke through it, breathed forth its Holy Spirit, and wrought miracles by its power. God Himself lives in it, and by its Wisdom He created the universe; and it is now spirit and life to all the universe of things. And, therefore, no man, angel, or spirit, either in the flesh or out of it, is a reliable teacher of Divine Truth, who does not teach it from this Divine Revelation.

This is a fact, important to be known and regarded, at the present day, that men may not look, for spiritual wisdom, to broken cisterns that hold no water; that the traditions of men may not, in the coming age of spiritual commotion, make the commandments of God of none effect. For the written Word is the Great Rock of Ages, and no new things can ever supplant, or overreach, the Eternal Wisdom of the Great Jehovah, revealed to man for his spiritual life both here and hereafter.

Let us, then, come to it like little children to their father's table, for it is Divine food for human souls. Therefore Jeremiah saith to the Lord, " Thy Words were found, and I did eat them; and Thy Word was unto me the joy and rejoicing of my heart; for I am called by Thy name, O Lord God of hosts." (Jer. xv, 16.) And David says, " The Words of the Lord are pure Words; as silver tried in a furnace of earth, purified seven times."

CHAPTER IX.

WE are told, in the Holy Word, that God is angry, and that He is Love; that He is wrathful, and kind; revengeful, and merciful; provokable, and unchangeable; that He repents, and repents not; that He loved Jacob, and hated Esau, and that He is *no respecter of persons;* but maketh His sun to rise on the evil and on the good, and sendeth His rain upon the just and the unjust; that He curses people, and punishes them; and that He is kind unto the unthankful and the evil, and that His tender mercies are over all His works; that He forms the light, and creates darkness; makes peace, and creates evil. He says, "Is there evil in the city, and I have not done it?" thus plainly indicating that He does all the evil in the city. And to complete the apparently decided fatality of all things, the foreknowledge of God has been understood by some to pre-order and fix fast everything that occurs, whether of thought, feeling, or action; and to sustain this view, we are often cited to the Epistle to the Romans: "Whom He did foreknow, He also did predestinate." . . . "Whom He did predestinate, them He also called: and whom He called, them He also justified : and whom He justified, them He also glorified." "Therefore hath He mercy on whom He will have mercy ; and whom He will He hardeneth ;" that He "maketh one vessel to honor and another to dishonor."

Men have two ways of receiving ideas—by appearances, and by realities. And a glance at the Key of First Principles, will very soon decide which of the above characters of God must be the real, and which the apparent. And as the Principles which constitute this Key are Eternal Axioms, which all Christians must admit, they would throw much light upon all the doctrines of the Word, by distinguishing between the apparent and the real, if men would receive and use them. For there is a common consent and agreement, among all Christians, to the truth of the first general view of the doctrines of the Scriptures, which teaches that there is an Infinite and Eternal Being who created all things ; that the Bible is His revealed Word ; that in Him is a Trinity, called Father, Son, and Holy Spirit ; that He made all things good ; that man fell into depravity, and imparted his sinful nature to his offspring ; that, to save the fallen world, God was manifest in the flesh, and thereby opened up a way of salvation ; that, in order to be saved, man must be regenerated by the Spirit of God ; that, after death, we rise and go into the spiritual world, and there are judged, and are happy if regenerated, and unhappy if unregenerated. These great leading doctrines God, in His Holy Word, simply and clearly teaches : and, as here stated, they are indisputably true to the very letter, and the Christian world generally acknowledge them as here expressed. And yet those very people are divided into hundreds of different sects, and are at great variance upon the character and quality of these doctrines. They know them alike by outward terms, but not by essential principles. Thus they disagree as to what each doctrine is in itself, and are wavering in mystery, between the *apparent* and the *real*. But, by the Key of First Principles, as expressed in Chapter I, light may be thrown upon all the doctrines, the apparent may be distinguished from the real, and all may be brought together in harmony, and the watchmen see eye to eye.

Now, all things have their appearances and their realities. There is truth as it appears, and truth as it is; the literal sense of the Word as it appears, and that sense as it is; nature as it appears, and nature as it is; God as He appears, in His Word and works, and God as He is. And even the appearances are various, depending altogether upon the states of the observers.

Nature and its laws do not appear to the scholar as they do to the savage. The same forms of things fall upon the eyes of both, but they suggest very different ideas. The savage sees them only by the light of the sun; the scholar has the additional light of science. All persons, at first, look at nature as it appears. But, as their minds are educated, they lose thought of the appearance and see things more as they are, rising, as they progress, from the surface view to scientific laws.

And as with God's works, so with His Word; here too is the apparent and the real. When wicked men first turn their thoughts seriously toward moral and religious things, they see in the Word only the low appearances of God's character. Each man sees Him according to his state; the angry man as angry; the froward, as froward; the upright man as upright; the pure in heart, as pure. Thus He seems to come, " all things to all men."

Now it is much better that man should believe the apparently hard things that are written of God than not believe anything. When Galileo presented the solar system to men, the world, as to astronomy, was in the shade of appearance, believing that the sun daily revolved around the earth. But this was much better than no thought on the subject. It was far above what any animal could think. And though only an appearance, yet it was truth to those who could see no higher. And, as such minds are developed by science, they will see through the appearance to the reality. And so of spiritual things. We must first have them by appearances. Men are of all qualities, from infernal to heavenly. And God's Holy Word, in its Infinity, is adapted to all, from the highest to the lowest. In it, God comes to men with a disposition and passions apparently like their own; and of every shade of character, from the most furious and wrathful to the most gentle and merciful. And without so coming He could not reach all minds. For the elements of one mind cannot flow into another by outward instructions, without a medium or language for ideas adapted to their states. That medium, for the lowest and most vile people, is the "terror of the Law" in the literal and apparent sense.

Now it is much better that the Lord should appear to a very wicked, perverse, and ignorant people as an almighty, wrathful, vengeance-taking God, than as all-merciful and forgiving. For, as they are taught from infancy to fear this terrible Being, this character has a powerful influence over their conduct, in restraining them from vice. Such an apparent idea of God can reach and influence them when a real one could not be seen, and would not be feared if it could be seen. And all the scripture which so represents God is mercifully given for the use and benefit of all such barbarous and cruel minds. The world has had its ages of such benighted ignorance and tyranny. And it has its nations now, to whom such teachings are a blessing.

And, in the ages of great sin and ignorance, even a lake of fire and brimstone, apparently prepared by the Lord to torment wicked souls in forever, has been a blessing, just so far as it has restrained from sin, held evils in check, and caused men to keep the commandments. And with a people in a state of blind superstition, and fear of an awful unknown Power, this dreadful doctrine would have that influence, when nothing else would do it. And now, when we see the real, spiritual truth of this doctrine, and find that that burning lake is no fiction, but a dreadful reality, coming not from God, but from the transgression of His laws, and located in our own souls, if we are evil, and that it will torment us with the fires of hatred, revenge, jealousy, and ill will forever, unless removed by repentance and a good life; I say, when we see this, the same Holy Scripture may bless us also, and save our souls.

Thus we see that the Infinite Word of God is suited to all ages of the world and to all peoples : not only to the patriarchs, the Israelites, and the first Christians, but also to those of the New Jerusalem, the glorious light of which is now dawning upon the world; and if we apply it to our hearts and lives, it will lead our souls into the paradise of God.

But, it is asked, Is not this using deception, by making God to appear what He is not ? When those scriptures are properly considered, there will be seen nothing false in their expressions. It is not a falsity that the sun appears to revolve round the earth, or the grass to look green, or the snow white. These things are truths to a mind that can look no higher, though science speaks further to others. Every man must judge of things according to his state. All men must think and judge of God, not as He is, in His Infinity, but as He manifests Himself to them in His Word.

The bad man, therefore, sees God in the apparent truth of His Word as acting against thieves, murderers, and robbers, for breaking His Law, just as he himself would act against them if they had trespassed against him. He looks upon the Law as just. And when circumstances bring him under the influence of God's Spirit, he is afraid to break the Law. And upon this ground he can commence the work of repentance and regeneration, when otherwise he could not be reached.

And when it is seen that all the power in man to do either right or wrong is not man's power, but God's, constantly given him, and that man is free to use it, either for good or for evil, the apparent truth is that God hardens men's hearts, and blinds their eyes, and creates their evils, and torments them, and sends them to hell, because it is done through God's power. In this apparent light it is that God, in order to reach the low states of the wicked, is said in Scripture to do these things: whereas the reality is that men, by the abuse of God's power and their own freedom, run into vice and iniquity. Thus, by sin, they harden their own hearts, blind their own eyes, create their own evils, torment themselves, and send themselves to hell, when they have full power and privilege given them to take the other course. Indeed, the human heart is not unconscious of its freedom and responsibility to the truth.

And as to the foreknowledge of God, binding the destinies of men to an unalterable course of life, this is also apparent. God, being Infinite in Wisdom, must know all things at once. Foreknowledge with Him, therefore, must be the same as afterknowledge, and thus does not interfere with the freedom of man. It would be absurd to suppose that the knowledge we of this age have of the American Revolution was the means of its success, or was in any way connected with it. But it has just as much to do with it as our foreknowledge would have with the laying of the Atlantic cable, it we could see that it would be successfully done in two years. Simple knowledge of events, whether present, past, or future, does not necessarily affect the events at all.

God made man free, and therefore His knowledge of his acts cannot affect or destroy that freedom. For, though He knew that a man would sin, yet He also knew that he could do better, or else His commandments are not binding. And the declaration, " Whom He did foreknow He also did predestinate," does not at all affect the matter, or reach man's freedom. For predestination is only the decision of a general law, showing that certain effects must follow certain causes ; that misery must follow the transgression of the laws of either moral or physical life, and happiness must be the result of obedience, so that the predestination rests entirely upon the life lived. The freedom of man, therefore, is the grand pivot upon which he turns either to the right hand or to the left, and thus he determines his own destiny.

Now, there are everywhere, throughout the entire Word and works of God, two scenes, the apparent and the real. The Lord's written language always paints two scenes, or one scene with two sides—an inside and an outside. It is declared in Scripture that the Word is

5*

"written within and on the back side." Now, we cannot
see the beauty of the outside scene, unless it be made
transparent by the light which shines upon the inside ;
giving us, at the same time, a view of the inside picture
in and through the outside one, by analogy. The outside
picture or literal sense is seen as a lower light, like moon-
light compared with the real light. This lower light
gives many simple and plain commandments, and teaches
many important duties ; and it directs the soul to higher
things.

This is all the light man can at first bear from the
Holy Word. But, in man's fallen state, this light cannot
bring out the clear, distinct features and qualities of even
the outside picture, so as to show its true designs, and its
full symmetry and beauty. Indeed, as we examine it
closely in that light only, we perceive much irregularity
and confusion, and are left in much uncertainty as to
what the picture, as a whole, is intended to represent.
But when, by analogy, the inner light shines through it,
it infills and blends with the lower light, and the two
scenes become one. The inside scene, with its real light,
now fills up and supplies all the apparent deficiencies of
the outside one. All the dark places, deformities, strange
objects, and mysterious characters, which were scattered
more or less throughout the whole view, are now brought
out in new light, and in great perfection and beauty.

This Divine picture, as seen upon the inside, is a view
of spiritual things, or things of the mind ; but as seen
only upon the outside, without the spiritual light, it is a
view of natural things, as seen in the light of the literal
sense, which is often only apparent and contradictory.
Thus the Holy Word has its earth-side and its heaven-
side, or its apparent and its real ; just as man has his

earth-side or natural mind and body, and his heaven-side or spiritual mind and body. Therefore, when we look at the Word upon its earth-side only, and from the earth-side of our mind, we do not see the scene as it really is, but only as it appears to our selfish, external man. Consequently, many parts of it appear dark and indistinct; and some portions seem distorted and ugly, with things out of place and upside down. And thence we begin to doubt its being a scene drawn entirely by a Divine pencil, in the hand of an Infinite Artist.

But the difficulty is all in ourselves. The mental position or state in which we stand to view it, darkens and distorts our vision. The selfish and ignorant mental sphere which surrounds us, and through which we are looking, gives its own false coloring to the Divine Word.

But let our understandings be once open to the spiritual sense, so as to let in upon our natural mind, by analogy, the heavenly light of the Sun of Righteousness, and the fogs of our mental earth will soon disappear. And then even the earth-side of the Holy Word will be bright and beautiful.

Now, as before suggested, it is precisely so with God's Book of Nature, but on a lower plane of thought. The untutored savage, standing, as he believes, on the immovable, flat earth in the centre of creation, sees the lamps and torches of the heavens revolving around him in panoramic order; while a new and sublime scene passes before the learned, filling his soul with rational wonder and admiration. The first of these is a natural scene, viewed with the eyes of the body, in natural light. The second is a mental scene, viewed by the eye of the mind in the light of science. If, then, the two scenes in God's Book of Nature are so completely unlike in aspect, magnitude, and fact ; if the view becomes so vastly changed in beauty and grandeur, by the aid of only the light of natural science ; what must be the change of scenes in God's Book of Revelation, when we can look above and beyond all the clouds of appearances, and view it in the pure light of spiritual science—the science of the soul—the science of thoughts and feelings—the science of spiritual substance, of spiritual heat and light, of spiritual attraction and repulsion ; and, indeed, when we can have a rational conception and knowledge of the Science of Causes, and, to some extent, of God Himself, the Cause of all causes, and in the light of His Divine Wisdom can look down upon Nature, and see her, with all her apparent laws of gravitation, motion, heat, light, and production, to be but the mere blind and unconscious effect of the higher, the spiritual principles and laws, and as having existence, life, light, and action, only in and by the constant influx of these spiritual principles, as they flow from the Divine Fountain ?

To come into the blessed enjoyment of this Spiritual Light and Life is now the privilege of fallen humanity.

CHAPTER X.

In order to bring out the Spiritual Sense of the Word, by analogy, so that its principles may be rationally understood, and its importance appreciated, it will be necessary, first, to obtain clear ideas of the elements of that spiritual sense, and of the way those elements are to reach and affect the human mind. For, to look with facility for a mental thing that we have not got, we must have some idea of its qualities, and also of its application to us. Although these qualities have been frequently mentioned, yet they should be more specifically considered.

And we will open the subject by stating that the Spiritual Sense of the Word, which men now receive, is the Lord, at His second coming: that He comes as the elements of life, and that human minds are, therefore, the recipients.

But as the Word has a natural, as well as a spiritual sense, so also the human mind, which receives it, has a natural plane, and a spiritual plane, in each of which, there is a will and an understanding. These planes are called, in Scripture, the internal and the external, or the spiritual and the natural man, or mind. By the spiritual mind, we have communion with spiritual things; we think of God and heaven, virtue and holiness. By the natural mind, we have connection, through the body, with natural things, and think of the world, and its attractions. These two minds are often at variance; and we find ourselves halting between two opinions; one mind inviting us to sin, and the other prompting us to virtue. And when we enter our closet for self-examination, we often sit in judgment upon the thoughts, feelings, and actions of the natural man, and decide against them. Now this cannot be done by the same will and understanding that had been astray. For the same mind cannot be bad one moment and good the next.

Now, the external mind is first formed and developed through the means of the senses; it is natural and worldly; the internal mind is afterward formed by religious education and heavenly influences. The whole process of regeneration is a warfare between these two minds: the Spirit of Truth, and heavenly influences, sustaining the internal mind, and the temptations of the world, and evil influences, exciting the external mind.

These views of man's mind will introduce us to a true idea of the mind of the Lord, while in the flesh; and which we will illustrate by comparing the Infant in the manger with another infant: the first we will call Divine, and the second, human. The human infant had a natural father; the Divine had not. The human was a recipient of life; the Divine had self-existent Life, which was the Father. Not that God was limited, as to space. He was the Omnipresent Life of the universe. And yet there is nothing unreasonable, or contradictory to Divine Laws, in His thus assuming our nature. He, who is the Life of the universe, could certainly assume a human mind—the highest order of His creation. And there is no more mystery in it than in any other Divine act. It is just what might be expected from Infinite Mercy, if He could thereby better reach and influence our free minds.

This Divine Infant had, from Mary, besides the natural body, an external plane of the mind, with a will and understanding like those of any other infant. And though the self-existent Life of the Father within, was Almighty, and One with the universal Life—yet before the assumed mind and nature could become a medium of that life to man, they must be developed through the natural senses like those of any other infant. Thus the assumed natural body and mind grew up in the world, with a nature like ours, "tempted in all points like as we are." And when He spoke from the natural mind, He prayed to the Father, spoke of His inferiority to the Father, and said the Father within Him did the Works. But when He spoke from His Spiritual Mind, He declared His equality by saying, He and the Father were One: that He was the First and the Last, with all Power in heaven and on earth.

Now, the Word clearly teaches, that the object of this second coming of the Lord is to establish His kingdom on earth: that that kingdom is His church: and that, in that kingdom, He is to wipe away all tears from men's eyes; and they are to be His people, and He Himself is to be with them, their God. And that church, which He is to establish, is denominated the New Jerusalem, which is to come down from God out of heaven, prepared as a bride adorned for her husband. It is declared, in Revelation, that His *name*, at His second coming, should be

called "*the Word of God.*" At His first coming, He
came as the *Word*, which was in the beginning with God,
and which was God; and that Word was manifest in the
flesh, and came a *Light* into the world, or the Truth into
the human mind.

Therefore, though He comes again as the mighty God
—Father, Son and Holy Spirit,—yet, the feature which
He presents is the Word, or the Spiritual Truths of the
Sacred Scriptures. The higher elements of His nature
can only be approached through the Word of Truth—the
Father can be found only in the Son—the Goodness only
in the Truth. Therefore, God Himself comes to men, as
the Word. He came the first time, as the Word, in the
literal sense. He comes the second time, as the Word, in
the spiritual sense. True, there was an assumed finite
nature and body, like ours. But they were not the Lord
—the Mighty God. They were assumed only as a means
of bringing the Word, which in the beginning was with
God and was God, down to man's fallen state; that we
might have the Light of Life—the Spirit of Truth—and
become regenerated.

But, let us seek a true idea of the Lord's coming and
going. Where can He, who is Omnipresent, come from,
or go to? Certainly nowhere, as to space. There can
nothing exist, in which He is not, in some sense, present.
And there can be no coming or going, between the Father
and the Son, in God. The Father is God's Love, and the
Son is the Word or Truth, which that Love speaks. They
are always together. Could they be separated, they would
both be finite—neither of them would be Omnipresent.

What, then, is the coming and going of the Most High
God? It is simply the receiving and the losing of the
Love and Wisdom of God, by the mind of man. All

coming and going, of the Lord, have regard solely to the mind of man. The mind, that does not see and love the Truth of the Word, has not God in the understanding and affections. Yet, God, by influx, is really in that person, as his life, although that man does not receive Him into his thoughts and feelings. He is not with him rationally, affectionately, or reciprocally. Therefore, all God's coming and going is into, and out of, the affections of man. And this is done by man's loving the Truth, and rejecting it. The coming and going is, therefore, all on man's part, not at all on God's. Thus, by the "fall," we lose God; that is, we lose the love of Goodness and Truth —the Lord is gone from the mind. But, by regeneration, He comes again—those elements of His nature are received into the understanding and will. It is because man has freedom and rationality, that God can thus come and go. He comes and goes as to nothing else in the universe but the mind of man.

And, when the Lord thus comes and goes, it seems, by some of the literal expressions of the Word, as though He left the Father and returned to Him. Thus He says, "I came forth from the Father, and am come into the world: again, I leave the world, and go to the Father." But the Father Principle, in God, being the Divine Love, and the Son Principle, the Divine Truth or Word, we see that from love to man, and a desire to instruct him and bless him, God speaks, or gives forth the Truth, from His affections. Thus the Son comes forth from the Father. God, as Love, sends forth the Truth, or Word, into the world; but the Father comes in it. And when the human mind sees and receives that Truth, the Word comes into the mental world—the mind of man. And when man declines into evil and loses his love for that Truth, and deals in falsities, that Truth is said to leave the world; and whenever it ascends above man's comprehension, it is said to go to the Father.

That Truth says to man, " Behold, I stand at the door and knock." Thus the Lord, as the Word or the Truth, wants to get into man's affections. Man's understanding is the door to his will. The Truth addresses itself to the rational faculty, saying, It is wrong to steal, lie, covet, murder. Do you not see that it makes the world miserable and wretched to do these things? In this, the Lord is standing at the door and knocking; and man's yielding his will to that Truth, and obeying it, is what is meant by his hearing the Lord's voice and opening the door. And, as he loves the Truth, he sups with the Lord, by drinking that Truth into his soul. And, as he gives his affections to God, acknowledging, with gratitude, the Truth, the Lord sups with him.

Thus the Lord comes into the world—the mental world. And thus the Lord, as the Word, came into the assumed mind—the mind received from Mary. For, although the Father, or the Divine Love, is the inmost Life and Divinity of Jesus Christ, in the flesh; yet, as we have said, the natural plane of the mind, which He received from Mary, was a little empire of itself, as it were; with will and understanding, freedom and rationality, receiving life and power, from God, to act, in perfect freedom, the same as any other external human mind. And the Truth of the Word, from the Father, met that mind from without, in the Bible, the same as it meets any other mind. It stood at the understanding, or door of that assumed human nature, and knocked. And that nature heard the voice, and opened the door; and the Lord, as the Word, came in and supped with that nature, and that

nature with the Word. Thus that assumed nature received the Truth through the written Word, and acknowledged the Father as its Author, while the Father was still
within it. But as the Lord glorified His assumed humanity, by putting off everything finite, received from Mary,
and putting the Infinite, from the Father, in its place,
there could be nothing material, or finite, about the Lord,
when He returned to the Father, or ascended into His
Divinity, out of the spiritual sight of the disciples. Therefore, we are taught, in the Gospel, that that only ascended
up into heaven which came down from heaven, even the
Son of Man which is in heaven. The Great Jehovah,
therefore, did not add to Himself, by the assumption of
our nature. Infinity cannot be increased. He only
brought Himself nearer to us, by descending into the
natural plane of human life, and giving us the Gospel in
that plane ; and then, by putting off the finite, He returned into the Infinite with the glorified natural, but
Infinite, Humanity. And thus, having that Infinite,
Glorified Humanity, He could give the Holy Spirit, or
send forth the Comforter, so as to reach fallen man, after
the ascension. For the literal sense of the Word, like the
assumed Humanity, is filled with that Spirit ; and through
that Word comes the Comforter. For, in the ascension,
the Lord became, more fully, the Spirit and Life of the
Word to man.

Thus the Word now becomes the Mediator, to those
who receive it, the same as the assumed human nature
became it, at His first coming ; the letters and words answering to the material body ; the literal sense being in
man's language, answering to the finite sphere of the assumed mind ; and the spiritual sense, to the Divine Mind,
within the assumed. Therefore, after the Lord's ascen-

sion, the written Word became the obvious Mediator, through which the Comforter could be sent, from the Father, to man. For the Word, in its Spirit and Life, is the Manifested Lord, sending forth the Holy Spirit to all who faithfully seek the Lord, in the Goods and Truths of that Word.

But when, in the process of time, " the traditions of men had made the commandments of God of none effect," and they sought salvation, by faith in the Lord, *out* of the Word, and away off, in some distant aerial region called heaven; then, a true knowledge of the Lord was gradually lost; and it became necessary that He should make a Second Coming. This second coming was prophetically announced by the Lord Himself. And now, if we bear in mind that the Lord's coming or going is, always, into, or out of, the mind of man, and nowhere else; and that it is simply receiving or losing the knowledge and love of Him; and that this coming and going must always be the Word of Truth and Life into, and out of, man's will and understanding, we shall then see that the world of mankind must have lost a true knowledge of Him, and of the doctrines of His Word, or He would not have been absent from men; and, therefore, could not have made an advent. He could not come where He already was. And, as His First Coming, into men's minds, was by a New Birth of the Truth, received into their wills, and given forth into life, by means of regeneration : so, also, must be His Second Coming. No men really knew the Lord, at His first coming, but those who received His Spirit of Truth and Love, through the new birth. He made no other first coming to men than into their souls. True, before coming into their souls, He took our fallen nature, and brought the Spirit of Truth and Love, Infinitely into that, by

Glorification. But this work would do men no good, if He could not, thereby, approach and enter their minds. Thus His first coming, to men, was into their souls, as the Word of Goodness and Truth, received into their wills and understandings, by regeneration. And precisely so, is His second coming.

Now, it is prophetically declared, in Matthew (24th chapter), that the world would lose all knowledge of the Lord, and become so wicked, in His absence, that no flesh could be saved without a second coming. This shows that there would come a dark, selfish, unregenerate state of the world—a state without a true knowledge of the Lord, or of the doctrines of His Word. And it must be into the world, in such a state, that the Lord makes His Second Coming. For, when the world is not in that dark state, the Lord is already there. He is present with every mind, where the truths of His Word are seen and loved ; and absent from every mind, where they are not. Thus He comes, as the *lightning cometh out of the East and shineth even unto the West.*

Herein we see that the second coming of the Lord is like the first. For His first coming, as declared in the first chapter of John, was "*a Light into the world.*" He came as the Word of Truth, which was in the beginning with God and was God. And it is declared, in the Apocalypse, that, at His second coming, His name should be called "*The Word of God.*" His first coming was called "*The true Light, that lighteth every man that cometh into the world.*" He is the "*Sun of Righteousness*" for the human soul—the true spiritual light and life of all that will receive Him. His second coming is of a higher order than the first, and is suited to the scientifically advanced state of the world. He comes now, not only as the Literal, but also the Spiritual Truth of the Word. He now comes as the Word in its fulness, opening to us the nature of the spiritual world and the laws of our spiritual being, by opening the Holy Word, and revealing its Spiritual Sense; and giving a clear, rational, full and consistent view of the literal sense, and showing the perfect unity and harmony between the two senses.

Here the reader may ask what we have to say about the resurrection and the judgment, which the Bible teaches will take place when the Lord shall make His second advent? We answer, This is precisely what the Spiritual Sense of the Word is coming for. Many men, in this age, are dead in trespasses and sins, who cannot be raised from this death, without the coming of the Spiritual Light of the Word, to their souls, for Judgment. Nothing else will reach their head and their heart. Besides, the Lord never comes to men, but in judgment; and man can never be blessed, but in judgment. When man does not need judging, the Lord is with him. Therefore judgments are mentioned as blessings. The Psalmist sings, "Arise, O Lord, judge the earth." "The judgments of the Lord are true and righteous altogether." "Let Zion rejoice and the daughter of Judah be glad, because of Thy judgments." "I will praise Thee with righteousness of heart, when I shall have learned Thy judgments." "My soul breaketh for the longing it hath for Thy judgments, at all times." "At midnight I will arise and give thanks, because of Thy judgments." "When Thy judgments are in the earth the inhabitants will learn righteousness."

It is true, there is another feature to the judgment, when it says, "the ungodly shall not stand in the judgment;" and that God will execute judgment upon the wicked. But it does not hurt the wicked to be judged.

It only decides what they are. It does not punish them. Their evils punish them.

Now, the Judgment is an operation of the Truth in the mind of those that are judged. They decide whether they will receive the Truth, and go with it; or reject it, and go against it. For, it is written, "The Father judgeth no man, but hath committed all judgment unto the Son." (John v, 22.) And the Lord says, "I judge no man." (John viii, 15.) "He that rejecteth Me, and receiveth not My Words, hath One that judgeth him: the Word that I have spoken, the same shall judge him, in the last day." (John xii, 48.)

Thus the Word of the Lord, the Divine Truth, is now coming, the second time, with judgment. He came also the first time with judgment; therefore He said, "Now is the judgment of this world; now is the prince of this world cast out." Thus redemption, the establishment of the church, and all blessings, come with judgment: as it is written, "Zion shall be redeemed with judgment." "The Lord will establish His kingdom with judgment." He will purge Jerusalem with judgment. Here we see that the Truth of the commandments is the life and power of the judgment, in the mind. So, we are commanded to "keep the Lord's judgments." And this keeping of the judgments regenerates us, and unites us to the Lord; for He says, "I will betroth thee unto me in judgment."

Thus the spiritual sense of the Word is coming to raise us from the dead, judge us, purify us, fill us with new Light and Life, that we may be good and happy. And it comes, saying, "Awake, thou that sleepest, and arise from the dead, and Christ shall give thee light." And, in the Spiritual Sense of the Word, He comes "with power and great glory:" and if we yield to Him, His

Truth will enter and explore our entire memory, so that *the sea will give up its dead.* Every false principle within the shores of our knowledge, or understanding, will be judged and condemned by the Truth, and freely put away. Nor will the Light stop there, but will enter the will, and there, *Death and Hell will give up the dead that are in them;* or all the *evils of the heart*, which cause the fires of hell in us to burn with anger, revenge and malice, or with any unkindness, will be seen, repented of, and given up. And thus the Great Judgment which is promised at the Lord's Second Coming, will be performed in each mind that receives Him; all the *dead* principles of that mind, *small and great*, will *stand before* the Truth; the sheep and the goats will be separated, the evils and falsities rejected, and the whole mind will be brought into harmony and peace. Thus we live in the Great Judgment Day, which will be continued as long as there is any one to be judged. Through this judgment, the world is to be brought into order, until the Lord, as the Divine Truth, reigns in all the people of the Earth; when " all shall know Him, from the least to the greatest." And as His coming is through the literal sense of the Word, into the human mind, therefore the " clouds of heaven," in which He is to come, are the dark and mysterious appearances of the literal sense of the Word as seen in the mind —the mental heaven—until illuminated and explained by the Spiritual Sense.

CHAPTER XI.

GOD is the Universal Being, ever, unchangeably the same ; His Word is universal Light and Life, ever in, it-self, the same ; His Language, therefore, is universal and unchangeable in its Divine character and qualities. It is THE UNIVERSAL LANGUAGE. This is the Language of Correspondences. It is *the relative law of life* between the natural and the spiritual worlds. And being the uni-versal language, it is the basis of all other languages. No language could be formed without it ; and all people more or less use it in adulterated forms ; and they see some light from it, though they may know nothing of it as a science. Now, for a simple illustration : bring to-gether men of all nations of the earth, who know nothing of one another's languages, but are acquainted with the characters of animals ; then bring before them a most selfish, greedy, loathsome man, and point to him and then point to the hog, and they will all understand the man's character better probably than it could be described in their several languages. And it will be the same if we point to the most licentious, secret, and subtle man, and then to the serpent ; or to the most innocent and

6

harmless, and then to the lamb ; or to the most bold, strong, and fearless, and then to the lion ; or to the most watchful and cautious, even to cruelty against intruders, and then to the dog : and so we might go on describing various characters, not only by the animals, but also by other things ; by the hawk and the dove, the wheat and the tares, the olive and the thorn, the vine and the bramble, by things wholesome and things poisonous. Thus the universal language everywhere speaks, either in stronger or in fainter accents ; and neither the wisest nor the most ignorant could describe a thought or a feeling without it or ideas drawn from it.

At the time when the Lord said, in Genesis, " Behold, the people is one, and they have all one language ; " " the whole earth was of one language, and of one speech," then the people all spoke the universal language. The loss of that language, which occurred in building the tower of Babel, left men without any sure way of expressing ideas ; and consequently the world has become filled with a variety of uncertain languages, no one of which any two persons understand alike. This is because the language has no roots. True, the language we use purports to take root in many others. But even these languages themselves, and even those of them which are called dead or fixed languages, have, to men, lost their roots. Nature is the ground in which all true language takes root. And the law of analogy is the only light in which that root can be truly seen. We know the dead languages are not fluctuating and changing, like those in common use. But the reason is they are not used. It is to the conservative nature of the Hebrew and Greek languages, that we are indebted for so correct a knowledge of the Holy Word as we now have. And it is therefore of the Divine Providence that they became dead, that they could better preserve the Word. Those languages still take root in nature. But men, by the loss of the science of correspondences, see not where nor how that root exists. Hence the uncertainty which hangs over the precise meaning of many things in even those languages, and particularly in the Holy Word, where many things were written solely for the sake of the spiritual sense, and therefore where no shadow of a rational meaning can be seen without the law of analogy.

But the Lord says prophetically, pointing to this age of the world, " Then will I turn to the people a pure language, that they may all call upon the name of the LORD, to serve Him with one consent." Now what can this pure language be, in which all the people will call upon the name of the Lord, to serve Him with one consent, unless it be a language which will give them all the same ideas of God and of His Word? and also, unless it be that very language which the people had when the whole earth was of one speech, and all called upon the name of the Lord? And who, that sees the science of correspondences and, reads the Word by it, can doubt that the time has now come in which that prophecy is being fulfilled, when he sees persons of every nation, and kindred, and tongue, and people embracing this language, reading the Holy Word by it, and as they truly proceed, understanding it alike ; and beholding therein the Lord Jesus Christ, as the one God, whom they can all serve with one consent? And what other language can the Lord turn to the people, than the one they have before had, and which He gave them? He says He will turn to the people a pure language. What is a pure language? It is certainly something above human. Like its Divine Author it must be divine, definite, and sure ; the same yesterday, to-day, and forever. Such is the language of analogy ; and such is no other language. Therefore, in the primeval age the people read, in the book of Nature, the history of their creation, the character and laws of God, and the nature and quality of themselves. There was no truth which men needed to know that this book of Nature did not teach or indicate. It was to them a Fountain of infinite wisdom from the Lord. Upon what page soever their eyes rested, they saw, as by intuition, the true nature and character of the scene in its living aspect. So clearly did they look through nature up to nature's God, that the very names which they gave to the various objects of the creation indicated and expressed the peculiar quality and character of those objects. Thus it was a universal language, understood and read by all alike ; for it spoke from life, through qualities clearly indicated by their forms and uses. And for a long time the language of correspondences was the only language of the earth.

It was the first written language. When men first began to put their thoughts upon the barks and leaves of the trees, and the skins of beasts, they did it in the hieroglyphics of nature. They had no other language. Pictures of the objects in nature, instead of the living originals, became the expressive symbols of men's ideas. And there was no thought, feeling, passion, or propensity of the mind, which this language could not delineate to the life ; and much more correctly than any other language could do it ; because man's spiritual qualities had given the very forms to the objects in nature which would be selected to represent those qualities in man. The written language, therefore, could not possibly be mistaken by any one who understood the science of correspondences, even at the present day. Did the people of that age wish to express upon parchment any attribute or character of their Creator or of man, in the book of Nature, they saw their subject in living lines, and any expression of character could be delineated therefrom. And did they wish to correspond with their friends at a distance, or narrate a history of events, this mode of writing was amply sufficient.

But, in the process of inventions, the period arrived when a new language, from the use of sounds expressed by means of letters and words, was invented and introduced into use. But even in this language men still conveyed their ideas, as before, by natural symbols. For, though they did not paint any longer the objects of nature, yet they spelled and used the names of those objects, and therefore continued to look, by correspondence, through the objects themselves, for the quality of the ideas. For example: they had been accustomed to paint the lamb for innocence; the serpent for subtlety; the hand for power; the eye for the understanding; the heart for the will; the ear for obedience; the stars for knowledges; the moon for faith; the sun for love, and sometimes for the Lord, and so forth. But now they use the names of these things, which conveyed the same ideas. For the names of things always indicated their quality. So that the change in the mode of writing did not change in the least the character of the language. It was still the language of correspondences—the universal language. And the names of the natural things just mentioned now signify in the Word what is stated.

This is the true, original language. And in this language Moses, a man skilled in all the wisdom of the Egyptians, wrote the Pentateuch in the Hebrew dialect;

a language peculiar for the expression of the qualities of things by their names. In no other language than correspondences could the Bible possibly contain the Word of God, for no other language can have, in itself, " spirit and life."

But as man by sinful habits became less and less spiritually-minded, and gradually sunk into sensuality and naturalism, so this sublime language lost its beauty and glory, until its gold became as dross and passed away. But not without leaving its expressive memorandums upon the pyramids of Egypt ; in the records of the Druids ; in Oriental literature ; in the fabulous stories of antiquity ; in the idolatrous worship of the Gentiles ; in Heathen mythology ; in the poetry of all ages ; and even faintly in the present profane languages of the earth.

But from all these remains, the spirit and life have departed ; and the consequence of the loss of this science is " confusion of tongues " all over the earth. Men cannot now certainly understand each other. Their words have no definite meaning. They quarrel from the want of a sure way of expressing their ideas. The hottest mental combats often end in the perception of the fact that the parties both meant the same thing, but misunderstood each other's words.

It is therefore from false, and not from true views of the Word, that men are divided. Truths are eternal verities. They are ever and unchangeably the same. And all truths are in harmony, and sustain each other. About them, when seen, men cannot differ. It is about falsities altogether that the Christian world is contending. Falsities are all dark, unstable, deceptive, and mysterious ; fit grounds for contention and strife, and for the proud

display of self-wisdom ; and constant changes of opinion
are, and must be, taking place among those who build
upon such grounds : while those who build on the " Rock
of Ages "—the spiritual truth of the Word, rationally
seen in the light of analogy—never can change their
views, nor disagree in their doctrines, unless by sin they
lose their language. Analogical students of the Word,
therefore, so far as they receive the light, will come to
the same conclusions as to its teachings, because their
investigations will be carried on by a scientific Law, and
that Law divine ; and the reason they will not disagree is
the very reason why they differ not in mathematics : because in both instances the truths are indisputable. If, as
we believe, there are no two persons who, without the
light of this science, do agree as to the doctrines of the
Word, and no two who have it that disagree, the question as to its truth becomes a startling one.

Thus nature is the basis of all language. And, however lost we may now be to the true roots and laws of
our own dialect, we may soon know by rational reflection
that it is Dame Nature that has taught us all to talk.
We can lisp only her accents. True, her language has
become to us much adulterated, but that is our own fault.
We use it nevertheless. Of this we may be convinced by
trying to answer this one question : Had we no language,
how would we get one ? Now, we may think deeply, and
seek, as keenly as we can, the answer to this question,
and we shall find it impossible to see how to express a
single idea in speech without taking the sign from nature.
For illustration : Had we no words to express the idea of
innocence, how would we declare it ? By a harmless expression of the face, a soft tone of the voice, or a gentle
motion of the hand ? How should we know but it meant

gentleness, kindness, quietude, or some other grace or virtue? We could not certainly tell. We should have no other way than by seeking something in nature which was a symbol of innocence. And if we could read the book of Nature in correspondences, we should point at once to the lamb. But having lost the science of correspondences, the language we should now draw from nature, if we had none, would be very indefinite. Still we should go there; for the natural man has no other way, and can think of no other way to describe his thoughts and feelings, but in the use of words which have been drawn entirely from nature.

Take for instance the whole variety of adjectives, by which we express the qualities of mental things: bitter, sweet, sour, warm, cold, long, short, high, low, dark, light, near, distant, black, white, no matter what. They are all taken from nature. And yet we use them to describe the states and qualities of the mind. We speak of a warm or cold heart; a bitter, sweet, or sour temper, and of a long, deep, or shallow head; of high or low spirits; a dark and muddy, or clear and lucid understanding; a bright or cloudy intellect; a black character; a distant relative, a near friend, a knotty subject; and so we might go on and fill up our chapter. These expressions are used because there is no other way to express the quality of spiritual things but by means of words expressive of the quality of natural things.

Now, nothing short of the restoration of this science can ever draw out the deep truths of the Word, restore harmony to the minds of Christians, and bring the watchmen to see eye to eye. Well may the Psalmist sing of things of nature, saying, "There is no speech nor lan-

guage where their voice is not heard. Their line is gone
out through all the earth, and their words to the end of
the world." *

* See SILVER's Lectures, on the Symbolic Character of the Sacred Scriptures, Chapters II and III, from which we have made extracts in this chapter.

6*

CHAPTER XII.

MEN once saw that the outward creation or visible system—the Sun, Moon, Stars, and Earth, with all their varieties of things—was a symbol of the human mind. Before the science of correspondences was lost, this was clearly understood, from the very nature of God, men and things. For this reason man was called a microcosm or little world. And now, by means of that science, we of this age may see the propriety of the expression. For the science expressly shows that God has given His Word to teach us spiritual things through His Works.

For this purpose the things of nature are constantly brought up in His Word. Read where we will, they are ever before our thoughts. And though the Word is given by a Spiritual Being, to teach spiritual creatures spiritual things, and comes declaring itself to be Spirit and Life, yet it commences with the mention of natural things and natural events; and it talks about them continually, throughout the entire Bible.

It is no wonder therefore that, upon the loss of the science of correspondences, men became more and more natural until they saw, in the Word, little else than a history of natural things, and laws for the action of material bodies; as was the case with the Jews; but few of whom had any thoughts of spiritual things or of any existence above matter.

But we may now see that the Word so speaks, because natural things are the results of spiritual things, and correspond to them. For all natural things are the effects of will and understanding somewhere exercised. And those things must point, by certain and eternal laws, to the character and quality of the causes which produced them. Throughout the whole Divine Record, therefore, we may look, by analogy, through the effects to their causes, and see the nature and character of the thoughts and feelings which brought the natural events to pass. And we may thus read the spiritual, the real history. Who cannot read in a human production something of the thoughts and feelings of the artist who paints a picture, or of the man who invents a machine? Precisely so do all natural things suggest the mental nature and character of their causes.

And now, when we contemplate the spirituality of the Word, and see that the historical parts, besides the account they give of God, are a narrative of the various creations, falls and regenerations of the souls of men, in different ages and under various circumstances; and that the prophetical portions are a description of the same kind of things foretold; while the legal parts are given for the guidance of the mental action of those souls, and for their true illumination and life; and that even the Psalms, besides their reference to the glorification of the Lord's Humanity, are a description of the same kind of things, showing more particularly what men's souls pass through in their regeneration, and the influences which produce

it : I say, when we see this, and understand that the
things below man in the scale of being, are symbols of his
mental qualities ; and that the internal plane of man's
mind is his heaven, with its sun, moon and stars, and that
the external plane is his earth, with all its living creatures
of affections and thoughts, then there will be a view
opened, for a bird's-eye glance at the Word, whereby a
flood of light will flow into our minds to aid us in the investigations before us.   For it will give us a clue to the
true meaning of all those dark passages in the Word
which speak of the creation and passing away, at sundry
times, of the heavens and the earth, as well as to all other
strange things said therein ; for it will open the door for
a general exploration and understanding of the entire
Word, by correspondences.

From this view we may see that, as man is a microcosm, having within him all the living elements of the
macrocosm ; and as God, the Infinite Man, is the Author
and Father of all, is related to all, and is giving existence
and life to all ; so therefore the history and study of man
is the history and study of everything.   And God's Holy
Word embraces that whole vast history.   It is an entire
history of man ; past, present and prophetic.   Whatever
therefore may be the apparent subject of the letter of the
Word, we must look, by analogy, through what appears
on the surface, to matters of the mind—to things human.

Where the creation of natural things is mentioned,
the internal sense treats of the creation of the spiritual
things to which the natural things correspond.   This immense, and yet consolidated system of views, of God, man,
and the universe ; and of the Holy Word, as the medium
of light and life to all created things ; strikes many minds,
at the first view, as strange and novel ; and they turn

aside, saying, it is asking too much to request their attention to any such system. But let me ask them if it is asking too much to request their attention to the Word of the Most High God? And let me further ask, where they are, without the Word of God, and what light they can bring from any other source or system to show the use, beauty and harmony of that entire Word? Upon what other ground, than this language of analogy, can we possibly account for the propriety or use of many portions of the Sacred Word? What shall we do with the Pentateuch, and Joshua, or with the books of Ezekiel and the Apocalypse, or with many mysterious things scattered throughout the Word? Why is the vast universe, in generals and in particulars, so frequently brought before us? The sun, moon, stars, winds, rain, clouds, hail, snow, ice, frost, fire, light, darkness, calms, storms, thunders, earthquakes, floods, droughts, mountains, hills, valleys, seas, rivers—everything inanimate: beasts, birds, fishes, reptiles, insects—everything that flies, walks, creeps, swims, or crawls: trees, brambles, briers, shrubs, thistles, wheat, rye, barley, corn—everything that grows upon the earth: gold, silver, copper, brass, iron, lead, precious stones, rocks, clay, sand—everything in the earth; and even the earth itself: why are these things so frequently mentioned by the Lord, in whole or in part, to teach men the doctrines of the Word and the way of life? for "all Scripture is profitable for doctrine." Must it not be because they impart moral and religious instruction by a higher meaning that the letter which killeth? Why are these things mentioned as living and rational creatures? the floods clapping their hands, the hills rejoicing, the trees choosing a king, the mountains moving about, the hills skipping like young sheep, the valleys shouting and singing, the earth reeling to and fro like a drunken man, every-thing that hath breath praising the Lord, and God enter-ing into covenant with the beasts of the field and the creeping things of the earth,—why all this, unless they correspond to principles in man; so that it is man that reels to and fro, man that praises God by every living principle of his nature, man with whom God entered into covenant; man that shouts and sings, man that claps his hands, man that chooses a king, principles in man that skip like young sheep, mountains in man that are moved? It must be so: and by the science of correspondences it is clearly seen to be so. But without this science, what can we learn from such things of the Word as the Lord's shav-ing with a hired razor, and its consuming the beard from the feet? From the dragon's sweeping down a third part of the stars with his tail? From a chariot's being cast into a dead sleep? From Jehovah's riding on horseback or in chariots? From horses' coming out of the book when opened? From the locusts with shapes like horses, faces like men, hair like women, teeth like lions, and tails like scorpions. What can these things mean? Are they the Word of Infinite Wisdom? They are, most certainly; and they are beaming with truth, clear to the mind and filled with food for hungry souls. Come ye to the banquet! come with confidence and a teachable spirit, and you will find, in every passage, a well of living water springing up unto everlasting life, for all that thirst.*

Now, from this general glance at the subject let us next look at the use made in the Word of the sun, moon and stars. As these are called heavenly bodies and are said to be in the heavens, so in order for them to corre-

---

* See SILVER's Lectures, Chapter III.

spond to things of the human mind, that mind must have its heaven. And as the Holy Word is a history of the human mind, and commences by saying, "In the beginning God created the heaven and the earth," so, by the word "heaven" is meant the internal plane of the mind, and by the "earth," the external plane. And a little examination will show any one that this is what is meant by the phrase "the heavens and the earth," wherever used in the Word.

The Lord says, in Isaiah (lxv, 17), "Behold, I create new heavens and a new earth : and the former shall not be remembered, nor come into mind." Now by the former heavens and earth which are not to be remembered must be meant the very heavens and earth created in the beginning, for they can mean no other. And they must also mean the human mind, because by the new heavens and new earth mentioned, is meant, a new state of the human mind, with the internal and external mind brought into order ; for the prophecy continues, "Behold, I create Jerusalem a rejoicing, and her people a joy ;" where Jerusalem means the church or the human mind in order.

Now, this prophecy, in Isaiah, relates to the coming of the Lord in the flesh, for the establishment of the Christian Church, or of a new state of the human mind. And this state of the mind is the new heavens and the new earth, to which the prophecy refers : for the former heavens and earth, or good and true state of the mind, had passed away in the progressive fall of man ; and the new heavens and earth were to take their place.

And so, in the prophecy through Jeremiah, our Lord says, in reference to this dark state of the human mind or of the church, "My people is foolish, they have not known Me ; they are sottish children, and have none understand-

ing ; they are wise to do evil, but to do good they have
no knowledge.   I beheld *the earth, and lo, it was without
form and void ; and the heavens, and there was no light ;*
I beheld, and lo, there was no man, and all the birds of
heaven were fled."   Here we have the depraved state of
the Jews, at the time the Lord was to come in the flesh.
And how much it is like the description of the state of
the first people on earth, while in spiritual ignorance, or
before the kingdom of heaven was established in them !
for that narrative, in Genesis, says, " In the beginning God
created the heaven and the earth : and *the earth was without form, and void ; and darkness was upon the face of
the deep.*"   And so the Jewish mind at the coming of the
Lord was without form, and void, because it was not sym-
metrical, being deformed by sin, and void of goodness and
truth.   Its heavens or internal mind, as the prophecy declares, had no light, for it had ceased to be spiritual.
And the reason why it is said, " *there was no man,*" is,
because it requires the image of God to make a real man ;
and this the Jews had lost.   And so the reason why it is
said that all the birds of heaven were fled is because all
heavenly thoughts were gone.   The Jews had become a
low, sensual people.

Now in order to restore the Jews to the image of God,
the lights of truth must be set again in the heavens, to
give light upon the earth, and the fled birds or heavenly
thoughts must be called back.   And all this the Lord
did, in the establishment of the Christian Church.   He
even created man again in His own image after His likeness : or He created a new heavens and a new earth, or
the church in man, and illuminated it.   And He says to
it prophetically, " Arise, shine, for thy light is come, and
the glory of the Lord is risen upon thee ; and the Gentiles

shall walk to thy light, and kings to the brightness of thy
rising." Thus the Lord is the light of the mind or of the
church. The sun denotes the Lord as to love and wisdom, the moon denotes truth or faith, and the stars truths
or knowledges. These things are never mentioned in the
Word without having this signification. For as the moon
is a dark, opaque body, receiving all its light from the
sun, so the human mind is a dark opaque body, receiving
all its light of truth, or its true faith, from the Lord, the
Sun of Righteousness. And as the human mind shines by
the truths of faith from the Lord, so the moon shines by
light borrowed from the sun. The moon is therefore used
in the Word as a true symbol of faith. And the stars are
most beautiful symbols of truths or knowledges in the
mind. Being bright objects in the natural firmament,
they denote true principles in the understanding or mental firmament. What a beautiful mental constellation are
the ten commandments, when bright and clear in the firmament of the mind! Like beacon lights to the natural
mariner, they stand in our mental heavens as fixed stars
upon which we may ever depend, to mark our moral and
religious latitude and longitude in the ocean of life, as we
strive, in dependence upon the Lord, to guide our frail
bark of humanity, in its onward-bound voyage to the
haven of peace, our eternal home. Stars are therefore
said to fall from heaven, or to withdraw their shining,
whenever man loses his knowledge of the truths of the
Word.

In the prophecy in Joel, concerning a dark and depraved state of the world, the Lord says, "The earth shall
quake before them; the heavens shall tremble; the sun
and the moon shall be dark, and the stars shall withdraw
their shining. . . . The sun shall be turned into darkness,

and the moon into blood." (ii, 10, 31.) This is a prophetic description of the dismal state of the human mind when its sun of righteousness, its moon of· faith, and its stars of spiritual knowledges cease to shine. And how graphic is this description when the analogy is seen! No human language can compare with it either for fulness, definiteness or force.

What a pitiable state of man, or of the mental earth, is shown by the following language through Isaiah! "The earth mourneth and fadeth away. The earth is defiled. The foundations of the earth do shake. The earth is utterly broken down. The earth is clean dissolved. The earth is moved exceedingly. The earth shall reel to and fro like a drunkard." Now as the sun, moon and stars were not disturbed at the Lord's coming, when this prophecy was fulfilled, something else is meant. And we have positive proof, in plain and unmistakable language, what that something else is. For on the day of Pentecost, when the people "were all amazed, and marvelled, saying one to another, behold, are not all these which speak Galilæans? And how hear we every man in our own tongue, wherein we were born? . . . But Peter, standing up with the eleven, lifted up his voice, and said unto them, . . . This is that which was spoken by the prophet Joel: And it shall come to pass in the last days, saith God, . . . I will show wonders in heaven above, and signs in the earth beneath; blood, and fire, and vapour of smoke: the sun shall be turned into darkness, and the moon into blood, before that great and notable day of the Lord come."

. Here Peter quotes the very words of Joel (ii, 28–31), who declares that before the things, mentioned as occurring on the day of Pentecost, should take place, the sun should be turned into darkness, and the moon into blood. Thus showing clearly that, before the Christian Church should be established, the true light of faith would be gone from the human mind on earth. For by the sun's being turned into darkness is meant the loss of all true knowledge and love of the Lord, the Sun of Righteousness. And by the moon's being turned to blood is meant violence done to faith. There can be no question of the meaning of these prophecies left in the mind of any one, after candidly examining them in the light of analogy, in which they are written.

The same symbolic language is used in the prophetic portions of the New Testament, to express another dark, divided and distracted state of the religious world on the earth, and of the establishment of the New Jerusalem. For the prophet John says, in the Apocalypse, " and I saw a new heaven, and a new earth : for the first heaven and the first earth were passed away : . . . and I John saw the holy city, New Jerusalem, coming down from God out of heaven, prepared as a bride adorned for her husband. And I heard a great voice out of heaven saying, Behold, the tabernacle of God is with men, and He will dwell with them, and they shall be His people, and God Himself shall be with them, their God."

Now the whole 24th chapter of Matthew is a prophecy of the divisions, disorders and troubles which would arise in the Christian world, and of the coming of the Lord for the establishment of the New Jerusalem. The Lord there says, " Immediately after the tribulation of those days shall the sun be darkened, and the moon shall not give her light, and the stars shall fall from heaven, and the powers of the heavens shall be shaken : and then shall appear the sign of the Son of man in heaven : and then shall all the tribes of the earth mourn, and they shall see the Son of man coming in the clouds of heaven with power and great glory." All these wonderful things concerning the sun, moon and stars, were to take place before the coming of the Lord in the clouds of heaven and the descent of the New Jerusalem. And as the things written concerning the sun, moon and stars did not take place in outward nature at the Lord's first coming, as prophesied in Isaiah, Jeremiah and Joel, we therefore are not to look for anything of the kind at His second coming in the clouds of heaven, for it is declared that in both instances the same things would take place.

But all will be plain when men see that the clouds are the dark, literal sense of the Word, when not understood; and that the Lord, who is the Truth, will make His coming as the spiritual light of the Word, in those clouds, by means of the science of correspondences. Who does not see that without that science, the Scripture we have considered is a dark cloud in the mind? But by the use of that science, the Lord, as heavenly light, comes in this cloud with power and great glory.

The passage in Mark which treats of the second coming of the Lord, and of the state of the world, reads thus: "But in those days, after that tribulation, the sun shall be darkened, and the moon shall not give her light, and the stars of heaven shall fall." By the tribulation of those days is meant what we now see throughout the world, as divisions, and subdivisions, and contentions of sects, and parties, and creeds, called in the prophetic teachings of the 24th chapter of Matthew, wars, and rumors of wars, and earthquakes, and pestilences, and famines, and cryings of lo, here, and lo, there. But in Isaiah (lx, 18, 20), where it is prophesied of the coming of the New Jerusalem, our Lord says, " Violence shall no more be heard in thy land, wasting nor destruction within thy borders ; but thou shalt call thy walls salvation, and thy gates praise. Thy sun shall no more go down ; neither shall thy moon withdraw itself: for the LORD shall be thine everlasting light, and the days of thy mourning shall be ended."

In one of the prophecies of the New Jerusalem, through St. John, it says, " There appeared a great wonder in heaven ; a woman clothed with the sun and the moon under her feet ; and upon her head a crown of twelve stars." The woman denotes the crowning state of the church, when she is to come as a bride adorned for her husband. How cheering the thought that the church is yet to be clothed with light as with a garment—a light shining from heavenly love, so that her deportment will be pure mercy and intelligence ; that her understanding is to be filled with all spiritual knowledges, symbolized by a crown of twelve stars : that she will ever stand firm upon the eternal rock of true faith, denoted by the moon under her feet as a sure lantern to her paths !

There is another striking prophecy in the Apocalypse, concerning the disturbed and beclouded condition of the Christian world preceding the descent of the New Jerusalem. It reads thus : " The sun became black as sackcloth of hair, and the moon became as blood ; and the stars of heaven fell unto the earth, even as a fig-tree casteth her untimely figs, when she is shaken of a mighty wind ; and the heavens departed as a scroll when it is rolled together." Now while we cannot conceive of stars falling from heaven, nor the moon becoming as blood, we can conceive of truths becoming lost to the mind, and of violence being done to faith, while it is crimsoned with sins of every dye.

We have now given a brief explanation of the meaning of the heavens and the earth, the sun, moon and stars, from the very commencement of the Word to its close—in Genesis, in the Prophets, in the Gospels and the Acts of the Apostles, as taken from the Prophets, and in Revelation. The literal sense alone is against the reason which God has given to man, and consequently cannot teach him. But, by the divine science of correspondences, in which the Holy Word is written, we have a rational and beautiful view of the truth therein taught. And what is most important is, they show us our God, and teach us the way of life and salvation—the very things which we most need to know, and which the good God most desires to teach us.

Again, the mind has its mountains, hills and valleys. Mountains are our highest loves, whether good or evil. Therefore if the thing we most ardently love be goodness, that affection would be called a "mountain of holiness," a "mountain of the Lord," because a high state of love to the Lord. So if it be self we most love, manifested in some violent feeling of revenge or malice toward some individual who has injured or slandered us, that bitter feeling is also a mountain—the uppermost pinnacle of our mental earth. This mountain must be removed before we can find rest or peace of soul. This is the kind of mountain to which, if we have faith like a grain of mustard-seed, we can say, "be thou removed, and it shall be done;" for if we have faith to believe that it is wrong to feel unkind toward anybody; that we should love even our enemies and bless those that curse us, then we can remove this mountain of revenge.

Hills, in a bad sense, denote feelings not so high as mountains, not so bitter as revenge or malice, yet feelings

which are unkind and uncharitable. In a good sense,
they denote feelings of charity and good-will. From this,
we may form some idea of what is meant in the Word by
the moving about of mountains and hills. For the mountains of self-love, and the hills of the love of the world are
removed by regeneration ; and the mountains of the love
of God and the neighbor take their place.

Wherever in the Word, animals are mentioned, we find
in them a representation of the human affections ; in the
birds mentioned, we see a symbol of man's thoughts.
And the more closely we study the character and qualities
of the various animals and birds, in connection with our
own feelings and thoughts, the more strongly will we become confirmed in the belief that there must be some analogical law or connection between the human mind and
these creatures. We shall then understand why Herod
was called a fox, and Dan a lion's whelp or an adder in
the path. We shall also see why the Lord says, "The lion
shall lie down with the lamb, and the leopard with the
kid ; the cow and bear shall feed together, and a little
child shall lead them ;" for by this language we shall see
a beautiful description of the state of the regenerate mind,
when all the various feelings of the bosom, denoted by
the different beasts, are in harmony and love ; when the
strong lion and leopard of the mind are filled with the
spirit of mercy and truth, and are faithfully protecting
the lambs and kids of innocence and virtue from all
harm, and even lying down in their embrace. We shall
understand what is meant in the Word, by the beasts before the throne of God full of eyes before and behind.
For, as eyes denote the understanding, we shall see that
it is the affections of man filled with wisdom concerning
things future and past. We shall see why it is written that

the beasts give glory, and honor, and thanksgiving to the
Lord; why the beasts say, Amen; why, when the Lord
opened the first seal, it was a beast that said, "Come and
see;" and also why the beasts fell down and worshipped
God, saying, Amen, Alleluia. We shall see that the
human heart, the soul's affections, are what is meant by
beasts; that it is men and not animals that do these things.

Now, how like the thoughts the birds fly about from
spray to spray, and from object to object; now rising
toward heaven and now sinking to earth! One bird meets
the eye and is gone. We know not whence he came, nor
where he went. How like the coming and going thought!
Another appears dressed in beauty. 'Tis like the poet's
brilliant thought, flying to perch in the verse of fame or
affection. Another bird soars, in the morning, on the
wings of joy, warbling his joyous notes like the happy
Christian's thought, ascending to heaven in the morning
anthem. Some birds descend to the earth and feed upon
filth; fit symbols of the dissolute thoughts of the grovelling mind, indulging in sin. Some are birds of night,
which cannot bear the light of day. They denote the hidden thoughts of the thievish soul, afraid to appear before
the eyes of men. Some birds are fierce and cruel, armed
with beaks and claws for destruction. They point to the
malicious murderer's thoughts, seeking carnage and gain.
Other birds are as gentle and harmless as the breath of
heaven, and as joyous as the music of spring, corresponding to the thoughts of innocent children sporting 'mid sunshine and flowers. Some birds, in their union, are as
affectionate and as constant to each other as mercy and
truth. They denote the conjugal thoughts of faithful
souls, which no powers can sever nor adversities weaken.
Some birds are as black as darkness, and others as white

as the light; while others are mixed with black and white. How perfectly they symbolize, in color, the false, the true, and the adulterated thoughts of men! Birds are indeed most true and perfect representatives of thoughts, and throughout the Holy Word they always denote something of the rational or intellectual element.

It is remarkable that almost everywhere in the Word, where birds are mentioned, some other meaning than the literal sense must be given them, before the mind can be satisfied. If we go to the first chapter of Genesis, the first place where "winged fowl" is mentioned, we are confounded with the idea that the birds were made of water. But when we see that it is a spiritual history, and that water there corresponds to truth, and birds to thoughts, all is light: the mystery is fled. For we see that all the thoughts of the people, before the fall, to which birds correspond, must have been true; for the truths of the Lord brought them forth. And we also see that all the affections, to which the animals correspond, must have been good; for the will or goodness of God, to which the land corresponds, brought them forth. And as beasts and birds are there used merely for the sake of the spiritual sense, all is rational and clear.

That birds denote thoughts, we may see from the following illustrations: In Isaiah our Lord says, "As birds flying, so will I defend Jerusalem." This is the only way the Lord can defend Jerusalem or the church. When the church in ourselves or in the community is in danger, we must have true thoughts, and we must let them fly from mind to mind, or the church will not be defended. Again, in Jeremiah, the Lord says of the people, "How long shall the land mourn for the wickedness of them that dwell therein? the beasts are consumed and the birds."

7

Now, spiritually speaking, this was actually the state of the Jewish church; good affections and true thoughts were gone or destroyed. But the natural beasts and birds were on the earth, as usual. And the Lord again says, by the same prophet, " Mine heritage is unto Me as a speckled bird; the birds round about are against her." The speckled bird denotes an adulterated state of the mind, by mixing up truths and falsities together: the white spots indicating truths, and the black ones, falsities, so that the thoughts are presented, partly true and partly false—a speckled bird. A church or a professed Christian must be true, or the thoughts of the people round about, or out of the church, will condemn him. The community will be against a speckled bird. In Revelations, speaking of the church as a city, or rather, as to doctrine, it says, " Babylon the Great is fallen, is fallen, and is become the habitation of devils, and the hold of every foul spirit, and a cage of every unclean and hateful bird." How true it is that a fallen and corrupt mind is a cage of such birds !

Again, the Holy Word speaks much of horses, where every one must see that it cannot mean natural horses. Now if we will only admit that the term horse means the understanding of knowledge, and read the Word with that idea in the mind, connected with other correspondences, all the strange passages of the Word, where the term horse is used, will be rationally understood. But if we should adopt any other signification, the passages could not be understood. We could make nothing out of them. The Word speaks of horses and their riders. The horses signify the understanding of things, whether true or false. The riders are the persons themselves who have this understanding and knowledge. Without the understanding of divine truth we could not possibly make spiritual progress. We rest and rely upon the understanding and power of the truth, as we rest and rely upon the ability and strength of our horse; and there is a perfect correspondence between them. But if, instead of the truth, our understanding be filled with false, absurd and evil views, it will be like a wild, frantic, ungovernable horse, leaping all the fences or rules of law and order, starting at every new object, getting into mud and mire, and often jeopardizing our life on the way. A man with such a mind needs to keep a strong bit and a straight rein over his headstrong understanding, or it will surely run away with him, and throw him among the rocks of error, on the wayside of destruction, or down the precipice of vice.

Now, in prophesying of the future dark state of the Jewish church, it says, in Zechariah xii, 4, "In that day, saith Jehovah, I will smite every horse with astonishment, and his rider with madness: and I will open mine eyes upon the house of Judah, and I will smite every horse of the people with blindness." This prophecy has reference to the state of the Jewish church when the Lord should come in the flesh, and is already fulfilled; and yet every natural horse was not smitten with astonishment and blindness. But the understandings of the Jews became astonished, and were blind to the truths of the Gospel; and they remain so to this day.*

The correspondence, in the Word, of the vegetable kingdom to the human mind is no less striking than that of the animal; and it is as little understood without the spiritual sense. It generally refers to things of the natural mind: the grass upon which animals feed denoting natural good, upon which the affections live; and the trees,

---

* See SILVER's Lectures, Chapter VI, explaining the horses' coming out of the book. Rev. vi.

whose fruits are for man, denote more elevated principles of the mind ; thorns, thistles, nettles, briers, brambles and tares denoting false and evil principles ; and corn and grain, generally, good principles.

Much is said in the Word of trees. They often denote men, and sometimes God. By the Tree of Life is meant the Lord. In Judges ix, 8–15, the trees are represented as going out to choose a king over them ; and the trees throughout the parable denote people ; and the subject is beautifully applicable to men now. (Explained in SILVER's Lectures, chap. vii.) Great use is made, in the Word, of the olive, the vine and the fig-tree. In the 31st chapter of Ezekiel, a variety of trees are brought up, denoting men or principles of the mind. Here Pharaoh is called the Assyrian, and also a cedar of Lebanon. And he is represented as a wonderful tree ; the other trees envy him, and some faint, and some go to hell ; and all the fowls of heaven and beasts of the field are connected with him. Pharaoh, king of Egypt, represents the natural man in the love of science, and progressing in scientific wisdom and knowledge, and thereby gaining great power and influence, becoming envied and admired for his vast acquirements and superior excellence, until he becomes great in his own estimation, inflated with self-love, and thus he falls into ruinous evils. The various conditions of the trees, and birds and beasts, and the waters, show the operations of the various principles of his mind to which these natural things correspond, as he rises to the zenith of his glory, and falls into darkness and death. And in the sure language of God we may find it exceedingly interesting and instructive, as applicable to our natural man, by the rules of analogy. The spiritual sense is highly instructive ; but we have not room to explain it.

Let us now glance at the similitude between the earth
and the mind. The highest symbol of God in any one
thing, except the human mind—the highest symbol of
Him in nature—is the sun ; the heat denoting His love,
the light, His wisdom, and their action, His power. And
when we consider the sun as corresponding to God and
the earth to man, we have a broad field for contemplation, and one which throws much light upon the understanding of the Holy Word. The first general division
of the earth is into land and water ; that of the mind, into
will and understanding. The land denotes the good or
evil ground of the will ; and the water, the truth or
falsity of the understanding. The land can produce nothing without water : nor can the will, without the understanding ; goodness can do nothing without truth, nor
evil, without falsity. But even the land and water together can produce nothing of themselves, alone. They
must have the heat and light of the sun. So also must
the will and understanding of man have the love and
wisdom of God—the divine influx—or they can do nothing. The land and water of the earth denote the will and
understanding of the external mind, or the natural good
and truth which are in them. To be truly alive and pro-
ductive in heavenly things, this natural will and understanding must receive spiritual goods and truths from the
internal mind. This internal mind is represented by the
natural heavens, with the sun, moon and stars : the sun
denoting the Lord, the moon, faith in Him, and the stars,
knowledges of His commandments. And how forcibly
does the power of these divine principles, from our internal mind operating upon our external, correspond to the
influence of those heavenly bodies upon the earth, without which it would be utterly unfruitful.

Thus the correspondence between the physical universe and the human mind is everywhere most perfect, not only in generals but in particulars. And it is necessarily so, because the elements of the human mind are the living elements of the universe, by regular influx. These are the glorious truths which will yet lift the veil from human hearts and minds, and bring the world together in wisdom and love. Then will the knowledge of the Lord cover the earth as the waters cover the sea, and tears will be wiped from off all faces.

CHAPTER XIII.

NUMBERS, like everything else of the Word, always have a spiritual signification touching the soul or life, which is their essential meaning. Sometimes they mean also what is numerically expressed in the literal sense, and sometimes they do not, but can only be understood in the spiritual sense. To number people or things is to ascertain their general qualities.

Now, in order to prepare our minds for looking into the spiritual signification of numbers, let us first throw our thoughts back to the primeval age, when everything seen, said, or done, meant and declared something mental or spiritual. We shall then see that numbers would naturally and necessarily be used to denote the qualities of thoughts, feelings, and principles.

And beginning with number *One*, it would of course mean God: He is First of all; First in quality and in quantity; the All in all. And this *quality-signification* of number one has never been wholly lost. Thus, we say of a person, he is the first man in town, or the first scholar in the class. He may have been the last man that moved into town, and the last that entered the class.

Moreover, when we leave individuals and come to principles or elements, Love is number One. It is the Life principle, the spring of all action. And next to Love is Wisdom. Wisdom is number Two. But it involves number One. We cannot have two things without having one. We cannot be truly wise without being good. Two, therefore, denotes the dual principle, and signifies marriage, or Love and Wisdom, or goodness and truth in union. Next to Love and Wisdom is Power. Power is number Three. But it involves the other two. We cannot have three things without the two. We cannot have power without having love and wisdom, or will and understanding, either in true or in inverted order. Power, therefore, involves everything that is in it. Consequently the number Three signifies all, fulness, perfection.

Very many passages can be cited from the Word to sustain these statements. As in John x, 30, " I and My Father are One." The Father is Love; the Son, or Word, is Truth. And in Deuteronomy vi, 4, " Hear, O Israel : Jehovah our God is One Jehovah." Here the phrase *Jehovah our God* means the Divine Love and the Divine Wisdom, which are declared to be *One*. In all cases where God is mentioned by two names, His Love and Wisdom are meant. By knowing this, much light is seen. So the phrase Jesus Christ means the Divine Love and Wisdom, or Goodness and Truth. Again, in Psalm xxvii, 4, " *One* thing have I desired of the Lord, that will I seek after; that I may dwell in the house of the Lord all the days of my life, to behold the beauty of the Lord, and to inquire in His temple." Here the *one* thing desired involves *three* things, which it requires the union of will, understanding, and action to accomplish. It is the same in Mark x, 21 : " *One* thing thou lackest : go thy way, sell whatsoever thou hast, and give to the poor." *One* thing involves the three. A volume could be cited to sustain this truth.

Four, being the square of two, denotes also union ; and consequently the fulness of goods and truths, or evils and falsities, in the complex : as in Zechariah vi, 1, " And I turned, and lifted up mine eyes, and looked, and behold, there came four chariots out from between two mountains." Now this relates solely to things of the mind. It is a vision of the coming of the church into men. Chariots denote doctrines : four denotes fulness, and also conjunction of goodness and truth therein : a mountain denotes love ; two mountains, love to God and the neighbor. By the chariots being drawn by horses is meant that the doctrines were in the understanding ; coming from the mountains shows that they go forth from the heart. The whole vision is exceedingly beautiful, teaching the way of life ; but we are now only upon numbers, and have not room to give further illustration.

The number Ten denotes all a man has. Something of its quality-signification may be seen in the fact of man's having ten fingers and ten toes. It suggested the origin and rule for counting by tens. Therefore, any number obtained by adding ciphers to ten, as 100, 1,000, and so forth, signifies the same as ten, only extending more into particulars. Thus the ten commandments include the whole law—all. And a thousand commandments would mean not only what was in the ten, but would direct the thoughts to the particular commandments everywhere in the Word.

The number Five, the half of ten, sometimes signifies the same as ten, and sometimes a few, or much, or little,

7*

according to the subject treated of and the manner used. As in Matthew xxv, 1, 2, " Then shall the kingdom of heaven be likened unto ten virgins, which took their lamps and went forth to meet the bridegroom. And five of them were wise, and five were foolish." Here the Bridegroom is the Lord, as the Word ; the kingdom of heaven is the church ; the ten virgins are all the members, without regard to numbers ; the five wise ones are all, without regard to numbers, who loved the truth ; and the five foolish are all who do not love the truth : for truth, in the understanding, is the lamp, and love of that truth, in the will, is the oil in the vessel for the lamp. The reason the wise did not give to the foolish of their oil is, no one can be good in borrowed love. They must go and buy for themselves, which is done by giving up the love of deception, and obtaining the love of the truth.

Now, a few simple rules will aid a person very much to understand the Word, and particularly with regard to large numbers. For example : from number two arise 4, 8, 16, 400, 800, 1,600, 4,000, 8,000, 16,000, and so forth ; which numbers signify the same as two, but direct the thoughts more into particulars. From three arise 6, 9, 12, 24, 72, 144, 1,440, 144,000 ; also 30, 300, 3,000 ; 60, 600, 6,000, and so forth ; which numbers signify the same as three, but point to particulars. From five arise 10, 100, 1,000, 10,000 ; also 50, 500, 5,000, and so forth ; which numbers signify the same as five, but direct to particulars. From seven arise 14, 70, 700, 7,000, 70,000, which numbers signify the same as seven, pointing to particulars.

Seven is a number signifying holiness, or a state of rest after regeneration. Days or times, in the Word, always denote states of mind. The six days of creation denote the states through which we pass in being regenerated. And when the battles are all fought, and the victories won, we come to the sabbath of rest.

Now we have expressed the meaning of the four simple and radical numbers, two, three, five, and seven, from which all larger numbers arise, either by multiplication or addition, or by both together. By having a knowledge, therefore, of the signification of only the first ten numbers, and which we have given, the truth of which, from the spiritual sense of the Word, may be satisfactorily proved, we may ascertain something of the meaning of any larger number in the Word, by reducing it to the simple, primitive, or radical number, so that it is not so difficult to ascertain something about the spiritual meaning of numbers as might at first be supposed; and particularly when we are prepared to understand the spiritual meaning of the other parts of the subject where the numbers are used.

In verification of these general statements we will adduce a few examples, commencing with number Twelve, which is the common multiple of three and four. Three, we have seen, denotes fulness and perfection, embracing the triune elements of God Himself: four is the square of two—the dual number—which denotes the union of goodness and truth. Twelve, therefore, the product of three and four, must, from the very qualities they express, denote all goods and truths in the complex. And this is fully sustained by the very prominent use made of it in the Word.

There were twelve tribes of Israel, meaning all the church of God, the elements of which are goods and truths. Moses built an altar on twelve pillars. Pillars signify truths, and altar, worship; denoting that worship should be based on all truths. The breastplate of Aaron, the High Priest, had twelve precious stones, containing the names of the twelve tribes of Israel. Precious stones denote truths; twelve, all goods and truths; the plate worn over the breast denotes that the truths should come from the heart. Joshua set up twelve stones from the river Jordan, as a monumental memorial of the crossing, which signifies that, with all goods and truths in the mind, men will never forget God's mercies. In the temple, they built a sea or font for baptism, and set it upon twelve oxen. Oxen denote good affections, and there being twelve supporting the water, which denotes truth, signifies that all goods and truths attending the washing of regeneration, must come from the affections. There were twelve apostles, who represented all truths of the Word. In the crown of the woman, who denotes the church, there were twelve stars, denoting all truths in the understanding. The Holy City has twelve foundations of stones, denoting that it is based on all truths; and twelve gates, and at the gates twelve angels, which teach that we enter by means of truths and goods.

Again, *forty* is a number much used. And as it is the product of four multiplied by ten, we see that it represents fulness, extending to particulars in man, and would denote all the qualities and states of mind we pass through in the accomplishment of any mental revolution.

Now, the flood is said to have been brought on by a rain of forty days and forty nights; and the narrative declares that the flood was forty days upon the earth. And yet the water is said to have prevailed a much longer time. Now the days denote states of mind; and forty days mean all the states through which that people passed from the commencement of the fall until their minds were inundated with falsities. Thus in Numbers it is written, " Ye shall bear your iniquity forty years : ye shall search the land forty days ; " which means through all the states of their trials. The Psalms are a full prophecy of the states through which the Lord's assumed nature passed, on the earth, to its glorification. And in them He says of the Israelites, " Forty years long was I grieved with this generation." Now, what does He mean ? He did not live forty years on the earth. It means, then, all His states of temptation. Ezekiel was commanded to lie forty days upon his right side, to bear the iniquity of the house of Judah. The right side has relation to goodness, the left side, to truth. To lie upon the right side means to rest or rely upon the goodness of God, and forty days would be during all the states the church might pass through until their iniquity was passed away. Herein it is obvious why it was ordained, in Deuteronomy, that a wicked man should be beaten with forty stripes. It means that he would receive punishment for *all his sins*. And it is said that Moses abode in the mount forty days and forty nights, neither did he eat bread nor drink water, praying for the people. And so, the Lord was tempted in the wilderness forty days : and the children of Israel were forty years in the wilderness, to humble them and to prove them. But it is by no means certain that the Israelites were there forty years, or that the Lord was there forty days, or that Moses was praying forty days and nights without eating bread or drinking water. For forty here means, essentially, all the states of trial through which they passed.

Again, the Lord says, " As the hosts of heaven cannot be numbered, neither the sand of the sea measured, so will I multiply the seed of David, My servant." Now, this cannot be a natural fact, and can only be understood spiritually, by looking at David as the representative of the Lord, as the Word; the Truths of which are multiplied indefinitely, adapting themselves to the states of all people.

The Lord is said to tell the number of the stars, and to call them all by their names. To number or count means to examine the qualities of things, and see how good or how true they are. To number the stars is to examine the truths of the human mind, the stars of our mental heaven, and see their quality. He is said to bring out the hosts of heaven by number; which means that He arranges all heavenly principles in the mind, according to their quality.

Again, the Lord says, through John, "Here is wisdom. Let him that hath understanding count the number of the beast: for it is the number of a man; and his number is Six hundred three score and six." (Rev. xiii, 18.) Here is indeed wisdom: for none can count the number of the beast but him that hath understanding. And to have understanding is to see why his number is 666, and also why this is the number of a man. To have understanding in this matter is to know the spiritual sense.

Now, the quality of the human mind is the thing here inquired after. For the spiritual sense of the Word treats of nothing else but the Divine and human minds. And the mind of man is the complex of all created things. He is called a *beast* on account of his natural appetites and passions. He is called a *man* on account of his reason and intellect. It is his rational faculty which distinguishes him from the beast, and gives him the appellation of man; for the beasts are not endowed with reason.

" Here is wisdom. Let him that hath understanding

count the number of the beast : for it is the number of a man." To count the number of the beast is to ascertain the quality of man's appetites and passions. To count the number of the man is to ascertain the quality of his reason and judgment. To have the number of the beast the same as the number of the man, is to have his reason and judgment of the same quality as his appetites and passions; which is to have his appetites and passions such as his reason and judgment approve. All this is readily seen by any one who will candidly seek the spiritual sense of the subject. But why the number was found to be 666 is not so easily seen. But, by going back to the simple or radical numbers, whose meaning is fixed and certain, we find that two multiplied by three makes six ; and six, having the qualities of both two and three, would denote all goods and truths, the same as twelve : and 666 would mean the same extended to every particular and quality of the mind. But correspondences are to be taken either in a good sense or a bad sense, according to the subject-matter treated of ; and the way they should be taken is readily seen. Now we find that the subject of the thirteenth chapter of Revelation is the state of a fallen church, or of a depraved and beastly mind, destitute of goods and truths ; therefore, the number 666 is expressed in a bad sense, and denotes that the quality of the man has fallen to the depraved quality of the beast, and consequently, in this instance, that number, instead of meaning all goods and truths, extending to all the particulars and qualities of life, means all evils and falsities, extending throughout the whole man or fallen church.

Again, in Genesis vi, 3, it is said of man, that " his days shall be *an hundred and twenty years*." And, from a literal, sensual conclusion, it would be quite natural to suppose that, because of the wickedness of the people, God had determined to cut down their long lives to the period of one hundred and twenty years : or, from some cause or other, their days were thereafter to be limited to that number. But this seems not to be the fact. For, at the time the Divine decree was passed, Noah is said to be five hundred years old. (Gen. v, 32.) Yet he lived . another hundred years, till the flood (chap. vii, 6, 11), and three hundred and fifty years after it : in all, nine hundred and fifty years. (Chap. ix, 28, 29.) Shem also lived six hundred years (chap. xi, 10, 11) ; Arphaxad, four hundred and forty-three years ; Peleg, two hundred and thirty-nine years ; Reu, two hundred and thirty-nine ; Serug, two hundred and thirty ; and many others overran the one hundred and twenty years.

Now, nothing but the spiritual sense can reconcile such apparent discrepancies. But when we see that the number one hundred and twenty arises from the multiplication of ten by twelve, and look at the spiritual meaning, all is plain. For, as ten denotes all the principles of good which the people had, and twelve all the goods and truths which they could receive, and which the Lord would adapt to their states and wants ; therefore, the promise of one hundred and twenty years' life, instead of foreshadowing evil, was a glorious promise, because it declared that, notwithstanding the dark and dead state of the people, just before the flood, yet God would give them new life or new qualities ; thus pointing to a new or Noatic state of the church, whereby He would raise them above the falses and evils that threatened universal destruction, and would give them the qualities of spiritual life, denoted by one hundred and twenty years, but which had no reference whatever to time.

Thus, by a knowledge of the spiritual signification of numbers, and of the spiritual sense of the scripture immediately connected with them, all the objections, with regard to numbers, which Dr. Colenso or any others may raise against the entire truthfulness and holiness of the Scriptures, as given in their original tongues, are entirely groundless, because they reach not the Word itself. Their energies are spent in the shades of appearances, which the spiritual Light of the Word, when seen, readily dispels, leaving even the literal sense luminous and beautiful with the heavenly light, of which it is the perfect vessel and medium.

And as with numbers, so with weights and measures. They all have a spiritual signification, and are used to express states and qualities of the mind. And so also are all temples, tabernacles, altars, and works of art, mentioned in the Word.

To weigh a mental thing is to find out how good it is. To be weighed in a balance and found wanting, is to have no goodness. To measure a principle of the mind is to find out how true it is.

Thus, Revelation xxi, 17, the angel measured the wall of the city and found it to be "one hundred and forty-four cubits according to the measure of a man, that is, of the angel." Now, this is so said because the number twelve denotes all goods and truths; and one hundred and forty-four, being the square of twelve, means the same as twelve, extending to particulars. Now, goods and truths, affectionately and rationally received into the mind, are what constitute a true man or an angel. Therefore, one hundred and forty-four, meaning all goods and truths, would be his measure, or denote his quality. Any one may see that this has nothing to do with natural things. The city descends from God, out of heaven, into the human mind. By this city is meant the doctrines of the Word, in their spiritual signification. By its measure being twelve thousand furlongs, is meant that the doctrines comprise all truths, expressed in laws and rules of action, reaching every circumstance and condition in life. This is because twelve denotes fulness of all goods and truths, and ten, one hundred, or one thousand, denotes all a man has or can receive. Therefore, the city also is the measure of a man, because these doctrines in the mind would show what a man's qualities are, or what his measure is. And by "the length, and the breadth, and the height" of the city being equal, we are taught that the doctrines are equally good, true, and useful. Here it is remarkable that the wall which surrounds the city measures only one hundred and forty-four cubits, while the city, within the wall, is the enormous size of twelve thousand furlongs square. Thus the literal sense alone is a dense cloud of darkness. But when we behold the spiritual sense—the Lord, as the Word, coming in this cloud—all is luminous, beautiful, and rational.

Now, did Bishop Colenso see this spiritual sense pervading the entire Word of God, filling it with spirit and life, as the soul fills the body, how would the atmosphere of his mind clear up, and the heart glow with fresh gratitude and love to the Heavenly Father, as his spirit should read in every sentence clear, useful, and heavenly-instruction, offering to the hungry soul the blessed food of angels! And how gladly would he publish a new version of "*The Pentateuch and Book of Joshua Critically Examined*," with pages glowing with new light, and saying with joy and gladness, to the readers of his first book, that the sacred Scriptures are the sure words of the All-

Wise God, faithfully handed down, without contradiction or error. Then, whenever he should read the history of "*the family of Judah*," of which he speaks in chapter ii, he would not be seeking discrepancies in the letter, but the life and harmony of the spirit. In what is said of their numbers and travels, his thoughts would not be dwelling upon the count and movement of their bodies, but upon the qualities and states of human souls, which the numbers and movements signify. Whenever he should read therein, "Thy fathers went down into Egypt with three-score and ten persons: and now the Lord thy God hath made thee as the stars of heaven for multitude," he would look into the expression, "*three-score and ten*," not for the number of persons, but for the goods and truths of the soul which the number 70 signifies; and he would look into the expression, "*stars of heaven for multitude*," for the great increase of heavenly truths with which they had been blessed: for he would see at once that, as persons, they could not have become as the natural stars for multitude; while, as to the truths of the Word, to which stars correspond, they could be so; for the sacred truths are not only bright, but innumerable. And that history would then become to him the Word of God, and teach his soul practical lessons of regeneration, as doth all scripture when the spiritual sense is seen.

And the mystery which he sees in chapter iv, with regard to "*the size of the court of the tabernacle compared with the number of the congregation*," would be removed by the light of the internal sense. For the human mind is the true tabernacle of God, and is called in the Word "the temple of the Lord." And all the temples and tabernacles, cities and courts, mentioned in the Word, with all their measurements, dimensions, localities, vessels, ornaments, and uses, denote the minds of men, or qualities and things of the mind. And, as the Bishop should look into the world of mind for the things signified by courts, tabernacles, and numbers, he would find this scripture "profitable for doctrine . . . and instruction in righteousness," and applicable to his own mind, or to any number of people at any time, who would look to the Lord for light and life.

Wherever the court and tabernacle are mentioned, the tabernacle denotes the internal mind of man, and the court the external mind; and by the door of the tabernacle is meant faith in the truth. Therefore the Lord says He is THE DOOR, because He is the truth of faith, or is the Word, in the understanding, believed. And by the assembling of all the congregation at the door of the tabernacle, would be meant the bringing together of all the affections and principles of the mind of an individual or of a community before the Lord, in true faith, that the tabernacle of the soul might be entered by the Lord, as the Word, through the door of faith, for the establishment of His kingdom. In this way we become prepared to receive the Lord or the truth through the court or external mind, into the tabernacle or internal mind, where, in the light of that truth, we may begin truly to read and know ourselves, and in the power of the Spirit to become new creatures. In this way the minds of men are to become the temples of the Lord.

And the width of the tabernacle being ten cubits, and the length thirty cubits, and the court being one hundred cubits in length, and fifty in breadth, all these numbers show at once what should be the quality of the internal and external minds in order to receive the Lord and be prepared for heaven. For these numbers denote fulness of goods and truths.

And how much the value of the Holy Word is enhanced when we see that it is not given merely to direct the construction and arrangement of material things, and to prompt our actions with regard to them ; but to teach the soul, through their forms, sizes, and uses, the true qualities of the heart and the living lessons of the Word ; thus showing the proper states of mind necessary for true worship, and for the work of regeneration !

But here men seem alarmed at the apparent loss of the literal sense of the Word, as though their sheet anchor were gone. But let me quiet their fears by assuring them that the literal sense of the Word is everywhere true, as a sure expression or symbol of an internal or real sense, which is the soul's true life ; and what can we want more ? True, the Bishop finds great difficulty with the literal sense. But suppose he did not ; suppose everything in the letter had been differently written, and were just suited to his mind, and to all natural minds, so that they could see and understand it as well as they do a common note of hand ; what would be the result ? The Bishop would probably be satisfied with the literal sense, and would seek nothing higher in the Word, and men would seem to themselves to know as much about it as the Lord. The fact is, the difficulties men find in understanding the letter of the Word are what will eventually turn their attention to the spiritual sense. There is a holy sphere and power in the Word that men cannot give up. And when the Lord, as the spiritual sense, is once fairly "*lifted up*," He "*will draw all men unto*" Him.

There is much literal history in the Word, the general features of which are a true record of events as they occurred in this world; but, in making that record, many particular things were no doubt modified by the Lord to suit the requirements of the spiritual sense, leaving out such things as were not in correspondences, and supplying such as were, at the same time giving all the literal history necessary for the good of mankind, and making a perfect spiritual history of the church in man, or of mental and real things contained in such a literal sense as would perfectly express it by correspondences : so that we can go to this history to learn correctly what the souls of men have passed through, and also to obtain thereby the valuable instructions we need for the action and purification of our own souls.

Thus the history says the seed of Abram was to be *innumerable*—" *as the dust of the earth, and as the stars of heaven.*" (Gen. xiii, 16.)   Here the natural history, for the sake of the spiritual sense, is made to give up every appearance of truthfulness, and to state what no one believes naturally occurred ; and yet no one is hurt by it ; while that same literal sense, in the language of correspondences, is perfectly true and beautiful ; because Abram represents the Lord, and by the seed of Abram is denoted. all the truths of the Word, which are innumerable.

Much might be cited from the Word, wherein it is clear that the literal narrative was either interrupted by something foreign from the natural thread of thought, or modified by changes, for the sake of the spiritual or living sense ; and particularly with regard to numbers, which are ever used to express the quality of mental things . always, no doubt, giving a correct natural account of the number of persons or things referred to, whenever that number would express the true quality of the spiritual

things treated of: but if it would not, we readily see
that, if expressed in the record, it would not be a true
spiritual history. And most surely the words of the
Most High God, which are spirit and life, must be given
to spiritual beings for higher purposes than simply to
talk about the things of time, and teach men after what
fashion they should make natural tabernacles, and courts,
and temples, and high priests' garments, and their ornaments. They must be given to teach how the minds of
men—the true tabernacles of the Lord—are to be formed,
by means of things good and true, and clothed with the
" garments of salvation," having on the " breast-plate of
righteousness," and the " feet shod with the preparation
of the gospel of peace." And through the description of
these outward things, that instruction, by the science of
correspondences, is given ; and no doubt better than it
could be given, in the spiritual light, in any other way.
Moreover, when we see clearly that numbers are used to
express the qualities of things of the mind, and often
without any regard to the number of natural things referred to, many difficulties of the letter, which appear of
great magnitude to some men, but which, in reality, do
not at all concern us spiritually, are at once removed, and
the literal sense appears all right—the numbers answering
the full purpose for which they were used : as in the seal-
ing of the servants of God, from the tribes of the children
of Israel. (Rev. vii.) We find the whole number sealed
to be one hundred and forty-four thousand. This number, we have shown, signifies the same as twelve, of
which one hundred and forty-four is the square, and
which, as has been shown, was the measure of a man, that
is, of an angel. And as twelve denotes all goods and
truths, so we thereby see the true character and quality

of all the children of Israel who were prepared for heaven : which teaches that, to be sealed for heaven, we must not be opposed to anything heavenly, but must yield to the influence of all goods and truths, in their multifarious operations, even as to all the little particulars of thoughts, feelings, and actions, expressed by one hundred and forty-four thousand.

By this light are dispelled all the clouds of doubt that may arise from the idea that, of the enormous body of the children of Israel, able to send out six hundred and three thousand, five hundred and fifty warriors (Numbers i), there should have been but one hundred and forty-four thousand sealed for heaven ; and also from the fact that, though the twelve tribes were of various magnitudes, some containing more than twice the number of others, yet that each tribe should have had precisely the same number of good ones—twelve thousand. For, when we see that twelve thousand denotes simply the qualification of the members of each tribe for heaven, whether they were many or few, all is right. Therefore we learn from this spiritual sense that the one hundred and forty-four thousand saved were all that were good and true, without regard to natural numbers, and also that simply belonging outwardly to a body of the church does not save us. We must bear the seal of twelve thousand in the forehead. We must be good and true.

And so all the difficulties which the Bishop sees in the " war on Midian," noted in Part First of his work, numbers 169 and 172, would soon be lost in spiritual light, if he saw the internal sense and felt its importance. For he would then see that, whatever may have been the natural facts in the various wars mentioned in the Word, the narratives have been written and recorded for the sake of the spiritual sense, in order to teach men the way of life. And in seeing and receiving the spiritual light and life, his soul would be satisfied that he had found a true history of mental wars—of the combats of goods and truths against evils and falsities in the human mind. He would see that the various nations, tribes, and sexes engaged denote principles of the mind; that the numbers mentioned denote the qualities of those principles; and that the extent or size of the numbers is always governed primarily by the mental qualities of the nations, tribes, individuals, or principles mentioned, rather than by the count of them. And then he would see, by the spiritual rule of arriving at mental qualities, that, where thirty thousand are mentioned, there may not have been over thirty individuals, or where five hundred thousand, not over fifty, and so forth; and that the numbers had been extended for the sake of the innumerable qualities, combinations, and shades of the various goods and truths or evils and falsities engaged, conquered, or killed in this mental warfare; and of which the Lord, who ordered the record, could see the use that would eventually result from it. For we should consider that the Lord's Word must be eternal truth, and therefore adapted to all ages that are to come, and that its true spirit and life are yet to be clearly seen and felt.

And then, as the Bishop would see that, in the "war on Midian," the instruction is applicable to man's regeneration in the present day and in the ages to come; and that the Israelites denote good and true principles of the internal mind, and the Midianites denote evil and false principles of the external mind; and as he would further see that any human mind, of either sex, has both the male and female elements; that the female elements of

8

that mind are either goods or evils, or both, and that the
male elements of the same mind are either truths or falsities, or both; and that this war on Midian we must all
pass through in our regeneration—the Israelites, or good
and true principles of the internal mind, fighting against
the Midianites, or evil and false principles of the external
mind;—I say, as the Bishop would see and receive this
spiritual light and life of the Holy Word, he would be
satisfied that he had found a true history of mental wars
which purify the soul, and that the literal sense was in
precisely the right language to express it.

And having the understanding thus far opened, to behold the wonderful things written in God's law, the
Bishop would be able clearly to see that, by the *males* of
the Midianites, which we must all slay in this warfare,
are meant all the *falsities* of the natural mind; and the
females, which Moses or the law commands us to slay,
are all the *evils* of that mind; while the young females,
that we are to keep for ourselves, are all the remains of
good, all the good, conscientious principles we may have,
which have not been adulterated or perverted with falsities; and that these tender germs of heavenly affection,
which the Lord has mercifully given us and thus far pro-
tected, we are to take to our bosoms, and ever guard them
from all harm.

Thus seeing the beauty and use of the spiritual sense,
and also the divine object in giving it; and seeing, further, that God is often said, in the Word, to order or to do
what He only permits to be done; and, therefore, that
whatever was wrong in the "war on Midian," was from
the wickedness of man, and not from God, and was permitted in order to prevent some greater evil or to bring
about some important good;—I say, seeing this heavenly

light, how changed would God's Word appear to the
Bishop, and how flimsy and indefinite would become all
his objections!

And so his inquiring heart would rejoice to see everything apparently unkind or unjust everywhere removed
from the will of God in the spirit of His Word; and particularly from such passages as those of Deuteronomy
xxi, 1, 2. And here he would see that, as every part of
the body denotes something of the mind—the eye denoting the understanding; the ear, obedience; the nose, perception; the hands, power; the lips, language; and so
forth—so he would also see that the first verse points to
the *mentally* wounded or maimed; to such as have by
sin destroyed their ability to propagate spiritual things—
the goods and truths of the Word—for, without the ability
or willingness to be instructed and to receive the truths of
the Word into good ground, and to cultivate and bring
forth the fruits of righteousness, men cannot be regenerated so as to enter into the kingdom of heaven, or the
"congregation of the Lord." Thus, how completely the
apparent injustice of the letter is lost in the beautiful
light of the spirit!

And equally are we rejoiced to see all unkindness removed from the second verse. For, in the spiritual sense,
we see that any spiritual birth, springing not from the
marriage of goodness and truth, must, in the divine light,
be illegitimate and evil, and therefore could not enter
heaven or be happy; for, in order to do this, we must be
born of God, or of goodness and truth. The church is
goodness from God in the will: the Lord, as the husband
of the church, is truth in the understanding: characters
born of this parentage are the only true children of God.
If men embrace the truths of the Word in their affections,

and humbly carry them out in their lives, they will be born of the spirit; whatever may have been the character or marriage relation of their natural parents.

Much sorrow and gloom have pressed upon the minds of certain individuals of former ages, in consequence of these verses; but, as intelligence and reason have advanced, men have turned from such teachings and their gloom to the worse gloom of skepticism. Let them now return and embrace the spirit and life of the Word, and all their former and latter gloom will disappear. The Word will everywhere be found to be pure and holy, merciful and kind, just and reasonable.

But it is not my intention, with the spiritual sense, to follow the Bishop through all his statements of difficulties in the letter; but merely to glance at the fundamental principles of the Divine and human natures, and at the great living laws of creation and providence, laid down in the Holy Word, and sustained and illustrated therein through the means of His works, by the science of correspondences, whereby the truth and perfection of the Word may be irrefutably sustained, and the true interests of mankind rationally understood.

CHAPTER XIV.

As heat and light are the highest and most prominent things used in correspondences, it will very much aid the student of the Word to obtain clear and definite views of the relation which they bear to the Divine Love and Wisdom, that he may be able, as he proceeds in the divine study, to understand the beautiful analogy which exists in the Word between the influence of the Love and Wisdom of God upon the human mind, in the production of everything good and true in the soul, and that of the heat and light of the sun, in the production of the things of nature, which are brought up in the Word to express those things of the soul.

Now heat corresponds to Love or Life, and light to Wisdom or Truth; and the Lord is called the Light and the Life. Spiritual Light and Life, then, are infinite things, and can be rationally approached by man, at this age of the world, only by the science of correspondences.

Now there are various degrees of heat and light. There are spiritual heat and light, or love and wisdom, from the spiritual sense of the Word, for the internal mind of man, by which we look up to God and to the heavenly laws; and there are natural heat and light, or love and wisdom, from the literal sense of the Word, for the external mind of man, by which we look out to our neighbors, and to the laws of civil truth and justice. And there are also material heat and light, by means of which we see and feel material things, through the senses of our material bodies. This material heat and light are the physical expressions of the Divine Love and Wisdom, and are the sensible manifestations to man in the flesh of those principles by correspondences.

But the material heat and light are not real life and light, but only their effects and representatives. Yet, as the divine life and light are the cause, and are in the effect, the material heat and light are, therefore, perfect correspondences to the spiritual life and light of the Word. But the literal sense of the Word is also a body of natural Truth and Love higher than matter ; and which the spiritual sense infills, as its soul and life. Therefore, when our thoughts ascend above material heat and light to the literal sense of the Word ; we find in that sense a sure correspondence to a still higher or spiritual sense. That literal sense is the body which adapts the spiritual sense to our capacities by correspondence, just as the material heat and light are the material body which brings down those divine principles still lower, and adapts them to our bodily senses.

We are now in the flesh, and are so low and natural that spiritual things have to be presented to us by correspondences, so as to be apprehended, even through material coverings. It was in consequence of this low state that the Lord, in order to reach us, had to come down into a material body, and reach us through the senses.

Now the Divine Life and Light, or Love and Wisdom,

are, in themselves, Infinite. And man, being finite, can
never see them as they are. He can only look toward
them by correspondences. And these correspondences
through which he looks must all be finite and adapted
to his state. The divine Life and Light, therefore, have
mercifully clothed themselves, by correspondences, in
lower and still lower finite forms, adapted to the various
states of men and angels, till they have come down to
men on earth in material heat and light.

The next form of them, above material heat and light,
is the literal sense of the Word in its love and truth. But
even these heavenly principles, as men see and feel them,
are also finite. Yet they are filled with the infinite.
And, as we look through them by correspondences to the
life and light of the spiritual sense, we have a still higher
and more complete view of the divine qualities.

But no angel can see God, as He is in Himself. The
higher we advance in purity, the more exalted will be the
correspondences through which we look, and the more
clear and heavenly the view. We can therefore have a
rational but finite conception of something like the infinite life and light, through their effects, produced by
natural life and light in the universe of mind; and also
by material heat and light in the universe of matter.
Spiritual life and light are for the spiritual minds of men
and angels; natural life and light, for the natural minds
of men and angels, and material heat and light, for the
bodies of men on earth and material substances.

But each lower degree has to be filled with the next
higher, or it could not exist. The material must be filled
with the natural, the natural with the spiritual, and the
spiritual with the celestial—the Divine Essence and
Fountain.

Now, as spiritual life and light are far above all spiritual minds, and are the source of their existence and development ; and as natural life and light are far above all natural minds, and are the immediate source of their existence and development ; so material heat and light are far above all other material substances, and *seem* to be the source of their existence and development. But this is only an appearance. Material heat and light are mere instruments. But even as material substances, they are far beyond the reach of the natural sciences of the present age. We know not, from natural science, what are their intrinsic properties.

Is it not a little remarkable that so common material substances as heat and light should, at this enlightened age, still remain beyond the reach of human sagacity or scientific research ? There are many things in nature which correspond to love and wisdom, to which we can successfully apply the laws of analytical investigation ; such as land and water, or gold and silver, or oil and wine, which denote goodness and truth, and point us, by correspondence, to the two great divine elements—Love and Wisdom, or Life and Light. These natural substances can be analyzed, and their properties defined ; but who can bring into his laboratory a ray of light, and extract from it its heat, and tell us what are the elementary properties of the two parts, or of either part ?

Now heat and light are the first material substances in which the Divine Love and Wisdom clothe themselves, in correspondence, as they descend in the scale of being. But, as these divine elements descend, through spiritual substances, into material, and first clothe themselves in heat and light, they, even there in the robe of nature, leave us lost as to the nature and quality of the very matter in which they express themselves to our senses ; thus leaving the material dress as much a matter of wonder to us as is the life which infills it, and to which it corresponds. Heat and light being only the first step below spiritual substances, are consequently the highest material substances. They are so high and so near the divine qualities, that when we attempt, by natural science, to analyze them, they are lost in the unspeakable glory of the infinite which they express. And they stand before the mind, and even the senses of man, as the most perfect correspondences, or the highest material symbols of the divine love and wisdom.

As God Himself is Love, and as He, by His infinite wisdom, created the universe, and as He, in that love and wisdom, is the Great Heavenly Father who is ever warming and illuminating the hearts and minds of angels and men ; so material heat and light seem, in their united power, to be the great parents of the material universe. All nature seems *almost* to worship the sun, and to look up to him for support and nourishment from his heat and light. The planets, in their revolutions, seem almost to do him homage. In his apparent, parental affections, he holds them in their orbits from going astray. They daily turn their faces to his genial sphere ; and in fable they might seem individually to say to their animal and vegetable offspring, " Look up, my children, to your glorious father, who warms you, and nourishes you, and gives you life and light." And when these planets, in their wanderings and apparent forgetfulness of the source of life, find the cold frosts of seeming selfishness congealing their bosoms and stopping the vital action, then seemingly like the repentant sinner they turn their frozen sides to the parent sun, and yielding to the kind and creative sphere

8*

of his heat and light, he melts their frosts, warms their bosoms, fills them with animation and life, clothes them in new robes, adorns them with beautiful colors from his own beams, and blesses them with flowers and fruits; and the song of joy and praise ascends from ten thousand choristers. And how precisely do these influences of the sun's heat and light upon the world of matter correspond to the operations of the divine love and wisdom upon the world of mind!

Yes, the sun is the first and highest symbol in nature of the Great Jehovah. And how perfect the correspondence! No wonder that the heathen worshipped the sun. There he stands, in glorious majesty, in the physical firmament, an immense body of heat and light, filling the vast sphere of his system of worlds, with his own genial beams, holding everything in their places, and presiding like a father over his family. And while there in his splendor, meeting the gaze of an inquiring world, he is sending down his properties to every living thing; giving constantly to the material world the very elements of himself, the same as God gives His love and wisdom to the mental world. And yet, with all these generous contributions of the sun's nature, he remains the very puzzle and wonder of all human science. How he can exist and constantly give off a vast flood of material substances— how he can forever be giving himself away, and still remain undiminished, is yet the astounding problem of the natural man. Thus, like our Heavenly Father, the sun is ever giving, and yet is ever full. Material heat and light, then, are yet above the reach of human science. We can approach no nearer to physical heat and light than their effects. We behold the animal or the tree, when alive, and we look at them when dead. We mark the change. But we know not the quality nor the substance of the life that once animated them. Thus it is beyond the power of human reason and research ever to draw from nature alone the moving power and quality of her laws. She can never tell us how it is that she has life and light, nor what that light and life are.

But there is an Author to nature. There is a Source from which nature springs. Now, man is neither that Author nor is he nature. He is the uniting link between the two. Man is human. Nature is not human. Humanity is free and rational. Nature is not free and rational. Humanity can look upward or downward, backward or forward. Nature can look but one way—the way she goes. Man is designed for higher life. Nature is not. Man, as to his mind, is both spiritual and natural. That mind is, therefore, connected internally with the spiritual world and with its God, and externally with its material body and with nature. Man is therefore capable of giving his affections and thoughts either to the things of this world, which are low and perishable, or to the things of the spiritual world, which are heavenly and eternal. Therefore, man is not always obliged to remain ignorant of the nature and quality of life and light, because the natural sciences do not reach them.

Man has a higher Teacher than nature. God is his Teacher. And though God speaks to him and teaches him through nature, yet He has also spoken to him in a direct revelation. And in this revelation of His Holy Word, He makes known to us man's relation to nature, and also his relation to his God. And He gives him a science above all natural sciences—the science of correspondences, or of the relation of natural things to their causes—the relation which exists between mind and matter.

By this science He teaches us to look through nature up to nature's God; to read the invisible things of God from the creation of the world, through the things that are made.

Man, therefore, is capable of making unlimited progress in wisdom and knowledge. For, though he sees not, by natural science, what the sun is, nor what his heat and light are, nor how he gives them off undiminished, yet he may see, by the Divine truth of analogy, into higher regions of light; he may see that the sun is the effect of the Divine love and wisdom in their operation for the creation of physical things; that the Divine love and wisdom, flowing from the Great Jehovah, for the creation of lower things, first produce the natural sun; that that sun is the first material ultimate or effect of the Divine efflux in the production of nature. And as the Divine love and wisdom are spiritual heat and light, and are ever flowing into the sun, producing natural heat and light, therefore the sun is always full, though constantly giving itself away in material heat and light. For, though the sun is ever giving off its substances, yet it is also ever being created; because the cause which at first produced it is always producing it. For, as God is the same yesterday, to-day, and forever, so He is therefore a Creator yesterday, to-day, and forever. He is, consequently, from His love and wisdom, always creating the sun. And through the outflowing heat and light of that sun, as a means, the Lord is always creating the lower orders of things in nature. Thus the earth brings forth, and is ever teeming with new creations of animal and vegetable life. Suspend the influx of the Divine love and wisdom into that sun, and you would suspend the efflux of the sun's heat and light; and darkness and death would follow throughout the entire solar system.

But, it is asked, how this is known? We answer, it is known from the science of correspondences, seen in the spiritual sense of the Holy Word. God Himself teaches it, not man. We are taught many times in the Word that heat and light correspond to love and wisdom; by which we are also taught that love and wisdom are the direct cause of heat and light as an effect. From this simple fact alone may be drawn all the ideas we have advanced on the subject.

The Sun of Righteousness, of which we read in the Holy Word, is nothing but the concentration of the Divine love and wisdom in the spiritual world. And the natural sun, in our world, is constantly created and sustained by the Divine love and wisdom flowing from God, as that Sun of Righteousness, into the material sphere. God works by means; and these means are always according to the science of correspondences. The opening of the Holy Word, by this Divine science, discloses to the mind of man a new source and field of instruction. The march of humanity, therefore, in the path of wisdom, must henceforth be more rapidly onward; for the way must become more and more clear and bright. And the extent of the progress will be limited only by infinity. But to make this progress we must look up, and not down. We must look to God as our teacher. We must look into the science of correspondences, and the nature of the Divine language. We must seek a knowledge of the world of causes through the world of effects. We must seek a knowledge of our own internal will or heart's desires through the nature and character of our outward thoughts, feelings, and actions. And we should measure them all by the golden reed of truth, and weigh them in the scales of Divine justice. Thus we must become acquainted with the Divine laws, in their mental and physical application to ourselves. And we must strive, diligently and faithfully, to conform our lives to those laws.

A brief but comprehensive view of those laws may be always seen in their Divine summing up—*love to God and the neighbor.* And we may readily decide upon the character of any thought, feeling, or action, by applying this test: Was it done from love to God and the neighbor? And would a world of such thoughts, feelings, and actions, produce heaven? These are the test questions. And we must ever be conscious that we derive all our wisdom, power, and ability to conform to these laws, from the *life and light of the Lord.*

"*In Him was life, and the life was the light of men.*" (John i, 4.) Here the Word says the *light of men* is the *life of God.* The true light of men is the Divine truth. The life of the Lord is the Divine love, which gives all the Divine truth to men. To really have the *light of men,* then, so as clearly to see by it, we must possess the *life.* That life is the love of God and the neighbor: it is the love of goodness and truth. If we have not that life, the light, as declared in the Word, will *shine in darkness, and the darkness will comprehend it not.* If we have not the life, the light will condemn us; and we cannot clearly see by it. We falsify it. And thus the light becomes darkness in us. And the Lord says of such, "If the light in thee be darkness, how great is that darkness!" If we have not that life or love of good, we then have the opposite life, the love of evil; and this evil love falsifies the truth.

But men may have, to some extent, the love of good or love of right, and still not clearly see the truth, for the want of proper instruction. And the Lord mercifully regards the conditions of men under all circumstances, and adapts His dispensations to their wants in every age of life. And now, when the world most needs it, He is giving to men the internal sense of the Word, and clear views of its doctrines; that its light and life may be seen and felt; so that the light may no longer shine in darkness, and the darkness comprehend it not. And it is our blessed privilege to live in this age, when that life and light are clearly made known. May we be truly sensible of this inestimable privilege; and may we rightly improve it, by shunning all evils as sins against God, and letting our light so shine before men that they may see our good works, and glorify our Father who is in heaven. Then will our path grow brighter and brighter unto the perfect day. God will be merciful unto us, and bless us, and show us the light of His countenance; that His way may be known upon the earth, His saving health among all nations.

CHAPTER XV.

As the one great study of man is the study of the human mind, God being connected with that mind, from above, and nature, from below, man being the intermediate plane, and the first receptacle of life ; therefore, if we would study divinity, we must study humanity in connection with God. For we can truly know nothing of God, or of His properties, except as they are received into the mind, and there understood and felt. We can know nothing of heaven, or of hell, or of the spiritual world, but from the study of the human mind and of their operations there. Everything has to be learned there, whether good or evil, true or false.

The human mind is the first free and rational receptacle into which things flow, from the Infinite Fountain. For, by the human mind is meant all the minds of angels and men—universal human nature. Before things enter the rational sphere of the human mind, we know nothing of them. The human mind is the great laboratory, into which all things must be brought, and analyzed, before they can be rationally known by any being but God.

But as this human mind has both an external and an

internal, or a natural and a spiritual plane, so it is capable of exercising two forms of thought, by having two standpoints for looking at the same things, whereby the objects viewed are seen in either a natural or spiritual point of view.

Now, it is in reference to these things that our Lord says, "No man putteth a piece of new cloth unto an old garment, for that which is put in to fill it up taketh from the garment, and the rent is made worse. Neither do men put new wine into old bottles: else the bottles break, and the wine runneth out, and the bottles perish: but they put new wine into new bottles, and both are preserved." (Matt. ix, 16, 17.) For the doctrine or idea which we have of a thing is the bottle; and the truth, contained in the idea, is the wine. And as the doctrines or ideas which we first form of things, whether civil, moral or religious, are all natural, therefore, they are the old bottles; and the natural truth which fills them is the old wine. The new wine is the spiritual truth of the Word, which must be put into new bottles.

The natural or literal truths of the Word are adapted to the natural or external mind, and to time and space. And as time and space are appearances—and yet, to the natural mind, are as realities—so the literal truths of the Word, in order to reach minds that are thinking and acting as in time and space, have to be brought down into appearances. The external mind, connected as it is with the body, and thereby with time and space, and receiving all its first impressions through the senses of the body, cannot be, at first, educated and developed in any other way. But when the external mind is developed to manhood, and its higher faculties begin to be called into exercise, man finds his apparent truths involved in mystery.

They rest in the world of effects, and do not reach the world of causes. They need an interpreter, before they can satisfy his mental wants. This is because man has a higher nature, a spiritual mind within, designed for the spiritual world; and he desires to know the " whys " and " wherefores " of his being, and is asking for spiritual light —for new wine.

But the spiritual mind is yet young, like a little child; while the natural mind is " a strong man armed." And the spiritual truths require the strong man to give up his way of feeling, thinking, and acting, and to submit to the dictation and government of this child. The strong man is proud and selfish, and his mental appetites and habits are · such that he does not relish this new wine. True there is much mystery about his old wine : but he has so adulterated it, by adapting it to his selfish feelings and habits of life, that he loves it better, in all its mysteries, than he does the new wine. " *No man having drunk old wine straightway desireth new,*" saith the Lord. Anything that is to revolutionize the whole mind, in its modes of thinking, feeling, and acting, or which is to change it from natural to spiritual, can only be slowly received and loved ; and to many, when first presented, it cannot be seen at all. When our Lord said to the Jews, " If a man keep my saying, he shall never see death," they could not drink that new wine. The old apparent truth, that the death of the body was the death of the man, was better wine to them. They therefore answered, " Now we know that thou hast a devil. Abraham is dead, and the prophets," &c. (John viii, 52, 53.)

The Jews obeyed the commandments, in the letter ; but they kept them not in the spirit : they did not love them. And they were, consequently, bad men. And the world was perishing under their teachings. The Lord therefore came and established the Christian Church; and He told His disciples that His words were spirit and life; and that, if they would enter into life, they must keep the commandments. And now, after the lapse of more than eighteen centuries, how poorly are the commandments kept, even in the letter; and how little are they lived and believed in, in the spirit! True, in the simple letter, they are the way of life, and bring heaven into all souls that sincerely love and keep them. But how few, at this day, are willing to love and keep them! And fewer still are willing to see that there is a spiritual sense in those commandments; and that men can steal, and lie, and murder, and commit adultery, and break the Sabbath, and transgress every divine law with their souls, while their bodies are rigidly keeping those laws in the letter. Thus did the Jews.

Let us then consider the necessity of new bottles for new wine, and the impossibility of receiving it into old bottles. When the Lord says, " He that eateth my flesh and drinketh my blood hath everlasting life," the old bottle, or natural thought, presents us with the broken body and shed blood of the Lord as the ground of salvation through faith : but the new bottle or spiritual thought, presents us, by correspondence, with His offered goodness and truth, which the old bottle cannot receive, because it is a different idea. Therefore, from the new bottle, or spiritual thought, we eat the bread and drink the wine, as an assurance, that it is only by the actual reception of the goodness and truth of the Lord, into our souls, that we can be born again, or have eternal life in heaven : and also, that, by the continual reception and appropriation of these principles, we must grow up from small beginnings, into full stature of men in Christ Jesus—from spiritual infants we must become full-grown men.

Hence, a great change is gradually coming over the Christian world. And it must continue till the Lord, according to promise, make *all things new*. Many persons are now seeing many things in the Word, in a very different light from that in which they were seen fifty years ago. This change is in consequence of a change of state and standpoint. One state looks at things through the old bottles; and the other, through the new. Therefore, in the celebration of the Lord's supper, the thoughts and feelings of persons in natural thought differ very widely from those of persons in spiritual thought. For, in the literal thought, men receive the bread and wine as a memorial that Christ died for them; and, in that act, they do show forth His death till He come. But, in the spiritual thought, the Lord has come, as spiritual truth; so that we no longer partake of that supper, to show forth His death till He come: but we receive the bread and wine, as symbols of the Lord's goodness and truth, received into the soul, at this, His second coming, as the spirit and life of that soul. In natural thought men receive these aliments in commemoration of Christ's death and departure. In spiritual thought, we receive them as symbols of His life and second coming. In natural thought, men see the letter, only, of the Word, which is as a cloud, hiding the Lord till He come. Therefore, in His absence, they dwell much upon the death and sufferings of His body. In spiritual thought we see the Lord Himself, as the spiritual truth, coming in the clouds of heaven, or literal sense of the Word, and we receive Him with joy and gladness, dwelling upon His goodness and truth as the living God, manifest. In natural thought, men have done right, and their duty, in sincerely and piously worshipping the Lord, in this ordinance, according to their understanding of the letter, in showing forth His death till He come. And they will receive their reward. But, in spiritual thought, in order to do our duty, we now, instead of showing forth the Lord's death and absence, must show forth His life and presence; by manifesting His goodness and truth, in our feelings and actions toward mankind. In natural thought, men have placed the salvation of the world upon the natural death and sufferings of the Lord, as a substitute for man's future punishment; applying this salvation to the soul, by means of faith in the atoning merits of that suffering. While in spiritual thought, we place man's salvation upon the spiritual resurrection and life of Christ, in which He conquered death and hell in our nature, giving us precept and example, and the power of His Spirit, whereby we, through faith in His Word, can conquer death and hell, in ourselves, and rise from the spiritual death of the love of self and the world, to the spiritual life of the love of God and the neighbor, and thereby be washed, and made clean, in the blood of Christ; or, in the life and power of the truth, constantly shed abroad from the risen and ever-living Lord, for the salvation of the world.

In natural thought, from its darkness and obscurity, in their natural minds, men have become divided into various sects with conflicting views. In spiritual thought, from the clear and indisputable light, harmonizing the whole Word in its letter and spirit, all the people of earth will gradually be brought together, and will see eye to eye. In natural thought, men suppose the Lord says, of His natural blood, "This is My blood of the New Testament, which is shed for many for the remission of sins."

In spiritual thought, we understand by His blood, the truth
of the Holy Spirit, ever shed for the cleansing of souls.
For, as the Holy Spirit is declared in the Word to be the
spirit of truth; what can be the blood of the New Testament, which remits sins, but the life and power of the spiritual truth, operating by means of the literal truth, cleansing the soul from all its sins, by repentance, faith, charity,
and obedience? And what else can remit sins, or change
men's hearts and minds and remove their evils, but the
Spirit of the living God—the power of truth and love?
Christ remitted sins, cast out devils, and cleansed souls,
while He was here in the flesh. And He did it by the
blood of the New Testament, or by the power of the
spirit of truth, operating through the natural truth upon
their minds, until they saw their evils and, with great
faith, broke off from their sins by righteousness. This
great faith was faith in the blood of Christ; or, in other
words, it was faith in Christ's word and power. They
believed what He told them; and, *believing* it, they *did*
it. They had no faith whatever in the blood of His
natural body. It had not been shed. They had not the
least idea, or thought, of any blood, in their minds. It is
simply because the life and power given to the natural
body operate by means of the blood, that the word
"blood" is used, in Scripture, to denote the life and power
of the soul. Herein is true correspondence. Faith, therefore, in the power of Christ, is faith in the truth of His
Word, as the wisdom of the Most High God.

If, then, we have faith in the truth of His Word strong
enough to induce us to repent of our sins, and break off
from them by righteousness and, thereby, receive God's
laws into our hearts; we shall drink into our souls
Christ's blood of the New Testament; and, in the process,

it will, by means of the natural truth, cleanse and purify us from all sins. Therefore, the blood of Christ, which cleanses from all sin, is the spiritual truth of the Word, operating by means of the natural truth ; and we must drink this spiritual truth, or have no life in us.

Again, the common creeds of Christendom acknowledge the truth of a trinity in God. But one man sees that trinity in natural thought, as three distinct persons, and supposes that, in some mysterious way, they make one God ; while another, in spiritual thought, sees three distinct elements of the one, undivided Jehovah.

So, again, the one in natural thought, sees the Lord by faith coming again into the natural world in the natural clouds, to be seen by natural eyes : while the other, in spiritual thought, sees Him coming, as the Word, or spiritual truth, into the mental world, or human mind, in mental clouds, to be seen by the understandings of men—the mental eyes.

Again, the one in natural thought, sees a natural resurrection ; a body rising up out of the grave, thousands of years after it had been buried, and uniting again with the soul ; the other, in spiritual thought, sees a spiritual body, rising from the natural body at death. The one in natural thought, looks at the man's body as the man ; and speaks of the man's being dead when the body dies : the other in spiritual thought, looks at the man's soul as the man, and speaks of him as alive when the body is dead. The one in natural thought, speaks of man's introducing sin into the natural world by his body's eating the fruit of a natural tree : the one in spiritual thought speaks of man's introducing sin into the world of mind, by his soul's eating of what is evil and false. The one in natural thought, looks upon heaven as a place of rewards, by outward comforts and blessings ; and upon hell, as a place of punishment, by outward inflictions : while the one in spiritual thought looks upon heaven as a state of inward peace and happiness of mind, resulting from the love of good ; and upon hell, as a state of inward troubles and unhappiness of mind, resulting from the love of evil. Therefore, the one in natural thought looks upon the torments of hell as inflicted by God ; while the one in spiritual thought looks upon them as the result of the evils of the heart : consequently, the one in natural thought looks upon God as angry and revengeful toward the wicked ; while the one in spiritual thought looks upon the anger and revenge as being in the wicked man, who would judge of God according to what he would do himself. Thus, in order to reach angry men, and excite them to repentance and fear, God's Word comes down to them, presenting Him as He appears to them to be.

Again, the one in natural thought looks upon sin, as a wicked act ; upon repentance of sin, as sorrow for the act ; and upon the remission of sin, as the pardon of the penalty of the act : while the one in spiritual thought, looks upon sin as a depraved and evil desire ; upon repentance of sin, as sorrow for the desire ; and upon the remission of sin, as the removal of the desire : so that a person, whose sins are all remitted, is pure and holy—prepared for heaven.

Thus, we see that the change from a natural to a spiritual mode of thought, presents an entirely new view of all the doctrines of the Word. It turns the whole course of human life into a new channel of thought, feeling, and action. Well may our Lord have said, *No man having drunk old wine, straightway desireth new.*

The progress, therefore, of this mighty work, by which

the entire face of humanity on earth is to be turned upward from time and matter, toward God and heaven,
must necessarily be slow. For the spiritual principles
have to be embraced as a whole ; and that must be done
by a full surrender of all the old bottles or doctrines, as
unfit for the new wine. For, our Lord says, " No man
putteth a piece of new cloth unto an old garment ; for
that which is put in to fill it up taketh from the garment,
and the rent is made worse." (Matt. ix, 16.) The old garment is the old doctrine ; the new garment is the new.
The old is natural or apparent truth, adulterated by man ;
the new, is spiritual or real truth.

Now, you cannot take parts of two garments and put
them together. The Lord says, " The new agreeth not
with the old." If you take the new doctrine of the trinity, in one person, where " God is in Christ reconciling
the world unto Himself," you cannot bring into the same
garment the old idea, that God is out of Christ ; and
Christ is reconciling God to the world and the world to
God : for here are two persons. And Christ therefore
must be either a finite man, or else there must be two
Gods.

Nor will any part of the old doctrine or garment agree
with any part of the new. We must take the new, entire,
as the Lord's vesture, woven without seam. For this vesture, or inner garment of the Lord, denotes the spiritual
sense of the Word, which is one perfect system of truths,
harmonious and inseparable ; while the outer garments of
the Lord, which were parted among the soldiers, denote
the literal sense which has been parted among so many
sects.

And, in further confirmation of the same truth, our
Lord says, again, " New wine must be put into new bot-
9

tles; and both are preserved." Here, again, the new bottles are the new doctrines, and the new wine is the spiritual truth that infills them. This new wine cannot be contained in the old, perverted bottles or doctrines. For illustration :—Our natural idea is the bottle, and the truth in the idea is the wine. Now, the truth contained in the idea of the resurrection of a spiritual body, from the natural, at death, cannot be contained in the idea of the resurrection of a dead, natural body, from the grave. The spiritual truth cannot enter that natural idea or bottle. The moment that it does, the bottle is burst; the idea is gone—lost in mystery.

Now, we cannot, if we would, give up the entire old system of doctrines, and embrace the entire new system at once. "No man having drunk old wine, *straightway* desireth new." We first receive some leading feature of the new system. The reasonableness of its truth strikes us forcibly. But now all the various points, in the old system, are at war with it. But the new truth stands firm. And the more the old doctrines war against it, the stronger it stands, and the weaker they become. For the new is developing its powers, and the old are exposing their weakness. And thus the strife goes on, till every old bottle, one after another, is burst or cast aside, and the new wine is joyfully received into new bottles, and both are preserved.

But this takes time: for the new truth has all kinds of enemies to fight; enemies without and enemies within —the hosts of hell and popular prejudice, and pride of heart, and self-love, and all the evils of humanity. But that is the way everything new and valuable to our race has had to struggle into being. And he is a valiant soldier of Christ who faithfully fights the battle. Therefore the Lord says, "Work out your own salvation with fear and trembling, for it is God that worketh in you." "Come unto me all ye that labor and are heavy laden, and I will give you rest." "Be thou faithful unto death, and I will give thee a crown of life." And, in the doing of this work, the Lord says, "Behold, I make all things new." "Arise, let us go hence."

CHAPTER XVI.

Much and important instruction is given, in the Word, in the use of the term 'salt.' But that instruction cannot be rationally seen and felt by the soul, without a knowledge of the spiritual sense. Indeed there is much general obscurity and, sometimes, apparent absurdity in the natural ideas alone expressed. But, as the spiritual light is seen, the darkness disappears amid the glory and beauty of the Divine Wisdom. Thus, when the Lord says to us, "Have salt in yourselves," we have no light till we see the correspondence of salt: and to see this, we must find out what principle in the mind would perform the same use to the affections and thoughts, which salt does to natural things.

Now, we all know that salt preserves meat from putrefaction. The fibres of the meat denote truths; and the vessels denote goods. The salt cleanses these vessels and fibres, by removing all the lifeless blood and other impure substances, and bringing them into close union and embrace. Now, because salt does this, it denotes the union of goodness and truth by regeneration. This is the specific signification of salt, when used in a good sense, in the

Word. It denotes the union of goodness and truth in the human mind. For goodness and truth, united in the mind, bring together all the affections and thoughts; while, at the same time, they expel everything impure and uncongenial, and unite the whole in a state of harmony and preservation.

Now, as salt is the great preservative, in nature, of things from decay and rot, by its purifying and uniting qualities, so it is, therefore, the very thing in nature which denotes the union of goodness and truth in the mind. For, without this union, the human mind must inevitably fall into a state of spiritual putrefaction and death. Thus we see that new and important light beams from the Holy Word, by simply knowing the correspondence of salt.

We can now understand, specifically, what our Saviour means when He commands us to have salt in ourselves. He means that we must love the Word of Life; that goodness in the heart must be united with truth in the head.

Again, the Lord says, in Mark, "Every one shall be salted with fire." Fire denotes love; hell fire, love of evil; heavenly fire, love of good or truth. A person with truth in his head only, and not in his heart, should be salted with fire. Love is goodness in action. Let him unite love with the truth, and the work is done. When a person is in the possession of the truth, which does not satisfy him, let him obey it till he loves it, and he will salt that truth with fire; he will unite it to his heart, and all will be peace. And we read, in Judges, that Abimelech sowed a city with salt: so, we should bring our hearts into love and obedience to the doctrines of the Word, and thus sow our city with salt.

In Kings, we read, that the men of Jericho said unto

Elisha, "Behold, I pray thee, the situation of this city is pleasant, as my lord seeth: but the water is naught, and the ground barren. And he said, Bring me a new cruse, and put salt therein. And they brought it to him. And he went forth unto the spring of the waters, and cast the salt in there, and said, Thus saith the LORD, I have healed these waters; there shall not be from thence any more death or barren land." (2 Kings ii, 19–21.) Now we cannot see why salt put into the spring should make the land of a city fruitful. But when we look into the spiritual sense, and see that the city denotes doctrines, the water, the truth of the doctrines, and the land, the good of them; all becomes instructive, clear, and practical. For the water, or truth of the doctrines, was naught or worthless, because it was not loved; and the land, or good of the doctrines, barren, because separated from the truth. The soil or good of the human heart will not bear fruit unless the truth comes into it, or is loved, any more than natural land will bear crops without rain or water. But as salt denotes the union of goodness and truth; the putting of the salt into the water, by the prophet, denotes the union of goodness and truth in the mind by the Lord, or the Word. And then the Lord says, "I have healed these waters;" that is to say, the truths are no longer lifeless and unhealthy, for they are loved. And, therefore, the Lord continues, "There shall not be from thence any more death or barren land;" that is, the soul will no longer be dead in sin, nor the heart unfruitful. For goodness and truth are now united in the mind; the man is spiritually alive, and brings forth the fruits of righteousness.

Salt, like other things of the Word, is sometimes used in an opposite, or bad sense; as is fire, which sometimes denotes love of good, and sometimes love of evil; and

water denoting either truth or falsehood ; a city, either
true or false doctrines ; and so forth. But we may see at
once, by the light in which a term is used, whether it is to
be taken in a good or a bad sense. So salt, when used in
the Word, means either the union of goodness and truth,
or their disunion. It is used, in both senses, many times
in the Holy Word. In the case of Lot's wife it is, of
course, used in a bad sense, which is known from the fact
that Lot's wife disobeyed the command of the angel by
looking back. And, from that circumstance, she is said to
have become a pillar of salt. Now by this pillar of salt
is meant the disjunction of goodness and truth in the
mind of Lot's wife. These divine principles had been
united in her. She had loved the truth. But she disobeyed its commands, and thus turned away her affections
from it. This disjunction of her heart from the truth is
what is meant by the pillar of salt. That pillar stands
recorded in the pages of Holy Writ, as an eternal monu-
ment of the folly and wickedness of turning our affections
away from the divine truth, and thereby losing love to
God and the neighbor. God has made that pillar a
most bold and conspicuous mark, in the journey of human life, cautioning the wayward traveller against violating the laws of his God, and thereby separating his affections from the truths of the Holy Writ.

In examining the subject of Lot's wife and the pillar
of salt, about which so much has been written and said,
let us remember that we are not talking about natural
salt, nor a material body, but of that principle of the mind
to which salt corresponds, and which, in the Divine Word,
is called salt. And, in the first place, let us see what
really constituted Lot's wife, and forget not that it takes
a soul, as well as a body, to make a wife. And now, as

we see that the body without the soul would not be Lot's wife, and as mind cannot be transmuted into matter, therefore, we see, that it would be impossible for Lot's wife to become a pillar of natural salt. Besides, the Bible teaches that our material bodies are not really ourselves, but tabernacles of clay, in which we dwell.

They who elevate their thoughts above the dust they tread upon, must surely see that it was the understandings and the wills, the knowing and the loving principles in Lot and his wife, which became wedded, and which constituted them truly man and wife.

But let us view the subject from another standpoint; one which presents a very general mode of expression in the Holy Word. From this position we see that men are sometimes called foxes, sometimes bears, dogs, serpents, trees, rivers, and many other things. Now, it does not mean that the *bodies* of men are foxes, dogs, trees, or rivers, for they have men's bodies. It is then the state of their souls that is meant, for this is the divine way of describing the various affections, feelings, passions, and principles of the human mind. Now, if the Bible calls Herod a fox, and Dan a lion's whelp, and the king of Assyria a river, and Pharaoh a cedar of Lebanon, without meaning that their bodies are those things, could it not, by the same law of language, call Lot's wife a pillar of salt, without meaning that her body was transmuted from flesh and bones into salt? Indeed, if the expression, *pillar of salt*, does not teach something of the state of Lot's wife's soul, it contains no practical truth, and is void of spirit and life. And if there be no spirit and life in it, if it be not " profitable for doctrine, for reproof, for correction and for instruction in righteousness," it is not the Word of God. There must be some analogy, therefore, between the pillar of salt and the state of Lot's wife's mind ; and that analogy is the thing to be sought after in order to find out what the Lord teaches by the expression. And that analogy is clearly seen by means of the spiritual signification of salt, which shows, conclusively, that it means the separation of her affections from the truth. And that this was the case with Lot's wife ; that her heart had turned away from the truth, is clearly seen, in the light of correspondence, by the act of her *looking back*. The narrative says, " His wife looked back from behind *him*, and she became a pillar of salt." There is therefore a positive relation between the formation of the pillar of salt and the looking back. And as the pillar of salt denotes the separation of goodness and truth in Lot's wife, we clearly see its verification in the act of looking back. For truth is the male element of the mind, and goodness is the female element.

Now, every mind has these two elements. Their union in the mind gives spiritual life ; their separation, spiritual death. The man or husband is, by correspondence, a symbol of the truth ; and the woman, or wife, is a symbol of goodness. Sodom and Gomorrah denote a false and evil state of mind. Lot and his wife were going away from those cities. Lot was before his wife. Truth leads the way. She looked back from behind him. He, the husband, denotes the truth : she, the wife, denotes goodness. The face denotes the affections. When she turned her face or affections toward Sodom or Gomorrah, or toward things evil and false, she had her back toward Lot, or the truth. This act, by correspondence, signifies an entire disunion of goodness and truth in Lot's wife. For, as he was a symbol of the truth and she of goodness, it teaches that she had turned away from the truth, or

9*

abandoned it. Her spiritual state, therefore, according to the sure science of correspondences, would be emphatically expressed by a pillar of salt.

Besides, she looked toward Sodom and Gomorrah. These cities denote an entire state of the love of self and the world. The fire and brimstone denote the burning of anger, lust, revenge, and hatred, of the people of those cities; or of false doctrines. In that act of Lot's wife we have a view of the fall. And it seems, by the narrative, that the change in her state was sudden, like an act of turning around. But it takes years to separate entirely the affections from truth. So the Fall in the garden seems to be sudden, like the eating of an apple; and yet the Fall which there commenced was not completed till the Lord came in the flesh. And both of these Falls are of the same character—the separation of goodness and truth. The will, or female element, first moves. One is symbolized by eating forbidden fruit, and the other by looking back to things evil and false.

Now if salt, in the Word, does not mean what I have here stated, what does it mean? The Lord has endowed us with reason, and says, "Come now, let us reason together." And He says, to good people, "Ye are the salt of the earth." Now, let us reason:—Does it mean salt?

Again, He says, "Every sacrifice shall be salted with salt;" and that "The sacrifices of God are a broken spirit." Does it mean salt? Again, "Have salt in yourselves." Does it mean salt? Joshua speaks of a city of salt. Does it mean salt? Moses says, "The sons of Ammon shall be a forsaken place of nettles, and a pit of *salt*." Does this mean salt? Moses, again, says, "Lot's wife became a pillar of salt." Does *this* mean salt? No. The spiritual sense of these passages opens to us a new and rational light, and presents us with living, practical truth. And how pointed and impressive is the lesson which we are taught in this event of Lot's wife, and by the meaning of salt! For when we examine poor human nature in the present age, by this spiritual light, how conspicuously do the pillars of salt stand out in the highway of life, as impressive statuary of caution, admonishing us to turn, neither to the right hand nor to the left, from the path of virtue. For every individual, whoever he may be, and whatever he may profess, who has the truth and who knows his duty, but who turns away from that truth and refuses to love and obey it, may see himself in the history of Lot's wife. For it is for this purpose that the narrative was recorded. Such a person is, *spiritually*, a pillar of salt, with his face toward Sodom and Gomorrah.

But, though sad the picture of fallen and perverse humanity when we look at its dark side, yet a brighter day for the race is dawning. And as it is generally darkest and coldest just before sunrise ; so, many, who are now in states of doubt and apathy, may, ere long, behold with joy the glories of the rising sun of an eternal day. For the seals of the Holy Word are being broken, and light is coming forth, suited to the wants of the age. It comes, not only to show us our evils and their nature, origin, and effects ; but, also, a rational way to get rid of them, and a conviction that, unless we do get rid of them, they will surely be our ruin. Thus a new and living way is opening before us. We can now see what to do, and how to do it. The fogs of mystery, which have so long darkened the path of life, are passing away before the beams of the rising Sun which ushers in the glorious day of peace and love ; a day when the human race will have salt in themselves, and thus be the salt of the earth. And for the furtherance of this object we now say, in the beautiful words of the apostle, " Let your speech be always with grace, seasoned with salt." Or let your words be always true, gently spoken, coming from the heart. " Have salt in yourselves, and have peace one with another."

CHAPTER XVII.

ONE of the leading features of the Word is water. This is because water is a symbol of the Divine truth—the great element of the human mind, of which the Word everywhere treats. Water is sometimes mentioned as a means of life, and sometimes of death. This is because, in a bad sense, it denotes falsehood; and in that sense it is spoken of as destroying men by a flood, as in the Mosaic deluge. And so in Ezekiel, where, prophesying of the church and its doctrines, the Word says, "Thus saith the Lord Jehovah, When I shall make thee a desolate city, like the cities that are not inhabited; when I shall bring up the deep upon thee, and great waters shall cover thee; when I shall bring thee down with them that descend into the pit, with the people of olden time." (xxvi, 19, 20.) Here we have a flood similar to the Mosaic: the city denoting the doctrines of the church; the people, the members; and the waters, falsehoods. And the prophecy declares that they shall be destroyed like the people of olden time, alluding to the flood. And as the Jewish church was not destroyed by a natural flood, and yet

shared the same fate of the people in the days of Noah, so
both floods must have been by falsehoods. And in many
other places waters are mentioned as inundating and destroying the church.

Now the sea, when mentioned in the Word, denotes
knowledge in the human mind, whether that knowledge
be true, false, or mixed. Every man, therefore, has his
sea of knowledge within the shores of his memory. This
sea is made up of all that he knows. All the sources of
information which he has are as springs or wells of water;
and the knowledges he is gaining from them, whether scientific, civil, or religious, are so many streams running
into the sea of his memory.

In this sea of knowledge he lives and moves, as a fish
in the ocean. Out of it he could not stir nor breathe; for
he would know nothing, and have no life. And so a
community has its sea of knowledge, out of which it cannot move. This human knowledge was the sea in which
the apostles were to fish, when the Lord called them to
be fishers of men. For men can be caught only within
the sea of their own knowledge; because the net or hook
of truth must take hold of their free wills and understandings. Thus there is no stratagem in this fishing. Men
are brought within the stronghold or power of the truth
rationally and voluntarily. When we clearly understand
the scripture where Peter was told, by the Lord, to go to
the sea and cast a hook, and take up the first fish that
came up, and that when he had opened his mouth he
would find a piece of money, we behold a beautiful illustration of the effect of the Divine truth upon the human
mind that heartily receives it. For the fish denotes a
man affectionately receiving the truth of the Word. This
truth is spiritual riches, represented by money. And he

who heartily receives this truth—these riches—will gladly open his mouth and speak the truth. The precious treasures of the Gospel will be ever found upon his tongue and his lips. Yes, whenever Peter, the rock upon which the Lord builds His church—the Divine truth—comes to the sea of man's knowledge, and takes hold of his heart by the power of the Word, that man will open his mouth and present to the Lord the *tribute money* of praise and thanksgiving, of truth and justice.

This mental sea is the real one from which we are to be spiritually instructed, where the disciples were commanded by the Lord to " cast the net on the right side of the ship." For, whatever the outward transactions may have been, we must look through them and above them into the world of mind. There we must find the sea of knowledge, the ship of doctrines, and the net of the truth ; and thus we must see the fishers of men going, by means of the doctrines of the Word and in the power of the truth, to the understandings of the people, to draw them, by the spirit of the Lord, into the kingdom of heaven.

As the natural ship, which is a beautiful symbol of the doctrines of the Holy Word, by which we are carried across the troublous sea of life to the peaceful haven of heavenly rest, floats upon the surface of the natural sea, so we are taught that the doctrines were above, and not in, the sea of knowledge in which the apostles were to fish, or to teach, in order to catch men. But as man receives the doctrines of love to God and the neighbor, he will be raised above the sea of natural truth into spiritual light, where he will feel the influence of the Holy Spirit, as the natural ship feels the breeze. While man is immersed in the things of this world, in the sea of self-wis-

dom, he cannot feel that heavenly influence. But as he
is elevated, he comes from the love of natural things into
the love of spiritual; he is in a new atmosphere of
thoughts and feelings: the spiritual plane of his mind is
opened to understand the truth, and to feel the power of
the spirit.

The net with which the apostles were fishing denotes
the power of the Spirit of Truth. All the varieties of the
principles of truth, in the whole doctrines, are there represented as brought together and interwoven into a net
as one. And when the truths of the Word, in their combined strength, are seen and understood, and are thence
brought to take hold on the heart, to circumscribe, control, and direct the actions; there is great power in them,
and men feel and acknowledge their force and influence.

But why are we commanded to cast the net on the
right side of the ship? The natural body is the proper
representative of the mind. And, throughout the entire
Word, the right organs of the body have relation to
things of the will, and the left organs to things of the
understanding. Now, as the ship denotes doctrines, and
the net the combined powers of doctrines, and as the
right side of the ship denotes the love of those doctrines,
and the left side the understanding of them; therefore, to
cast the net on the right side of the ship would be to
teach the truth of the doctrines from the heart—from the
love of those doctrines and the love of the neighbor.
Therefore, we are here taught that if we would come
effectually to men, we must come, not only to their intel-
lects, but also to their hearts. The net cast on the left
side of the ship, or from the understanding only, will
have no controlling power. The reason is, there will be
no life in it, no love, nothing to win the heart, nothing to

induce men to enter. Men do not like to have the cold cords of restraint and dictation thrown around them, against their wills. Truth alone is always inefficient. It must come from the heart, in kind, persuasive, and gentle influences. It must reach the feelings and the sympathies by carrying with it the feelings and the sympathies. The net must be cast on the right side of the ship.

The narrative says, that when Peter heard that it was the Lord, he girt his fisher's coat about him, for he was naked, and cast himself into the sea. Now, coat means outward deportment. A true fisher's coat is a heavenly robe of true sincerity and kindness. It is a sphere of goodness and mercy which we like to see in the conduct of a teacher.

Peter was naked, that is, his self-righteousness was exposed. He had not on the robe of true righteousness. He was teaching from his own understanding alone—from the left side of the ship. The Lord was not in his heart.

But when the Lord stood upon the shore, there was a new state of things. For the Lord upon the shore was the truth in the heart. The land corresponds to the will. Thus the truth began to be loved. And when the truth was really in the disciples' hearts; when they loved and depended upon the Lord, and acted from His spirit, they cast the net on the right side of the ship: then Peter could ·put on the robe of truth and love, and go down into the sea of the people's minds, and meet them according to their states. While the Lord was not on the shore, while Jesus was not in their feelings, the robe was not on, and it was mental darkness and night with them. They had been fishing all night, and had caught nothing. But the Lord on the shore, or the truth loved, brought the morning light into the soul, and they were now ready to approach men aright, or from the heart. Before the Lord was on the shore, the disciples were in spiritual hunger, as well as in nakedness and darkness. For the Lord said unto them, " Children, have ye any meat ? They answered Him, No." But when the Lord was in their heart, and they had cast the net on the right side of the ship, and it was filled with fishes, and the disciples had come to the land, or to the love of goodness, " they saw a fire of coals there, and fish laid thereon, and bread."

Now it is worthy of note that these things are mentioned as occurring after the Lord had risen from the sepulchre, and that this fire and fish and bread are of the Lord's providing, and not the fish that they had caught; they had not yet drawn the net to land. The fire denotes the Divine love ; the fish, scientific truths of the Word, and the bread, the good of those truths. Now, as fishes denote scientific truths, so the fishes caught in the net of the Holy Word denote persons receiving those scientific truths of the doctrines. Such persons represent fishes, because their minds are being exercised with the scientific truths to which fishes correspond. It may be asked why fishes denote scientifics. We answer, It is because water denotes truth, and water is said in Genesis to bring forth the fishes ; therefore they must correspond to something that truth brings forth. And as all real sciences are produced from truth, so sciences are nothing but truths brought down into rational forms or rules of thought, for practical illustrations. And fishes are beautiful correspondences to those scientific truths ; because all sciences are developed and exercised in the sea of man's knowledge, the same, by correspondence, as fishes are developed and exercised in the natural sea. And how much science it must require to understand the form and use of simply the bones that are in fishes and their application to the water for movement. There is nothing else in nature that so fully represents scientific principles as the fishes do. Ichthyology, therefore, may be called a science which looks into scientific principles. The net, which holds the people caught, denotes the combined strength and power of those truths, when received from the right side of the ship, or from the influence of the love of those doctrines. And the disciples, now on the land with the Lord, or, in other words, feeling the good of the Lord's love in their hearts, are enabled to see the coals of fire, and fish laid thereon, and bread ; that is, they are in a state to understand that the Lord gives, from His love, scientific truths and goods to men. And while their minds are in this clear state of perception, they feel a yearning love for the people in the net, or for persons interested in the doctrines. This feeling is denoted by the Lord's saying, "Bring of the fish which ye have now caught." They feel a yearning desire for their salvation. And from this high state of spiritual affection and power, they can reach the heart of those in the net ; and they are thus drawn to the land, or come into the love of the good of the doctrine. And under this state of things the disciples feast their own souls upon these scientific goods and truths. This is denoted by its being said that "Jesus then cometh and taketh bread, and giveth them, and fish likewise."

Now, this mental sea is the one into which Jonah was cast when he was swallowed by a great fish. Jonah was commanded by the Lord to go to Nineveh, and cry against it for its wickedness. But Jonah disobeyed this command, and started for Tarshish, from the presence of the Lord. We must now try to forget Jonah's body, and look into his mind for all the things that take place ; remembering that all natural things denote things of the mind, and that places denote states of mind : heaven, a happy state ; hell, a miserable state ; Jerusalem, a true state. And that to go from one place to another means to advance from one state of mind to another.

As a city denotes doctrines, so Nineveh, in this chapter, denotes a state of mind in false doctrines, which can be overcome, if man will go to Nineveh, or look into his state, and cry against his falses, or fight them. This we may know, because Jonah was commanded to go there, and cry against its sinful principles. It was Jonah himself that was in this false state of mind denoted by Nineveh. He had some good natural principles, but they were asleep. God wanted him to arise, wake up, and go to Nineveh ; that is, to examine into his condition, and fight against his false propensities. And so the Lord now says to all who are resting quietly in their falses and evils, " Arise, and go to Nineveh, that great city, and cry against it."

But, instead of going to Nineveh, Jonah rose up to flee unto Tarshish from the presence of the Lord. Now Tarshish denotes an external or natural state of mind, which trusts in man's goodness. This we may see, because, in going to Tarshish, it says he went *from* the presence of the Lord. The presence of the Lord is a state of mind looking toward the Lord. And as Tarshish was *away* from the Lord, it denotes a state of mind looking away from the Lord toward self. Therefore it says he went to Joppa, and took ship for Tarshish.

Now, ship denotes doctrines, because it is a universal law of correspondences that anything by which our bodies are carried denotes doctrines, by which our souls progress.

Ship for Tarshish denotes doctrines of naturalism; trusting in one's own wisdom and goodness : doctrines which lead away from the Lord. This we may see, because it says he entered the ship, and paid his fare. To pay his fare is to give his consent to the doctrines. Joppa denotes a state of mind prepared to embrace those doctrines, because it was here that Jonah entered the ship, or embraced those principles, which were to take him to Tarshish, from the presence of the Lord.

Thus Jonah was fairly on board the ship of naturalism, sailing for Tarshish, or going away from the Lord. The mariners, to manage the ship, were all the best natural principles of his mind. They were principles which still had in them some natural good—some regard for nature's God. The sea upon which he was sailing was the general sea of his own knowledge. And while thus going his own way, in the absence of God and His laws, a storm of warring elements arose, in the sea of his self-wisdom ; and doubts and darkness came over the horizon of his mind. This condition called up into action all the remaining principles of good in his soul. These principles of good began to feel that their ship of naturalism was trembling, and ready to break to pieces. But Jonah's self-wisdom overruled. By this we are taught that Jonah's natural judgment was losing all confidence in any religion whatever. The mariners—the better, active principles of his natural heart—were contending against his skepticism of the head and its evils ; and the sea of his whole mind was in commotion. Thus it is that when we deliberately turn away from the Lord, and disregard the better principles of our heart, and let the external and selfish judgment rule, we come into great darkness and distress. Such was Jonah's mental condition.

In this state of mind he says, " Take me up, and cast me forth into the sea." That is, the external man, the natural reason, says to the deeper and better principles, Let me go my own way—cast me into the sea ; I will rest in my own wisdom ; my own self-knowledge is sufficient for me —I know best. Thus the selfishness of the natural man ruled ; the better principles or remains gave up, and Jonah became immersed in the sea of his own false views. In this condition, the narrative says, " The Lord had prepared a great fish to swallow up Jonah." But the Lord is often said, in the Word, to do what He *permits*, only, to be done. So the Lord permitted Jonah to be swallowed by the fish of his own production ; by his own skepticism. For this great fish was false science. It was complete infidelity. Jonah may be said to have come to the conclusion that the outward senses of man tell us all that we can know ; that the Bible is a dark fable ; that nature is all there is ; and that man ends his existence with the death of the body.

How long a period of time Jonah spent, in passing through his changes, and embracing his infidelity, we know not. But he had come to a most wretched spiritual condition. And for the want of a true mental philosophy—a rational science of theology—how many strong minds, within the last century, have passed through Jonah's experience, until they found themselves engulfed in infidelity ; in the very belly of false, self-derived intelligence. For theology has not been looked upon as philosophical or rational. The reasoning faculties of men have had but little to do with it. And yet, theology is, most truly, a philosophical science ; the most beautiful of all sciences. It is only by the science of theology, that we can truly learn and understand the science of the human mind. There is no mental philosophy without it. For that philosophy is based upon the science of correspondences—the true science of all real sciences—showing the relation between mind and matter, God and nature, the soul and the brain, the mind and the body. It was the want, therefore, of a rational knowledge of first principles, or of God and His laws, as revealed in His Holy Word, which left the human mind to wander in the mazes of its own wisdom, till lost in doubt and darkness. When, therefore, we see a man who has not become acquainted with the philosophy of theology, but who, by the strength and activity of his own natural judgment, has reasoned himself, by a false, natural philosophy, into the belief that there is no life after death ; that man dies like the brute ; or that the Bible is the work of cunning priests ; or that there is no God, but Nature ; or that man is governed by circumstances and motives beyond his control, and is consequently irresponsible ;—I say, when we see this, we find a Jonah swallowed by a great fish. We find a man buried in the darkness of false science ; in the gloom of self-wisdom. But we find, indeed, a wretched creature, with no ray of hope before him ; nothing but darkness, and death, and extinction. He is truly in the midst of a great fish, at the bottom of the sea of his own wisdom ; with no light of truth to see, and no air of heaven to breathe. And we know of no way of escape from this condition, but to turn, as did Jonah, to the Lord, and pray out of the depths of this hell. But, in this age of skepticism—this age of Jonahs, swallowed by great fish —such men can be reached and led into this prayerful state, only by the exercise of the rational faculty, in the light of the true language—the Divine Language. I know of nothing else but the power of the Spirit of God's

Holy Word, rationally brought to bear upon their minds, that can possibly reach their case. But the Lord has mercifully provided for their wants, in the spiritual light of His Word.

Now, it is by no means my object to teach, that Jonah either was, or was not, swallowed by a fish. That is a matter that does not concern us. God gives us His Word, essentially, for spiritual teaching. But it *is* my object to show what practical truth God would teach us, by this history. For, whatever may have been the condition of Jonah's body, it is certain that the spiritual sense of the narrative gives the state of his soul; and for this purpose it has been given to man, that other minds may escape from infidelity, who are now in the same condition that Jonah was. That the history of Jonah's *mental* condition is here taught, we might know from his own language, when he says, "*I cried unto the Lord and He heard me; out of the belly of hell, I cried.*" Now, a natural fish is not hell. Nor is false science hell, unless a man embraces it, and brings thereby hell or misery into his soul, as did Jonah.

Again, Jonah says, "The waters compassed me about, even to the soul." Now, natural waters cannot come to the soul of man. But falses, to which waters correspond, can come into his soul and produce hell there. It is remarkable that, while Jonah is represented as in the fish, he makes no complaint, whatever, about his body. He does not allude to any physical wants. He mentions no struggles for breath, nor want of light or air, neither of which he could have had. But it was his soul only, that he was troubled about. He says, "When my soul fainted within me, I remembered the Lord: and my prayer came in unto Thee, into Thine holy temple." And he shows the former skepticism of his mind, when he says, "*They that observe lying vanities forsake their own mercy. . . . Salvation is of the Lord.*" Thus it was salvation, not physical life, that he was now seeking.

Again, he says, " The earth with her bars was about me for ever : yet hast thou brought up my life from corruption, O LORD, my God." This Jonah said, while he was still represented as being in the fish. It must, therefore, have been the life of his soul, which he felt was being brought up from the corruption of sin.

By the fish's giving up Jonah, is also to be understood Jonah's giving up the fish. As Jonah gave up his infidelity, his false science gave up him, as a matter of course. And it left him on dry land ; or with a heart free from the waters of falsehood. His external mind, of course, was not yet free from falses ; but the internal, the heart, the land, the new affection, was good, not false. This was good dry land. But in order to accomplish this state, he had to be in the belly of the fish three days and three nights ; that is, he had to pass from three states of darkness, or nights, into three states of light, or days, before he could come into a state to oppose his infidelity. Days, in the Word, denote states of mind. Three days or states have relation to first principles—Love, Wisdom, and Power : or, Charity, Faith, and Works. Before we commence regeneration, we are in the night of darkness upon all three of these principles. Each one has its night. And, by regeneration, we pass through the night of each principle, into the Gospel light of day. And, by that light, we see that faith, charity, and works must be united, that each may have life. Jonah, therefore, could not be placed in a condition to become freed from his skepticism, short of three days and three nights ; or, without coming

10

into those three states of light from those three states of darkness. He must see his duty, and see also that he must do it and love it.

But when Jonah *had* thus seen the true light of faith, charity, and works; and had resolved to walk by that light, the Lord said, again, unto him, "*Arise, go unto Nineveh, that great city, and preach unto it the preaching that I bid thee.*" And the narrative says, "So Jonah arose, and went unto Nineveh, according to the word of the LORD." Jonah was now ready to look his falses and evils full in the face, and to fight against them. He was ready to go to Nineveh. He had now only been brought to his senses. He had seen the light of truth, and the way of life in which it leads; and the whole work of purification was before him. In his internal mind, a good work was commenced, a little kingdom was begun. But his external mind still contained Nineveh, that great city, with all its selfish inhabitants. And it was the business of his life to subdue them.

Let us, then, profit by its instructions. Let us arise and go to the Nineveh of our self-love, that great city, and cry out against every false principle of the heart, as God, in this scripture, bids us. So shall we avoid the sea of falsehood and the fish of skepticism.

CHAPTER XVIII.

The Science of Correspondences lost in the building of the Tower of Babel, and restored in the loosing of the Seven Seals by the Lord, through EMANUEL SWEDENBORG.

In order to understand the subject before us, we must bear in mind that all the Holy Word contains a spiritual sense, and then, as we read the narrative in the first paragraph of the second chapter of Genesis, and see men building a city and a tower, in order to make themselves a name, lest they should be scattered abroad upon the face of the earth, we must look into human souls for the real city and tower. And, when we find them, we shall see that this city and tower-building are precisely what all unregenerate, selfish, ambitious persons are now doing, some on a larger and some on a smaller scale. For as a city denotes doctrines, or rules and principles of action, whether good or bad, and tower denotes worship and defence of those doctrines, therefore, every man who, in his self-wisdom and worldly ambition, sets out upon some new project or speculation, whether civil or religious, in order to obtain wealth, or power, or distinction, to make himself a name, that he need not be scattered abroad over the face of the earth; or, in other words, be mixed up and lost sight of in the common mass; every such man, in his new schemes, is striving to build a city and a tower, that he may reach the imaginary heaven of his ambition, and thereby satisfy his selfish aspirations to gain a notoriety above his fellows.

And a glance at the history of mankind, sacred and profane, presents a vast variety of these cities and towers, of every character and magnitude, from the molehill to the mountain. For every division and discord, political or moral, civil or religious; every crime, of every hue; all persecutions and abuses of the race, originate in the building of such cities and towers. And God has mercifully recorded the one in Scripture, as a common mirror, into which we may all look and behold the little cities of self-wisdom, and towers of pride and presumption, which we have been more or less building, in various ways, in our own hearts, and which we can now see to be wrong, and may abandon.

Now, in looking at the city and Tower of Babel, in this, their true light, how much darkness is removed from the clouds of the literal sense, which seem to teach that heaven, instead of being a happy state of the mind, is really a natural place, up somewhere in the sky; and that men believed they could actually go there by building a tower to reach it; and that God, in order to prevent it, came down and confounded their language, so that they could not understand one another, and thus He put a stop to the work. Besides, if they were really intending to build a natural tower up into the sky, to a place supposed to be heaven, they surely would not have commenced the work in a valley or plain, when they could have saved the expense of building through much space, by commencing on a mountain.

But now, inasmuch as the light of the Gospel is fast removing the darkness of all such clouds of the letter from the atmosphere of Christendom, and men of all sects are beginning to see and believe that heaven is anywhere where angels are, and that angels are everywhere where men are ; and that, to find these angels and this heaven, we must become angelic and heavenly ourselves : I say, inasmuch as this clear Gospel light is abroad in the land, we need give ourselves no anxiety about the literal sense of Scripture, which looks unintelligible. For we may rest assured that every apparently dark and strange passage is a divine casket, containing within it precious jewels of truth, to adorn the souls of those who shall look into this casket, and find and wear these jewels.

Then let us bless the Lord for the literal sense, and humbly look up through it, to the clear, divine instruction offered for our salvation. The grand idea, then, to be constantly and vividly kept before our thoughts, when we come to this Holy Word is, that it is a history of the human mind, and a rule for its guidance and development. That, as a history, it is perfect, glancing upward for the origin of man to the Infinite form and quality of humanity in the Divine Being ; and then downward to its finite form and quality in man : and then, tracing the formation of that mind, most minutely, from its first beginnings in the finite form, onward to the age in which we now live, and still onward in eternal progression, toward the divine perfection. Thus it is a history of man, for time and for eternity ; a history of the whole man, and a whole history. It is not only a general history of humanity as a whole, but a particular history of each individual ; so that any person, of whatever character, may read himself in it. For it paints minutely all the lights and shades, the elevations and depressions of our mental being, through all its various changes and developments, from its beginning, onward. It is a perfect history, because recorded by Infinite Wisdom.

The reason why it is a history of every individual is, that every possible state of human nature is described in it. Therefore, no life can be lived that is not entirely within its descriptions. But nobody can read there the peculiar life of an individual in all its particulars but the Allwise God, and the individual himself. As a person becomes regenerated, and the Word becomes opened to his mind, and his mind to the Word, his various states and shades of character are brought to his view in the Divine Records; and as he progresses he finds every sin, every shade and quality of his life depicted, and the sure remedy for every evil pointed out.

But all this history, we must remember, is a history of the soul; a history of the feelings, thoughts, and intentions; that the soul and its wants and world are the things here looked after. And the glorious epoch, in the history of our race, has now come when finite humanity has reached that stage in its mental development which calls for a reasonable knowledge of the soul, and of the peculiar relation between mind and matter. Yes, the time has arrived when, without this higher knowledge, humanity would soon perish in the darkness of materialism and the evils of self-love; for the light of Divine Revelation would be lost to mankind amid the ruins.

But our Heavenly Father, whose Divine Mercy is ever ready to meet the wants of every emergency, has, in this inquiring age, graciously offered us that needed knowledge in His Holy Word, through the clear symbols of nature in the sure Law of Analogy. But when men had this law of the Divine Language by intuition, they saw clearly the light of the Law by Divine Influx. But they saw it without the full, independent exercise of their own reason and judgment, and therefore they lost it. They are now to receive it through the free and open exercise of their rational faculty, so that they can thereby make it a part of their own mental being; and then they will never lose it again.

Man is, therefore, now on his intellectual way back from the dark world of effects to the bright world of causes. He left that luminous world in the undeveloped childhood of the race, by looking downward and outward in his own way—as children always do, to things of time and sense—till the clouds of his own self-wisdom shut out the higher light from his mind. But now he is to return to that world of causes, in the manhood of the race, through the exercise of his reason; looking upward through the fogs of the mind, to the inner world of his being, where the Lord is the Light thereof.

Now, it was the loss of the symbolic Light of the Word, the loss of the true character of the Divine Language, and thence of the character of God, which produced the confusion of tongues at the Tower of Babel. When they commenced the building of this tower, there was but one language on the earth. For the Lord said, " Behold, the people is one, and they have all one language; let us go down and confound their language, that they may not understand one another's speech." Now, the Lord is said to do what He only permits to be done. He did not confound their language Himself: but He permitted them to do it. It was their sins that did it. And it was done by their building, in their own minds, a false city of base principles, and a proud tower of arrogance and selfishness. This vile work created all their diversities of views and feelings. For now, they spoke no longer one another's sentiments and wants. Thus their real life-language was confounded. For all true human language is the language of the heart. It is what the heart wants, that the soul really speaks. And it speaks in looks and tones as well as in words and actions. And when the heart really speaks, no one, who knows the soul's speech, can mistake its eloquence or its wants; for it speaks to every sympathizing heart. But when hearts are divided by selfishness, and diversified in taste, they speak different emotions or languages, according to their various feelings and wants; and therefore they cannot work together upon the same mental tower. They do not understand one another's speech. Each one wants his own will and word to be law. Each wants the last word. They will not receive the words of one another as truth or justice. There is nothing confuses the language of the mind, in a community, like individual self-will in its various members. Look at a dozen men in hot dispute, and mark the confusion of tongues. They do not understand each other's speech. They will not, because their hearts are not prepared for it.

The narrative commences by saying, " And the whole earth was of one language, and one speech. And it came to pass, as they journeyed from the east, that they found a plain in the land of Shinar, and they dwelt there." Now, going from the east is, in true symbolic language, going away from the Lord, from light, from life, from love, from heaven. And dwelling in a plain, away from the Lord, would denote a low, selfish state of mind. And here, in this low mental condition, they built that famous city and tower, which have filled the world with opposing sects and parties, anger and ill will, sin and suffering. Here was lost the one universal language—the language of pure symbols—the language of the Holy Word—the language of the heart. Before this, the whole earth was of one speech. The mental earth spoke from the heart. The minds of the community were one. Love was the golden bond which harmonized the thoughts and feelings, and made their words one. Their words were a perfect index to the feelings which gave them forth. And they saw, in the sure light of analogy, the indisputable meaning of every utterance of the soul. For the divine language of the heart wears no disguise. It knows no deception. It is pure symbol. Throughout all nature it never lies. Fallen man only, of all the creatures of God, says one thing and feels another. Only man's language is confounded, and that, by the Tower of Babel in his soul. All other creatures perfectly understand one another's speech. There is no falsity nor equivocation there. Wicked man is the arch-deceiver.

Now, it would seem from the general history, that this city and tower were not commenced until after the time of the flood, and by the descendants of Noah; but the spiritual history is above time, reaching the states of men in all ages. Preparations for the building of this tower commenced with the commencement of the fall, and the first false, selfish principle, received into the human heart, was the first brick laid. And, therefore, our subject embraces the great theme of the fall of man and its consequences. As we stand aloof in silent contemplation, surveying the awful magnitude and consequences of this subject, it points us back to the calm and genial sphere of Paradisiacal days, where the imagination beholds the mental world, in its primeval beauty and innocence;

10*

where all was harmony within, and brightness without, and the whole earth was of one language and of one speech; when pure affection was sweetly manifest in every look, and tone, and act; when men's hearts were one and their speech one.

In passing the eyes along the brighter portion of this mingled picture, we next behold this happy people leaving their halcyon Paradise, their heavenly groves and sunny climes, to take a journey away from the glorious East, from whence had come all their joys. Yes: we behold them turning their backs to the light, the life, the joy, the heaven, the God and Father of all their blessings. For their own selfhood is now beginning to feel its importance, and to become active. New things are exciting their curiosity, and new experiments must be tried. And as they journeyed on in their selfish way, we follow them along their devious paths, down from the sunny hillsides of truth and love, where the fruits of righteousness and peace grow spontaneously on all the trees of the garden, except that of their own self-knowledge; and now we come to the gloomy plain of error and unkindness, where they feed upon the bitter fruits of their own depraved devices. And here, in this low, dark, selfish valley, they built that city of falsities and tower of arrogance which have spread consternation, distress, and woe over the whole face of the earth.

From the brief account, given in the Word, of this journey and tower-building, one would suppose it was all accomplished in a short time; at least, within the common age of man. And yet, it must have taken thousands of years—many generations. For slow must be the progress, whereby a pure and spotless people could become evil and false, so as entirely to lose sight of the true law of the heart and light of the mind ; and thus become blind to the symbolic language of the universe, in which they were educated—that beautiful analogical relation of cause and effect, which ever exists between the world of mind and the world of matter—their own and only native language. But such is the wonderful character of the Holy Word, that one divine idea grasps the whole ; for even the parts are infinite.

Let us then come to the Holy Word, for a true knowledge of humanity in the present age of the world, the age which most of all concérns us. And let us study it from the heart. For this is, indeed, an age of Babylonian cities and towers. Every sinful heart has its Babel, and every wicked people, their base city and tower. There is now no civil or religious government on the earth, that is entirely free from that diabolical city and tower, built in the land of Shinar. But although we behold these false cities and gigantic towers all over the world, and see poor humanity writhing under the pain and anguish of dominant cruelty ; yet, let us take courage, for the remedy is also at hand, and the promise of a glorious age to come is bright. Pure symbolic light, from the Holy Word, is now freely offered us, whereby we can rationally test the character of all cities and towers ; and, in the divine power of this light, we can abandon the cities of the plains and flee to the mountains. We can come back to the Paradise of God, and feast our souls upon the Tree of Life. All the gates of the heavenly garden are thrown open for our reception. The various flowers give forth their odors, and the breath of the morning comes laden with love. Angelic arms are open to receive us, and heavenly choirs will chant praises to God. Let us then build no cities nor towers ourselves, nor accept any of man's building. But let us freely enter the Divine City which cometh down from God out of heaven; whose builder and maker is God: where grows the Tree of Life, whose leaves never fade, and whose fruits never decay. Then shall we be able truly to "praise the Lord for His goodness, and for His wonderful works to the children of men."

Now, since the loss of this science, the church and the world have passed through many changes; until the time has come for the absolute necessity for a knowledge of this science, for the continuance and salvation of the human family on earth. And the peculiar manner in which it has been revealed is this:—The time had come, in the age of the world, when human nature had grown up to natural manhood; when the natural faculties and powers of reasoning were greatly developed; and when the religion of the world was of every caste and character, and involved in great mystery. Nothing in theology reached the wants of the free, reasoning, thinking, truth-desiring minds. They were asking for light in matters of religion, as well as in science. They were hungering and thirsting for something to satisfy the wants of the longing soul. These minds could begin to receive the spiritual sense of the Word, if it could only be brought scientifically before them. This sense was the only thing that could lead their thoughts to the true God, give them right views of His nature, and faith in His Holy Word. The lost science of correspondences was the only key to that spiritual sense that would fit their minds. If that science could be brought rationally before the minds of men, so as to enable them, from their low, natural position, to look understandingly up through the world of effects to the world of causes—through natural things to spiritual, material to mental—so as to see and receive spiritual light from the

Holy Word, then the human race on earth could be gradually elevated to heavenly order and happiness; otherwise man must perish. "Except these days should be shortened, no flesh should be saved."

By the use, then, of the key of correspondences, the seals of the Word could be broken and the Book opened. But who was able to do it? None but the "Lion of the tribe of Judah could prevail to open the Book, and loose the seals thereof." The seals were all in the human mind. It was sealed with seven seals; that is, every state of the human mind was closed against spiritual light. Man was altogether natural. But there were some minds in a religious state of natural good, and in such a state of natural rational freedom as to have their minds opened by instruction from the Lord, so as to see spiritual light through natural symbols, could they be so instructed.

But how was this mighty work to be done? How was the human mind to be opened and instructed, so as to behold the wonderful things written in God's law; to see the glory of the world of causes, and to look down upon effects, and see them as they really are? There was but one way to do it; and that was, for a man to take the Holy Word, give it his supreme time and attention, and work out its wonderful problems step by step; proving every operation, as he went along, by the truths of the Word itself, looking to the Divine Master for instruction. Thus, the mind, in this new study, would have to be as gradually opened, enlightened, and expanded, in spiritual science, as minds are naturally in the pursuit of natural science.

But a mind, to do this work, must be a mind in a state of strong natural truth and good. It must be a mind possessing rational and unwavering faith in the Lord, in the divinity of the Word, and in the work before him; a mind humble, prayerful, open, and confiding toward the Lord. But where was the mind to be found competent to the task of going to this Fountain of wisdom, working out its spiritual problems, and spreading out before the world a clear and satisfactory solution of the work, proved and authenticated by the Divine Truth itself?

EMANUEL SWEDENBORG was the man, in the Divine Providence, for this work. But what peculiar qualifications had he for entering upon a study so high and heavenly? From his youth, his training and education had prepared his mind for just such a work. With always a conscientious regard for the Bible, and a love of truth and virtue, he had mastered all the human literature of the age; deeply investigated the laws of matter in the mineral, vegetable, and animal kingdoms; had traced the economy of the human body up to the soul, and nature up to God; and had rationally seen something of the relation between mind and matter, and of the laws of creation. In this way, his natural mind had become a sincere and open vessel, adapted to the reception of spiritual truth; and his active soul was thirsting for something higher, and looking up to receive it. And thus, at the mature age of fifty-five years—ripe in natural goodness and truth, and in scientific and literary wisdom—he was prepared to enter upon the divine study of the Holy Word in its spiritual sense.

This study rationally opened his mind to the laws of the spiritual world; so that he gradually came, while in the flesh, into a state of free, open, and sensible consciousness of spiritual society and scenery, and this by a process of such perfect mental growth and development, according to divine order, that, when his spiritual senses had become clearly opened to the spiritual world, they were permanently so ; because his views of that world were not surface and uncertain views, presented from a disordered or inflated imagination, but they were scientific views. He saw and understood the law by which spiritual forms are manifested, and this law he found in the Holy Word. It is the SCIENCE OF CORRESPONDENCES, in which the Word is written, and which he labored to make known to the world ; and, in the ardent exercise of this benevolent desire to give it freely to his fellow man, his soul was rationally opened to receive it from the Lord.

Twenty-nine years of intense application were devoted to this work, in which he presented to mankind twenty massive volumes, opening and expounding the Sacred Scriptures, and specifically recording his illustrations, and the science of correspondences by which they are explained. This he did in the most modest and quiet manner, without any startling miracles, or outward displays of power, but in a deep, calm, and contemplative state of mind ; looking prayerfully and confidingly to the Lord while reading the Word.

In this way, the science of correspondences, and the spiritual sense of the Word, and its doctrines, have been presented to the world. But who has done it ? Certainly not Swedenborg, but the Lord Himself. Swedenborg never, in all these volumes, gives us so much as a single opinion of his own upon the meaning of the Word or its doctrines, or of the science of correspondences ; but the illustrations are so given as to make the Word itself its own interpreter. It is the Lord, therefore, and not Swedenborg, that speaks to the heart and the head of the reader of these volumes. Yet Swedenborg was not in-

spired. He acted not as an amanuensis, as did the
prophets. He freely saw and understood what he wrote.
He knew it was true ; but he knew, also, that it was not
one particle of it his own wisdom ; and he was far from
claiming it.

These twenty volumes, therefore, in their explanations
of the Word and its doctrines, become to the understanding reader, positive and conclusive evidence of their own
truth and the truth of the Holy Word. They call in an
array of testimony, which carries everything before it.
They call our own internal selves on to the stand, with all
our evils, and all we know of human nature and make
them cry out, Amen ! They call in to their support all
the truths of science and art. Indeed, they call in everything—the vast universe of mind and matter, and the law
of analogy between them. Everything in nature, from
the smallest dust of the earth to the sun in the heavens,
bears testimony in these volumes to the truth of the
Word, and the divinity of its Author ; proving beyond a
doubt, that the Creator of the universe is the Author of
the Holy Word ; that the spiritual truths of the Word
are the Divine Wisdom by which God created and sustains the universe ; and that the universe now stands in
relation to that wisdom, as effects to causes. All this is
satisfactorily proved by the law of analogy which pervades
the whole Word.

Thus the Lion of the tribe of Judah, according to
prophecy, has prevailed to open the Book, and loose the
seven seals of God's Holy Word ; and has mercifully
given to the world the divine science of correspondences
—the grand key which opens the door to that fountain
of wisdom which is to bring the world into order.

CHAPTER XIX.

By the science of correspondences men are enabled to ascertain what writings have an internal sense, and what have not; what are of God, and what are of men : which books of what is called the *"Bible, containing the Old and New Testaments,"* are plenarily inspired, and which are not.

The analytical investigation of languages, by this science, is exceedingly interesting, ever pointing, as with the finger of God, to the marked distinction between what is Divine and what is human, and thereby bringing out the Holy Word in bold relief, in its essential superiority over all other writings, because filled with living thoughts and feelings, evolving throughout a new and consecutive sense, far above the letter, breathing a Divine spirit expressive of a peculiar relation to human souls, touching their understandings and wills, and plainly directing their actions ; each part of the Word evincing a sensible connection with all the other parts, and even, by correspondences, with all the things of nature. Such is this wonderful book of God : whereas the same analysis, applied to any merely human composition, fails in all these particulars.

A language having only a natural sense gives, at once and fully, to any mind which understands the terms used and the grammar, all the ideas it contains; and any attempt to evolve an internal sense fails at every step. For, notwithstanding every natural thing mentioned, even in such language, corresponds to some spiritual thing, yet, as the other parts of the sentence are not arranged in relation to this correspondence, there can be no spiritual sense. This any one who examines the subject may see. And what in the Holy Word is most wonderful is, every part seems to involve all the rest, because it contains the Lord, who is perfect in the least things as well as the greatest; so that there is no part, however intricate or obscure, that is not rendered by the spiritual sense profitable for doctrine, reproof, correction, and instruction in righteousness.

In the general features of correspondences, the science appears plain, but in extending it to the particulars of the Word, men have thought it too obscure. But they should know that in looking, by analogy, into the interiors of the Word, in their minute particulars, the science of correspondences becomes, as it were, a spiritual microscope, bringing out, in their perfect order and beauty, thousands of otherwise hidden features and qualities of things, with their various relations and uses: the *lens* (permit the term) of this Divine instrument becoming more and more powerful as we progress in a practical knowledge of the spiritual qualities and powers of the Word, and as our mental vision becomes adapted to the new light. For, as the constant improvement in the natural microscope is bringing out more and more, to the astonished beholder, the perfect order and organization of the infinitesimal things in the interior of God's works, leaving the imagination yet room to play amid unseen wonders, which may lie still deeper within; so, as we progress in a knowledge of the science of correspondences, and look, by Divine light, through its increasing powers, into God's Word, we find the same cause for wonder and delight at its order and perfection in the infinite and minute varieties, relations, and combinations of its goods and truths, leaving us still ignorant of the extent and quality of the unseen glories yet remaining.

For, as the science of correspondences shows the relation between God's works and His Word, so these two great productions must, in their degrees, be alike perfect in their interiors; both speaking of the goodness and perfection of their Infinite Author in sure and responsive words, expressing His goodness in accents loud upon the surface, but becoming more and more gentle from within, till finally lost in the whispers of their own sweetness, as we lose sight of the interior excellences of the Word in the infinity of its perfections. No one, therefore, with a glimpse of the law of analogy, can doubt the complete distinction between the written Word of the Lord and all other languages.

Now the Pentateuch, and the book of Joshua, and that of Judges, are written according to the science of correspondences, and therefore have a complete spiritual sense. And they all purport to come from God. He speaks in them, and they are His Word.

But the book of Ruth has no spiritual sense, and the science of correspondences cannot be applied to it. Neither does the book anywhere claim to be spoken or directed by the Lord. He nowhere utters a syllable in it.

The two books of Samuel and the two books of Kings, are the Word of life, everywhere containing a spiritual

sense. God speaks in them, and the science of correspondences and their holy sphere prove their divinity.

The two books of Chronicles cannot be read by correspondences, and are, therefore, not *spirit* and *life* like the
Word. They are merely what their name indicates—
chronicles. God nowhere claims them, nor do the books
themselves claim Him as their author. In what they say
of David they quote one of the Psalms, which, with any
other quotations from the Word, has an internal sense.
The Chronicles, with the book of Ruth, are a mere record
of natural events ; and as such they often speak of what
God has said and done. But God's spirit is not manifest
in these books, speaking and directing present and future
things ; telling men how to speak, write, and act, as in
the other books.

The books of Ezra, Nehemiah, and Esther are of a
similar character to Ruth and Chronicles, having no spiritual sense. God has neither credit for them, nor does
He directly speak in them, or call them His Word.

The book of Job is a work by itself. It is of a higher
order and character of language than those without an
internal sense ; for it is written in correspondences. But
it is not of so high a character as the Word of God, because it does not everywhere refer to the Lord and contain His spirit. But it treats of spiritual things through
natural symbols.

The Psalms are a peculiarly sublime book. They
contain a spiritual sense, and God's Spirit breathes in
them throughout. Some of the literal sense is very beautiful, and some appears harsh and unmerciful. But in
the light of correspondences, the letter entire becomes a
beautiful casket of precious mental jewels. David is
everywhere in them a representative character denoting

the Lord. Not that David was personally a good man.
He was far from it. But the Psalms have a peculiar prophetic spirit, taking as a basis a certain character representing the Lord, who is called David. And this character is represented as passing through everything which
the Lord's assumed nature passed through in its life,
temptations, crucifixion, and glorification; and also
everything which men pass through in their regeneration; and also all the abuse which the Word, or the
truth, received from the Jews, or receives now from any
one who rejects it. Thus David is said to say in them,
"All they that see me laugh me to scorn : they shoot out
the lip, they shake the head, saying, He trusted on the
Lord that He would deliver him : let Him deliver him,
seeing He delighted in him." "They pierced my hands
and my feet." "They parted my garments among them,
and cast lots upon my vesture." (Psalm xxii, 7, 8, 16, 18.)
Here, because David represents the Lord, the things
which were long afterward done to the Lord were said
to be done to David. Now herein is a true spiritual
sense, and the literal sense is a true symbol of it; and
this is all the soul needs to know. Whatever occurred to
David's natural body is of no consequence to us. In the
spiritual sense it is a highly beautiful work; very devo-
tional, instructive, and refreshing to the soul. By the
enemies so much denounced, threatened, and hated therein, are always meant evils, not persons. And whoever
will read the Psalms, and put the Lord, in His assumed
humanity, in the place of David, will see much beauty in
them which he could not otherwise see. But to see them
in their perfection and glory, he must behold the spiritual
sense. Then will his soul, rejoicing, bless the Lord.

The Proverbs, Ecclesiastes, and the Song of Solomon
have no spiritual sense.

The Proverbs are what they declare themselves to be,
"The Proverbs of Solomon, the son of David, king of
Israel." Thus Solomon claims them as his own, and neither the Lord nor any one else says anything to the contrary.

Ecclesiastes is declared to be "The words of the
Preacher, the son of David, king of Jerusalem." Thus
this book does not claim to be the Word of God, nor does
God say it is His Word.

The Song of Solomon commences by saying, "The
Song of Songs, which is Solomon's." It is a highly
figurative book, but not in correspondences. In these
three books by Solomon, God utters not one syllable.
Indeed, in the last, God's name is not even mentioned or
alluded to.

The prophecies from Isaiah to Malachi, inclusive, have
all a spiritual sense. God is everywhere speaking in
them, and the writers constantly declare them to be "the
Word of the Lord," which came to them, "saying."

In the New Testament, the four Gospels and the Revelation have the spiritual sense. The Acts and the Epistles have not. In the Gospels and the Revelation the
Lord is ever present in word and in spirit. The Revelation commences by saying, "The Revelation of Jesus
Christ."

The Acts are simply what they are declared to be,
"*The Acts of the Apostles*." And so of the Epistles.
They are entitled, The Epistles of Paul, James, Peter,
John, and Jude. They are not the Gospel, but explanations and instructions concerning the Gospel : nor do the
apostles teach that these Acts and Epistles are God's acts
and epistles. They are highly valuable writings, and the
writers were devoted and godly men, chosen of the Lord

to teach and preach the everlasting Gospel which He had given them.

Now it is remarkable that no books of the Bible, except those in which God speaks, and which the writers acknowledge to be from Him, contain a spiritual sense. Indeed, the books seem to tell us in the very letter, upon their very face, which are God-breathed and which are not. But men had not noticed this distinction, and also the wonderful difference in their character, and the structure of the language, till they saw the spiritual sense. By this chapter we may be thought by some to be treating some of the books of the Bible lightly, because we declare them to be without a spiritual sense ; yet let such persons remember that we place as high a value upon those books as they do upon any part; while we esteem the other portions to be infinitely more valuable.

We are now able to see why the first and last parts of the Holy Word—the fore part of Genesis and the Apocalypse—are so wonderfully obscure. It is because they belong to states of human life on earth which have passed away, and which have not yet returned. But the day is coming when those Scriptures will be brilliant with heavenly light, and all the Holy Word will speak one voice, and that, the voice of mercy and peace.

CHAPTER XX.

THE church is the kingdom of Heaven. Its elements are goodness and truth. It cometh not with observation; neither is it here, nor there, as to space, but within the souls of men. It is a spiritual kingdom. The Lord is the King, and the commandments—the golden rules of life—are the laws of the realm. The establishment of this church is the creation of man. For the elements of the church, in man, are what make him a man. The church, therefore, is a human mind or a society of minds in true order.

Now, the Holy Word is a complete history of man or of the church; describing all its lights and shades, from its infancy in the Garden of Eden, to its full age in the millennium. All the things of nature, and their apparent histories, are mentioned in the Word to teach these spiritual things. They symbolize and set forth, by analogy, the mind of man, or the church, and its history. Consequently, whether we say man or the church, it spiritually means the same thing. For goodness and truth make us men by giving us the image and likeness of God—the Infinite Man. In losing goodness and truth, therefore, we cease to be either men or the church, and are said to be destroyed or dead in sin. It is goodness and truth which God gives man, when He *breathes into him the breath of lives*, and man becomes *a living soul*. For the breath which He breathes into him is the Holy Spirit— the Spirit of Truth and Love. Man receives this goodness and truth in his spiritual creation or regeneration. These divine elements are contained in the *words* of the Lord, which He declares are spirit and life. They are received into the will and understanding of man as he sees the truth, yields his heart to the laws of God, through faith and repentance, and obeys those laws till he loves them. This, and nothing else, makes him a man and a portion of the church of God.

Now, by the creation of man, in the first chapter of Genesis, is meant the creation of the race—mankind— males and females. And as the Holy Word is a manifestation and description of the elements and qualities of God, and a history, past, present, and prophetic, of the church or the human mind or soul, and its qualities, given through natural symbols; so it commences with the history of this mental creation—this spiritual humanity. And as all language is taken from the things of nature, there being "no speech nor language where their voice is not heard," and as no quality of the mind can be described, but through natural things, by correspondences; and as the human mind is a microcosm, to which the macrocosm corresponds; so the creation of the human mind, or mental universe, is described by an apparent history of the creation of the natural universe. This history is so composed as beautifully and rationally to describe this creation. And whether it gives also a real history of the creation of material things or not, is in no

11

way essential to us. We cannot understand it if it does. To be told that a thing was done so and so, without giving any rational idea of the powers used and how applied, conveys no food for the soul. For that can be fed only through the rational faculties. But the spiritual history we can understand, and apply it to our salvation. Therefore, in this, we get the things which God designs for us. And what do we want more?

In the expression "the heaven and the earth," we see the internal and the external planes of the mind; in the "light" used, we see the truth for those minds. In the first three days, we see the process of educating and developing the external or natural mind, that it may become a basis or vessel for spiritual things. By correspondence, we see, in the water, natural truth for that mind; and in the grass, we see natural good growing in the affections; and in this growing, we see action; and in the trees bearing fruit, we see good works. Here are the first three days or states, produced in true order, embracing the faith, charity, and works of the natural mind. This prepares man for spiritual or higher work; for through these states he can look up and desire spiritual things. And through the exercise of this desire, looking to the Lord by faith, while bearing the natural fruits of righteousness the truth gradually enters the internal will or heaven of the mind, and spiritual love to God is felt in the soul; thence comes spiritual faith; and from this love and faith comes spiritual knowledge, thus producing the fourth day or state of mind. This love, faith, and knowledge are what is meant by the sun, moon, and stars placed in the mental heaven, to give light upon the mental earth.

In this state man begins to be truly spiritual, and the

natural man begins to be governed by spiritual influences, so that it can bring forth something more alive than grass and trees. Therefore the intellectual and scientific faculties of the mind are next excited by heavenly light, and the thoughts and scientific reasonings begin to be spiritual, which is what is meant by the waters bringing forth fishes and birds. Next the *will* of the natural man comes under spiritual influences and the affections become heavenly, which is what is meant by the earth bringing forth animals and living creatures.

Under this state of things, which is called the fifth day, the internal and external minds can be brought together for mutual action, so as to be in the image of God; and the union of these minds brings man, or the real males and females, to the sixth day, or state of creation.

Thus we have the church, or men and women, in God's image: but they have much yet to do for the proper growth and development of their minds, before they reach the seventh state. They are therefore, as mental beings, commanded to be fruitful and multiply in spiritual things; to replenish their natural mind or earth and subdue it; and to govern all their thoughts, affections and propensities, which is what is meant by man's having dominion over the fish of the sea, fowl of the air, and over every living thing that moveth upon the earth. And as he gains this dominion, replenishes and subdues the natural mind, and gets the complete control over himself, he is prepared to enter upon the seventh state, or sabbath of rest from the six days' labor. God is said to rest because it is His Spirit that does the work.

When the labor of the sixth day is finished, man has become a spiritual man, and is prepared for something higher. As a spiritual man, *truth* predominates, and he holds this dominion by seeing his duty. But the wants of his nature are not satisfied; and there is a further development awaiting him, which we find described in chapter ii. This chapter introduces him into the celestial state, wherein *love* predominates.

Now, it is said in the second chapter, that "*there was not a man to till the ground.*" (ver. 5.) And yet the human race had been created—"male and female"—we know not how many; and they had increased and multiplied, and replenished the earth, and subdued it. Thus there were men enough to replenish and subdue the earth, but none to till the ground. This is because, by replenishing and subduing the earth is meant, supplying and controlling the natural mind by the truth, which is spiritual work; while, by tilling the ground is meant, warming and cultivating the natural mind with love, which is celestial work. Thus, subduing either the natural or the mental earth makes it good ground for tilling. Therefore, the reason there was no man to till the ground is, there was then no celestial man. The people had advanced only to the spiritual state. They could then subdue the natural mind, by the power of the truth, but they had not learned to till that mind, and fill it with celestial love, by the cultivation of merciful and kind affections. Thus the *earth* here means the external mind made spiritual; while the *ground* means the external mind made celestial. Men subdue the mental earth by the truth, or because they *see* it to be right. They till the ground by love, or because they *feel* it to be right.

It is because the work of the first chapter was simply a spiritual work, that the word "God" only is used; by which we are to understand, that the human mind was all the while under the direction and control of the truth, and was thus becoming spiritual; whereas, in the second chapter, it is Jehovah God, or Love and Truth operating in the heart together, which till the ground, or make man celestial. Thus, the second chapter takes men where the first leaves them, and it advances them on to the celestial state. And the process of the work is described in the following words: "And the LORD God made man (mankind) of the dust of the ground, and breathed into his nostrils the breath of lives; and man became a living soul." Here we see that the celestial state is produced by bringing love or good will down into the lowest, smallest things of the external mind—into the very dust of the ground. This is accomplished by doing all the little things of life kindly, from love to the neighbor. For dust denotes the lowest external things of the mind. This work of mercy and kindness is what forms man of the dust of the ground, because it makes him manly in the least things, and fills the whole mind with love to God and good will toward men. This makes man a " living soul," because it makes all his natural affections alive with love. In this way the true church—the kingdom of heaven—is formed.

But the work stops not here. Men are now prepared to make a garden of their mind, because they can now till the ground. Therefore, it is next said in the record, that " the LORD God planted a garden eastward in Eden." Planting the garden is bringing the truths into the warm celestial ground of the mind. This garden of Eden, therefore, is the human mind, not of one person only, but of all the human family then upon the earth, who were far enough advanced. They could, now, so till the ground as to produce good mental fruit-trees. Thus the trees of this garden were all the mental principles, growing from the ground of love. The rivers of the garden were all truths flowing from the Lord.

Here the human family, in this state of paradise, were commanded to dress and keep this mental garden. Herein all the principles of the mind were made new, and put on the celestial aspect. The very affections of the soul were all made new, or celestial, and the people understood their quality, and could read their own hearts. This we are taught in the following language: " Out of the ground the LORD God formed every beast of the field, and fowl of the air, and brought them to Adam (or man) to see what he would call them ; " that is, the people were enabled to know the quality of their thoughts and feelings.

Here it may be noticed that, in the first chapter, *water* brought forth the birds ; that is, the thoughts were spiritual : in this chapter they are formed of the *ground;* that is, they are celestial or flow from love. And so we may see why the trees and the beasts are said to be created over again : it is because, in the first chapter, these principles of the mind were created by means of the truth, and the earth produced them. They now have a higher creation, by means of love, and the *ground* gives them forth. Here we have the highest state to which the human mind advanced before the fall. It is a true celestial church, with everything orderly and heavenly.

We have now given the process of the creation of celestial men, who act in all things from pure love to God and the neighbor. And it is applicable to men in all ages. It is the way celestial men are now created. The phrase " in the beginning," is just as applicable to one period of time as another. There was no beginning with God; but there is a beginning with everything that is created; and, as it regards the thing itself, it is created *in the beginning.*

And, as God never *began* to be, so He never *began* to feel, think and act, or create; for He is "the same yesterday, to-day, and forever"—a Creator always.

Of this happy celestial family the history is brief, and we know but little about it. But we have much ground of belief that it was very numerous; for, from what we know of the process of the mental growth and decline of nations, it must have taken a long time to advance the human race from a state of entire ignorance, when "darkness was upon the faces of the *abyss*" of the soul, up to this high state of celestial light and life. Nor could they have suddenly or rapidly declined into evil.

But the time came when they found that "*it was not good to be alone.*" To be alone, as individuals or as a people, was to be single minded, one in heart and mind, and one with the Lord. It was to have no two sides or parties in anything; but for all to yield implicitly to the Lord's will. Thus they began to get tired of their oneness of state, and to want some variety, and to act more as many than as one alone. They wanted the privilege of saying either yes or no.

This uneasy state of mind is the germ of "the fall." God saw that man felt that "it was not good for him to be alone." Therefore, it is written that "the LORD God caused a deep sleep to fall upon Adam,* and he slept."

---

* It is important here to remember that, in the Hebrew language, there are two words to denote man; one of which is '*Adam*,' and the other is '*Aish;*' that the word Adam, or man, denotes a human being in general, without regard to sex—humanity—the race; and the word 'Aish,' or man, denotes a male human being only; and also that where it says, that "it is not good that the *man* should be alone," or that "the LORD God caused a deep sleep to fall upon Adam," and in all other previous instances, where the word 'man' is used, in these two chapters of Genesis, that word, in the original, denotes mankind without regard to sex.

Now the Lord is often said, in Scripture, to do what He only permits to be done. The deep sleep man brought upon himself; and it was this: The human race, in trying to reason from their own proprium, began to fall into a state of darkness and doubt as to whether their wisdom were all from the Lord, or partly from themselves. This darkness was the sleep. They were no longer awake or alive to the Lord's will and their duty; their understandings were becoming dark and their affections cold.

But, to understand the Scripture record of the process through which the church or human nature passed, during "the fall," we must have clear and distinct ideas of the male and female elements of the mind, in their general nature, without regard to individuals or sex. And we see that there must be these two spiritual elements, or there could not be the male and female ultimates; and that these elements must pervade the entire universe, by influx, or all nature would not present the male and female qualities. In God, they are Love and Wisdom; in man, they are truth and goodness; in animals, they are thoughts and feelings; in vegetables, they are light and heat, all coming from God, by means of the living Divine Influx. Woman is so organized as to express more of the goodness, and man more of the truth. Therefore, the woman manifests, of this influx, more of its gentleness, mercy, tenderness, and goodness; and man, more of its truth, justice, judgment, and power. Thus we learn, from the Holy Word, that the truths are male principles, and goods, female. Hence the Lord, as the Truth, is called the husband of the church, as goodness. And as truths are for the understanding, and goods for the will, so, spiritually speaking, the understanding is the male department of the mind, and the will, the female department.

Therefore, every person must have male and female elements; male, for the thoughts; and female, for the feelings. For, without the united action of the will and the understanding, man could do nothing. These elements, in their origin, are the root and source of all creation and action, being in the Divine Love and Wisdom of the Great Jehovah, and going forth " the Life of all things."

Now, by keeping the idea of these general male and female elements in the mind, without regard to sex, we shall see that a community of people as a body must have its male and female elements pervading all its parts as though it were one mind: the general understanding being the male department, and the general will, the female.

From this view we see that the *darkened understanding* of the people of Eden, was the *Adam*, or *male principle*, which was *asleep*. Sleep is a term often used in the Word to denote a state of doubtfulness, and indifference of mind. To such persons the Lord says, "Awake, thou that sleepest, and arise from the dead."

Now, that primeval people had turned their thoughts away from the Lord toward themselves, and had studied so hard to find out what there really was of them, independent of God—what their very selfhood was in itself— that their understanding, or Adam principle, had become beclouded with mystery. This was their deep sleep. Their understanding, or male department, was in darkness, and their will, or female element, had become cold. Hence the will did not ardently love the things of the understanding, for they were gloomy and doubtful; and the understanding saw nothing very inviting in the will, it was so indifferent.

But the Lord, who is ever in effort to help men out of their difficulties, by coming to them, under every trial,

11*

with something adapted to their state, took this coldness away from the affections of the people, and this darkness away from their understandings, by teaching them that men had a selfhood, and what it was, and that they were free to exercise it and love it as their own, and therefore, to be no longer "alone," provided they would acknowledge that all the power to act, and everything good and true, were given them from the Lord.

This was a new truth to them, and just what their state wanted; and it produced a new state of mind, giving them much joy. For this new truth in the understanding, or Adam department of the mind, could be received and warmly embraced by the new affections in the will, or Eve department. Thus the general mind of the people, which was before dark and cold, was now light and warm.

Now this cold and indifferent state of the will toward the darkened understanding, and toward the Lord as the Truth, is what is meant by the rib which was taken away; and the warm affection which the people received for the new truth, is what is meant by the woman, or flesh, which took the place of the rib : flesh denotes goodness.

This new truth in the understanding of the people, is the Lord as the Word, the Husband of the church. And the goodness of these new affections, in the will, is the church, the bride. And this union of truth in the understanding with good in the will, is used in the Word as a symbol of the relation between husband and wife.

Now, it is because the will of the people received these new and joyous affections through the truth in the understanding, which showed them that they were free agents and need not be alone, that it is said that the woman was taken out of the man. For the new truth, which the Lord here gave to the understanding, contained within it the very goodness which made the will so happy ; and which the will or woman received from the understanding or man. And as the understanding and the will are now brought joyously together, it is therefore added that " a man shall leave his father and his mother, and shall cleave unto his wife ; and they shall be one flesh."

It may seem strange that the cold selfhood of man should be called a rib or bone. But it is because a bone has but little feeling. And for this reason it is often used, in the Word, in that sense. Thus the Psalmist says, " Make me to have joy and gladness, that the bones which thou hast broken may rejoice." Here, by broken bones are meant broken affections, or subdued selfhood. Breaking a bone, by the Lord, is the same as taking out a rib or destroying a dead selfhood.

Now, the state of man's selfhood is the state of the church in him. And a man's selfhood is either dead or alive. It is dead when he loves self solely for the sake of self. It is alive when he loves self for the sake of the Lord ; for then he loves his neighbor as himself. In the new selfhood which was given in the place of the rib, the people saw that they were not good in and of themselves ; and seeing this, and looking to the Lord, they loved Him for the goods and truths that were in them from Him, and they loved themselves also for what God gave them. Here we have the condition of the church, or the state of man, when his mind was first opened to a true knowledge of his own selfhood, giving him some ideas of what was right and wrong in his thoughts and feelings. This was an important and responsible position to stand in ; and no doubt much valuable knowledge was gained, as they looked to the Lord and followed His directions, in their new state of the union of goodness and truth in them. But the history leaves us in entire ignorance of either their progress, or of the time of their continuance in this happy state.

For we next find them, under temptations, eating of the forbidden tree. Their happy state, before they yielded to the subtlety of the serpent, is symbolized by a garden. In this lovely garden, all was sweet and fresh as spring. Not a thorn or thistle to mar the beauty of the human intellect. There stood the Tree of Life, laden with the fruits of eternal love. This tree was God Himself in His mercy and truth. It was the tree of Divine Wisdom giving forth goodness. Its fruits gave life, health, happiness, and peace to the soul. There, also, was the tree of knowledge of good and evil. This was the tree of man's selfhood; of man's wisdom, humbly acknowledged to be all from the Lord. It was then a lovely tree, bearing the fruits of peace, of knowledge, and of good will, all received from the Tree of Life. Both these trees were necessary for the cultivation and development of this mental garden—the human mind.

The tree of man's knowledge took root in man's selfhood. This selfhood is the human element given man by God, in order that he may know God and freely love Him. Man's selfhood, therefore, was a good tree, of God's own planting; and without its cultivation and growth, man would be only an animal, not a man. The elements of this tree were freedom and rationality. Without these elements, the human mind would be a machine. This tree, therefore, is what gives man his distinct individuality, and makes him human. But this tree alone would not make a man. It has no life of its own. Man is not a self-existent being. Therefore, in order to have a man in the image and likeness of his God, the Tree of Life must also be there, acknowledged and loved. Now, while man went to the Tree of Life for goodness and truth—while he looked to the Lord for wisdom and guidance—all was well: the garden of his mind was budding and blossoming with new beauty, the Tree of Life was exhibiting new flowers and fruits, or new wisdom and goodness, every day. And his own tree of knowledge was growing up, straight and beautiful, bearing the fruits of righteousness, and mercy, for his neighbors. But when man, in the exercise of his freedom and curiosity, turned away from the Tree of Life, and ate of the tree of his own wisdom, he forgot his God, and became wise in his own eyes. When he ate of his own righteousness—of the tree of his own selfhood—it began to bear fruits only for himself. Before this, it was a generous tree, bearing all its fruits of kindness for the neighbor. Now, it was a selfish tree, feeling kind only toward self; and, therefore, was feeding and inflating the mind with self-wisdom and self-righteousness. Thus he learned to value himself more than his God, and the world more than his neighbor. And from this tree of self-wisdom, bearing the fruits of self-righteousness, have sprung all the evils and vices of humanity. Had men never eaten of this tree, but always gone to the Lord for wisdom, it would then have remained ever graceful and lovely, because always modestly blooming with wisdom, drawn from the Tree of Life.

But man, by trying his own skill, by experimenting in his own way, and by gradually overreaching the divine rules of order and justice, began to imagine that he was really becoming skilful and wise himself; and this self-wisdom became pleasant to the eyes, or to the understanding, and a tree to be desired to make one wise. And his growing vanity began to think, and to desire to have others think, that it was all his own wisdom. And thus, step after step, in his own way, he grew daily in the estimation of his own importance, and finally took to himself the merit of all the wisdom and goodness that his God had given him. Thus he went to himself for knowledge ; depended upon his own sagacity ; and gave forth to others all that he knew, as the result of his own wonderful powers and prudence. In this way, he lost all true knowledge of his God, and even worshipped himself; and desired others to worship him. Thus came sin.

And now, every person, in the supreme love of self, inwardly desires the praise, adoration, and worship of all others. This selfish state of mind leads to all the strifes and contentions among men, for praise, and power, and property, and preëminence ; and leads men into every degree of sin and vice, for self-gratification.

But, as the people were falling, God was in effort to save them. Thus we find Him calling out to them, in the garden, saying to Adam, " Where art thou ? " At this time, the garden of their mind still contained many beautiful trees and attractive objects. And they sought to hide themselves among the remaining good principles of their mind and character ; that is, they sought to keep the good qualities of their nature in sight ; and to hide their guilt and shame behind them. For it is written, " The eyes of them both were opened, and they knew that they were naked ; " that is, their understandings were opened, and they knew their evils were exposed to the divine truth.

Now, from the expression " *the eyes of both of them were opened,*" one would suppose, from the literal sense, that only *two persons* were treated of : but the true meaning is, the understandings of both males and females were opened, as to things good or evil, true or false. For they had eaten of the tree of knowledge of good and evil. Adam and Eve therefore do not mean two distinct persons, in this history; but the men and the women; and they mean, also, the two great elements of the human mind, the understanding and the will, which every person possesses : for the subject relates to the condition of the human family. And as the word " Adam " is the proper generic name for the race, and means all mankind, males and females, it is therefore written, " male and female created He them ; and called their name Adam." (Gen. v. 2.)

Now the question, " Where art thou ? " was the Truth addressing itself first to the understanding, or male element. And the people reasoned among themselves, as to the cause of their sins. And they finally came to the conclusion, that the fault was in the will, or female element; that they knew better than to sin, but that they could not help it. And how common it is for people thus to excuse themselves at the present day! They want some way to get rid of the blame. For illustration : a person sins, whether male or female : he reflects upon it ; and his judgment or male element acknowledges the fact ; he sees that the law of order is broken. But he comes to the conclusion that he is not to blame ; that it was *in his will* to sin. " The woman," he says, or the will, " that thou gavest to be with me, she gave me of the tree, and I did eat ; " thus casting all the blame entirely from himself, on to God. For he says to himself, I did not make my will—my disposition—God gave it to me. " The woman whom *Thou* gavest to be with me, *she* gave me." Thus men reasoned in the garden, and thus they reason at this day.

But as they continued to examine into, and to reason upon, the subject of their troubles, the question, by the light of truth, came up, as to where the will got the disposition to sin?—whether God gave it? For "the LORD God—the Truth—said unto the woman, What is this that *thou* hast done?" And, after mature deliberation, they changed their minds, as to the disposition to sin being originally in the will, and decided that it was in the senses. Thus they, in their will, answered, and said, "The serpent beguiled" the will, and the will sinned. Or the will says, "The serpent beguiled me, and I did eat." And here they put all the blame away from both the will and the understanding on to the senses—the serpent principle. So man now says he is not to blame for his sins—that he did not make his senses—that, if the temptation had not been in his way, he should not have sinned. If he had not seen the property, he should not have stolen it. If he had not heard the man's language, and seen his actions, and thus got angry, he should not have murdered him. Thus, he says, the senses of hearing and seeing beguiled the will into these acts of stealing and murder; and the will overruled the understanding. "The woman gave," and man sinned. Thus the blame is all laid upon the serpent. And so now, God, or the Truth, says to man, "Where art thou?" And these are his selfish replies, and flimsy excuses; when he might readily see, that all that comes from God must be good and true; and that man therefore must have depraved his own senses, corrupted his own will, and beclouded his own understanding.

Thus we see that the first effect of sin is to make man ashamed; he feels like a naked man, and wants to hide himself from the scrutiny of Truth, behind a fair outside. Next comes deception, which is mental darkness: he

avoids the light. And the next thing is to justify himself, and to cast the blame, first upon one thing and then
upon another, and lastly upon his God. Then follows
hatred to God and man ; and the love of nothing but what
contributes to his own selfish gratification.

Thus the race fell into sin. And the narrative
next declares that God " drove them out of the garden."
The garden being an orderly and happy state of the mind,
it was their sins that dispossessed them of it. But it was
the Lord, as the Truth, that apparently drove them out,
or rather, that showed them that they were out, and rendered them unhappy from a sense of their guilt. And
now they find themselves becoming more and more con-
tentious, depraved, and miserable. This is a sad state of
the church : and they see that it cannot be long endured ;
that it must lead to destruction. Something must be done
to restore harmony and peace among them. To accomplish this object, the understanding and the will of the
people—the Adam and Eve of the church—set themselves
to work to devise some doctrine or means which they
could use for their good or the benefit of the church.
They needed some rules of life. And they conceived
and brought forth the doctrine of faith, and called its
name Cain.

Faith was the first-begotten of the church. They resolved that they would not forget their God ; but would
believe on Him, and acknowledge His supremacy and
laws. But they found that one rule of life was not
enough. And they brought forth and established another
doctrine, which was charity ; and they called its name
Abel. Thus, Adam, or the understanding of the church
or people, in connection with Eve, or the will of the
church, brought forth and established, for the guidance

and government of the community, these two fundamental doctrines or rules of life, Faith and Charity, called Cain and Abel. These rules taught them that they must believe in the Lord and regard His laws; and also love one another and live in peace.

In consequence of the fall, these rules had become absolutely necessary for the order and safety of the community. They had eaten of the forbidden fruit—the tree of knowledge of good and evil. Their eyes or understandings were opened. And they had become wise in their own eyes, proud of their own wisdom. This brought discord. Each wanted to rule. And they were under the necessity of looking to the Lord, by faith, and exercising the laws of charity, in order to make life agreeable. And to accomplish this, the church established these two doctrines. They had now faith in the Lord, and charity toward the neighbor. And so long as they regarded these doctrines, all went on well, of course. This was the best that the Lord could do for them.

But, as selfishness increased, some ceased to be satisfied with the life of charity. It was more duty to the neighbor than they were willing to perform. And they gradually reasoned themselves into the belief that faith in God was all the doctrine that it was necessary to exercise. So long as they had charity, they offered the firstlings of the flock, or their best affections, to the Lord. But the faith of the head began to reason against the offerings of the heart, and these people said to themselves, It is not necessary to our salvation to love our neighbor: faith in God is far better. We need not give away any longer the firstlings of the flock—our best affections—for an offering; we want them for ourselves. Surely, if we give the fruit of the ground, or true faith in the Lord, that will be all-sufficient. Love to the neighbor cannot save us. Salvation is of God. We can do nothing. If we believe in the Lord, He will save us by that faith.

Thus the head reasoned against the heart, and the will and the understanding became separated. A strong contention arose between the judgment and the feelings, or between faith and charity, and eventually the selfishness of the natural, earthly man overruled the better feelings of the heart, and finally destroyed the love of the neighbor.

Thus Cain, or Faith, slew his brother Abel, or Charity. The good affections of the heart were destroyed. Faith alone was the cold and selfish state of a portion of the church. The church was therefore divided into two parties. Thus the Cainites, or faith-alone-people, had their own peculiar views, distinct from those who still adhered to the principle of charity. But they were unhappy creatures, as all must be who have no true love for one another.

"And the LORD God said unto Cain, Where is Abel, thy brother? And he said, I know not. Am I my brother's keeper?" Thus, in a reflective moment, the Lord, as the Truth, entered their minds, and they said to themselves, Where is my love to the neighbor? They saw and felt their coldness, and they answered, I know not where my charity is gone. And they answered truly, for they had ceased to be their brother's keeper. Their love of the neighbor was dead. They felt condemned under the light of this truth. They saw that they were not what they should be. And, as said by the Lord, when they should till the ground, or cultivate the mind, it would not yield its strength : for faith without charity can produce no good fruits. The mental earth cannot be cultivated by truth without goodness. And in their luminous moments, they saw that they were fugitives and vagabonds in the earth. And they were fearful of becoming entirely destroyed or wretched. But the light which thus showed them their condition, did not reach their hearts so as to enkindle benevolence, but only to excite selfish fear. And as the truth had failed to call them back to goodness, the next effort of the Lord was to keep them from falling lower. And He therefore said, " Whosoever slayeth Cain, vengeance shall be taken on him sevenfold : " that is, the Lord told them by the Truth, in their minds, that if they should destroy their faith in Him, or cease to believe in Him, they would be sevenfold more wretched than they were then. Their faith still gave them some connection with the Lord. There was something living in it. And if they should lose that, then, indeed, they would fall into the lowest wretchedness.

He who disbelieves in a God whom he can love, is spiritually or mentally most miserable. He has no hope of future existence or heavenly joys. All he can see before him, when this life ends, is darkness and extinction. And even this life loses its brightness and its true delights. These Cainites, therefore, settled down in the doctrine of faith alone. They became a portion of the church that differed from the main body. And the Lord set a mark upon them, that they might be known and preserved. That mark was *Faith.* The ensign of the church from which they sprung would be *Faith and Charity.* Name or mark means *quality.* Faith or Cain was the quality or name of the new sect. That was their mark of distinction. And so long as they should wear that mark—so long as they should have faith—they would have some spiritual life. But, being without charity, the light of their faith in time grew dim and feeble. Thus it is said that Cain went out from the presence of the Lord and dwelt in the land of Nod. They receded from the light and sunk into a vagabond state. Places denote states of mind; land of Nod, a vagabond state, or a state destitute of goodness and truth.

"And Cain knew his wife; and she conceived, and bare Enoch: and he builded a city, and called the name of the city after the name of his son, Enoch." Now Cain was a society of men and women who believed in faith alone. Cain also means the understanding, the male element of that body. And as soon as these Cainites had cultivated a real love of the idea of faith alone; when the feelings of the heart had become fully wedded to that sentiment of the head; those feelings were the wife—the will and the understanding of the people were wedded in that doctrine. And then followed the birth of Enoch. This church of Cain could have offspring, as well as the church of Adam. Thus these Cainites, through the union of their wills and understandings, gave birth to a whole system of doctrines of faith alone. Enoch, the child born, means these doctrines. This is known because city means doctrines, and name, quality; and it is said they builded a city, and called the name of the city after the name of their son, Enoch. The birth of Enoch, therefore, is the establishment of these doctrines of faith alone. And the building of the city is the arrangement of these doctrines into a system of faith.

But the loss of Abel could not be made up by all the devices and powers of the mind. Where charity, the very soul and life of society, is lacking, there is a want which nothing can supply. And this want was fast pervading the whole Adamic people—all the human race of that age. Under this state of things, something further must be done. Matters could not go on much further in this way, and be endurable. Therefore it is written that "Adam knew his wife again, and she bare a son, and called his name Seth. For God, *said she*, hath appointed me another seed instead of Abel, whom Cain slew." Here the general church devised a new doctrine, or way, which would supply the place of their lost charity, or Abel. This new son or truth of doctrine, brought forth by the united wisdom and love of the church, was *good works.* This son, Seth, which was given by the Lord instead of charity, was not charity itself; if it had been it would have been called Abel. But it was given for the purpose of restoring to the people charity, for it was given in Abel's stead. And the divine object was thereby accomplished. For the history says that to Seth was born a son, and they called his name Enos ; and that *then* began men to call on the name of the Lord.

Thus Seth, or good works, brought forth love to God and the neighbor. For to call on the name of the Lord is to desire, and to receive, His quality. And this quality includes mercy and kindness toward all. Thus we see here verified the great truth, taught by our Lord, that, if we would enter into life, we must keep the commandments. The Adamic church could not stand without the doctrine of works, as a basis. When they found themselves rapidly falling, they established the doctrines of faith and charity ; and supposed these were rules of life enough. But faith and charity cannot stand unless they are ultimated and grounded in works. Unless the works of faith and charity are kindly performed, Faith will surely slay his brother Charity. We now see why Adam gave names to only three children, Faith, Charity, and

Works. It is because he was the church, and faith, charity, and works embrace everything of the church. They are from the three great fundamental principles, Wisdom, Love, and Power. The doctrine of works is the doctrine of charity, in action. And if we are not charitable, but have natural faith enough to see that we ought to be ; and will then do the works of charity, we shall become so. We now see the necessity of protecting Cain, or Faith, after he had slain his brother. For, without the natural truth of faith, we could not perform good works, and thus be brought into the love of the neighbor, and thereby obtain charity, and thence true spiritual faith.

The lesson we draw from this history is twofold. First, that if we cease to give to God the firstlings of our flock, or our best affections, and trust to our own faith, we shall lose our charity, fall into a false and lifeless state of mind, and establish ourselves in false doctrines. Or, what is the same thing, we shall slay our brother Abel, remove from the presence of the Lord to the land of Nod, marry a wife, and build a city. And from this deplorable condition we can never be removed unless, in the second place, there is born unto us Seth, or good works, and we return to the presence of our God, in humble obedience to His commandments.

Thus the Lord arrested the downward progress of the race for a season. But the people had become divided in sentiment, and changes were frequently made, and new things devised or begotten, by the church, in its various branches, under different names of persons as offspring, until the people had become so depraved that " the sons of God saw the daughters of men that they were fair ; and they took them wives of all which they chose." (Gen. vi, 2.) This state of things brought on the flood. For by the sons of God are meant truths in the minds of the people; and by the daughters of men are meant their *evils.* Any truth from God's love is *a* son of the Father. All truths in the complex are *the* Son of God. All affections that come from man's selfish proprium are evils; and are here called daughters of men. Therefore, for the truths of the head to think the evils of the heart fair, and become wedded to them, is to falsify those truths, and fill the mind with deceit. Had these sons of God seen the daughters of *God* to be fair, and been wedded to them, all would have been well, for by daughters of God would have been meant good principles.

In this flood of falsities, which inundated the mental world, the most ancient, or Adamic church, with all its branches, came to an end on the earth; and the destruction of all good affections, thoughts, and principles of the mind is signified by the destruction of animals, birds, &c., and a new order of things had to be introduced. Among the people called Noah, there were minds that could receive these new instructions from the Lord, and become the church on a lower plane than that of the Adamic church.

By Noah and his family are meant all those who were willing to receive and regard the Lord's new instructions. By the ark is meant the church, or the new state of order which the Lord was establishing in their minds, as to doctrines and life. The church is now often called the ark of safety. By the materials and dimensions of the ark is meant the character and quality of the doctrines and principles of the church. This may at first strike some as strange and incredible. But this is a rule which holds good, by correspondences, throughout the entire Word. Much is said of the building of tabernacles and temples.

Look at the materials and dimensions of the Holy City or New Church Doctrines—a city 1,500 miles square, with gates, and walls, and foundations, and precious stones, and gold, and silver, and pearls, and glass, and trees, and rivers, and fruits, all coming down from God, out of heaven, into the human mind. Is the description of the ark, as applied to the principles of the church or the mind, any more strange than this?

By the building of the ark is denoted, the practising and establishing, by faithful and humble obedience, these new principles of life in the mind. For these doctrines and rules are various principles of goodness and truth, adapted to the states and wants of that age. And when these principles are received into the mind, that mind is the ark or the church. And though Noah and his family are said to be in the ark, yet the ark is also in them. Men are truly in the church only when the church or kingdom is in them. "I in thee and thou in Me," saith the Lord.

The three stories of the ark denote that the people were taught something of the three degrees of the mind— celestial, spiritual, and natural. The window, in the top, denotes that they were taught that the understanding is the receptacle of the truth of the Word, the true light of heaven. The door in the side denotes that they were taught that they could also receive the truth by hearing and obeying the rules of the church.

By their entering the ark is meant their coming under the power and influence of these doctrines and rules of life. By the animals, birds, and so forth, entering the ark, is meant the bringing of all their various affections, thoughts, and propensities within the control of the new divine rules. The clean beasts and cattle denote the good affections of the mind, and the unclean, the bad affections.

12

For on entering the ark, or coming under the influence of the doctrines, they took with them all their mental principles, good and bad. And here, in the church, the bad were to be subdued. The good are said to go in by sevens, because seven is a holy number, denoting purity.

What is meant by its raining 40 days and 40 nights may be seen in chap. xiii, on numbers.

At the time they entered the ark, we behold the people of that age in a state of profound darkness and error : their whole mental earth inundated with falses. In the midst of this general gloom and wretchedness, we see a little band, called Noah and his family, hearkening to the new teachings of the Lord, and forming a little church. They call this church the ark. And they enter into its worship and instructions, bringing under its influence all their wayward and various thoughts, feelings, and propensities—every living creature of their mind and heart—and they feed them there with food from heaven, or with divine goods and truths. In this ark or church, they keep their falses under, and thus the ark is raised in their estimation above their own and the surrounding waters of error, until its doctrines rise to the very summit of their affections. They truly love them. The ark rests on the Ararat of their hearts—their love to God and His truth. And as they were purified, and came into states of true thoughts and feelings, they felt a sincere regard for the salvation of the world of mankind lying in darkness around them. And they kindly sent forth the dove to see if the waters or falses were abated from their minds. The dove corresponds to the Holy Spirit—the spirit of truth and love.

This little church then sent forth that gentle spirit to the world of mind around, to see if the darkness of error had subsided, and they would accept the truth. But all was still false—dark as night. The dove found no rest for the sole of her foot, for the waters were on the whole face of the earth. No mind could receive the truth. What Christian heart that has a new and heavenly truth has not experienced the same thing, in his efforts to present that truth to other minds? How often the gentle dove has returned unto him, into the ark of his own bosom, for a place to rest her foot!

Noah first sent forth a raven, a bird denoting very external truth. This flew to and fro in their external understandings, till their falses had so subsided as to receive it. But they could receive nothing higher. It was necessary that they should have the external truth first, denoted by the raven. "First that which is natural, afterward that which is spiritual."

But Noah, after the return of the dove, waited seven days, or till they had come into new states of mind from the exercise of the natural truth; and he sent forth the dove again, or offered them the spiritual truth once more. But their perceptions were still too dark to receive her; and she returned: "And, lo, in her mouth was an olive leaf plucked off." The olive tree, from its oil, denotes celestial love: the leaf denotes the truth of faith from that love. The return of the dove, with the olive leaf plucked off, denotes that they would receive some little of spiritual truth, or some faith, but could not yet receive the love. The leaf was plucked off, or separated from the tree. Noah waited yet other seven days, or for new states of mind, and sent forth the dove again, and then they received the spirit of truth. And now the church began to spread among other minds.

Thus was established the Noatic state of the church—

the second distinct feature of the Lord's kingdom among
men, symbolized by an ark. There the little society called
Noah and his family were the church, in the light and life
of new Divine Truths; while all the community around
them were immersed in falsities. But Noah instructed
them in the Divine Truth. This we are taught by his
sending forth the dove, which denoted the Holy Spirit
—the Spirit of Truth.

And Noah planted in their minds a vineyard; or, in
other words, the people of this church cultivated their
hearts by the reception, propagation, and giving forth of
spiritual truths. But in process of time Noah or the
church fell in love with his vineyard, instead of God who
gave it; and they became drunken with the mental wine
of their own raising; or, in other words, they took to
themselves the merits of the vineyard, considered the
truths their own wisdom, and became intoxicated with
the errors of selfishness. Thus the second state of the
church was lost, and man sunk into naturalism.

Noah, like Adam, ate of the forbidden tree—the tree
of his own wisdom.

Men had now become so low that the Lord could no
longer approach them and teach them without written
laws and rules, rites and ceremonies. He therefore gave
them the commandments on Mount Sinai, and established
the church or the peremptory law of obedience. This
was the third or Jewish church. This state of the church
was symbolized by outward religious rites and ceremonies.
It was simply a church of works, in which men were to
fear God and keep His commandments. Men had become entirely natural; they had none but the most vague
ideas of a spiritual world, or of a life after death. They
looked only for temporal rewards and punishments. They

were to fear God and keep His commandments. All their rites and ceremonies were in true correspondences. And so long as they humbly performed them, and kept the commandments because God had commanded it, they received spiritual life, and could be prepared for heaven. But in time they lost their reverence and respect for God and His laws, and kept the commandments and performed their religious ceremonies entirely from selfish motives. Thus they fell into the lowest state of perverted humanity. A state denoted by whited sepulchres, generation of vipers, stiffnecked people, scribes, pharisees, hypocrites.

We have now traced the decline of humanity or of the church from its highest state of purity and innocence, as a garden of Eden, down to its lowest state of sin and selfishness, as an unfruitful wilderness; a state in which God could no longer reach men without assuming their nature. The fall was now completed: humanity had gone down to the very verge of complete destruction. Step after step it had declined, and the merciful Lord had followed it, until the last spark of life was about to expire.

To this little spark the Lord, through the virgin Mary, united Himself, wrapped around as it was with all the depravity of the race, so that, in the assumed nature, "He was tempted in all points like as we are." Thus He met the enemies and the evils of humanity on their own ground, rescued the race from destruction, turned the face of humanity upward, purified and glorified the assumed nature, and made it a Divine Mediator or Medium between the Father within and the wicked world without. And through the power of His Spirit, proceeding from His Divine Humanity, He established the Christian church, and gave us the blessed Gospel.

Herein He brought life and immortality to light;

taught them of heaven and of hell, of the resurrection, of the judgment, and of the future life.

But He told His disciples that that was not His last dispensation; that He would come again and establish the New Jerusalem. And He gave them the Apocalypse, which is a clear and distinct prophecy of the passing away of that state of the church, and of the coming of the new one.

Now, what was the first coming of the Lord? It was the Divine Truth or the Word, which "was in the beginning with God," and which "was God," assuming our nature and coming thereby into the minds of men. It was the Divine Truth filled with the Divine Love, spoken from the material body of the Lord, and also from the written Gospel.

What is the second coming of the Lord? It is the same Divine Truth filled with the same Divine Love, in its spirit and life, coming through the written Gospel into the minds of men.

The first coming was to the lowest possible state of mankind, when they had no thought of anything higher than matter. He therefore had to come into their depraved nature and in a material body. For thus only could He reach their low state; and then only by the literal sense of the Word.

But now, at the second coming, having put off that material body and everything depraved, He comes into the minds of men, as the Divine Word, not only in the literal sense, but also in its spirit and its life. The "many things," therefore, which at the first coming, He had to say to His disciples that they could not bear, He now reveals, showing us "plainly of the Father."

Thus we have in the Holy Word an account of the coming of the Lord to establish the New Jerusalem, the last and highest state of the church, the crowning dispensation of the Holy Word. The state of the Christian world, at this coming, is symbolically and prophetically described in the 24th chapter of Matthew, as háving passed through immense tribulation ; such as divisions, persecutions, wars, pestilences, earthquakes, and famines, until the Sun of Righteousness, in many minds, had become darkened, and the moon of faith did not give her light, and the stars of true knowledge had fallen from their mental heaven : i. e., until they were in doubts and darkness as to what to believe, and saw not the bright truths of the Word which they needed. And who can look through the present state of the Christian world, in all its various and conflicting aspects, from the gross Mormonism of ignorant Joe Smith, up to the views of learned doctors, who are now representing the Sacred Word of Light and Life as in the shades of error and contradiction —who, I say, can look at this picture and not see this prophecy being fulfilled ? Well may our Lord have said, "Except those days should be shortened, there should no flesh be saved." (Matt. xxiv, 22.)

In this condition of the church on earth it is declared that there should be seen the sign of the coming of the Son of Man ; and that He should come in the clouds of heaven, or in the letter of the Word, as seen in the beclouded state of men's minds—their mental heaven. The full description of this final church is given in the Apocalypse, which closes the canon of Scripture, and therefore the Divine history of the church. This description we find in the 21st chapter of Revelation, under the similitude of a Holy City, coming down from God out of heaven, prepared as a bride adorned for her husband.

Now, what is this Holy City ? It is a pure system of doctrines, teaching clearly the nature and character of

God and His laws ; and of man and all his duties. The city is said to be " pure gold, like unto clear glass," because the doctrines are all good and clearly seen, and make us rich unto salvation ; gold denoting goodness or heavenly riches, and clear glass meaning truth understood. A city is a beautiful symbol of doctrines, because it is used for the indwelling, comfort, intercourse, instruction, protection, support, and happiness of its inhabitants. Here they perform their labor, treasure up their wealth, build their houses and churches, attend their worship, sell their merchandise from man to man, and perform the duties of this life. Thus a city, in order, completely represents those heavenly doctrines, or rules of life, through which our souls may be brought together, to dwell in mutual love, use, and benefit, accumulating heavenly riches, and, as we need, passing from soul to soul, the precious goods and truths of spiritual life. A good man spiritually dwells in such doctrines of the Holy Word, as he naturally dwells in a city.

This Holy City of pure gold, like unto clear glass, is the doctrine of the Word in its spiritual light, shining through the literal sense. It is said to have twelve foundations of precious stones. Now, what are these foundations ? They are all natural truths. All natural truths whatever, whether scientific, civil, or religious, are the basis of spiritual truths. When, therefore, from the spiritual light of the Word, are clearly presented to the mind the beautiful doctrines of the trinity, atonement, fall, regeneration, resurrection, judgment, heaven, and hell, they strike the natural mind as true, for they are rational and consistent. This is because all natural truths are in harmony with spiritual truths. And when the natural mind, which is exercised with natural truths, is open to the reception of spiritual truths, those spiritual truths are seen through the natural truths, and rest upon them as a foundation. And while the foundations of this city are natural truths, the Light of the city is Spiritual Truth. There is "no need of the sun, neither of the moon, to shine in it : for the glory of God did lighten it, and the Lamb is the light thereof." The spiritual truth of the Holy Word, in the human mind, is the light of the doctrines, the glory of this city.

The gates of the city are introductory truths, denoted by pearls. Doctrines are things for the understanding. And to see the inner light of this city—the spiritual light of the doctrines—we must pass the gates ; that is, these gates must introduce to our minds the spiritual light. What then are these gates—these introductory truths ? They are the truths of analogy, seen by correspondences. They are the scientific light which shows the relation between the book of nature and the book of Revelation—between the works and the Word of God—between the literal and the spiritual sense of the Sacred Scriptures. Through these gates of pearl we enter understandingly into the Holy City. Pearls denote scientific truths, because things of the sea denote scientifics. There are twelve of these gates ; three on each of the four sides of the city ; the East, the West, the North, and the South. By the number 12, which denotes perfect fulness, we learn that these gates comprise all analogical truths whatever ; the entire circle of the science of correspondences.

But it is not necessary to understand all this science in order to enter this city. We can begin to enter on the East side, when the light of this science, like that of the rising sun, first feebly strikes us ; or we can enter on the South side, when we have a full blaze of the light, as at

12*

noon-day; or we can enter on the West side when we have neglected properly to use the light, till it is passing away; we can even then use the light and enter the city; or we can enter on the North side, where the light is dim and the feelings cool. Thus we can enter in the Spring of life, or in the Summer of life, or in the Autumn, or in the Winter. The gates of the New Jerusalem are never shut to man while he lives. And whether he has little light or much, if he uses the light he has, he can enter the heavenly abode.

But to enter, on either side, we must pass the three gates. These three gates are not side by side, but one within another, and united. To pass one or two will do us no good, unless we pass the third: for the number 3, in the Word, always points to the three great elements of life—wisdom, love, and power. These three gates, or classes of introductory truths, have therefore regard to our faith, our charity, and our works. When the spiritual light of the Word, by the law of analogy, enters our mind, we soon begin to see that in order to enter this city, or love these doctrines, we must *feel* right and *act* right, as well as *see* right: that our heart and our head must be in the work; that faith alone, or charity alone, or works alone, or any two of these together, will never bring us within the Holy City, or into the society of the pure and good. We must have goodness as well as truth, and we must do our duty. We must pass the three gates.

The streets of this city are the common paths or principles of life, wherein we meet our fellow men and carry out the golden rules of justice and mercy.

The form of this city is symbolized by a cube, because forms denote qualities. It is therefore said to be "four-square;" the length, the breadth, and the height of it being equal. Here again that wonderful number 3 comes in, with its heavenly instructions; for length has relation to goodness; breadth, to truth; and height, to use; thus teaching that the doctrines are as good as they are true, and as useful as they are good and true. And here also that full and perfect number 12 is again used, to define the extent and quality of this length, breadth, and height of doctrines; calling them each 12,000 furlongs; which means that they comprise all goods, truths, and uses; infinite Love, Wisdom, and Power in all their varieties and their fulness.

This city or doctrine is said to be measured by an angel with a golden reed. This is because, by measuring, is meant ascertaining the quality. And as gold denotes goodness, and reed, truth, so we are taught by this measuring, that it is only by truth from good through angelic and heavenly influences, that we can know the divine quality of these doctrines. Now, what, in the letter alone, seems strange, is, that though this city is declared to be 12,000 furlongs square, yet its wall is said to be the measure of a man; i. e., of an angel. But this is because a true man or angel loves the Holy Word, and is filled with these doctrines; they are therefore his spiritual measure or quality.

Now, for a man to enter this city, the city must also enter him. And we are taught that "there shall in no wise enter into it anything that defileth, neither whatsoever worketh abomination, or maketh a lie;" by which we are taught that, though we may have these doctrines in our understanding, yet we can receive them into our affections only as we put away our evils; that these pure elements will not mingle with falses and evils. Who then enters the Holy City? "He that overcometh." What does he find there? The Tree of Life. "To him that overcometh will I give to eat of the Tree of Life, which is in the midst of the paradise of God," saith our Lord. Here we are again, with the Adamites of old, in the paradise of God, eating of the Tree of Life, in the midst of the garden of the mind. But this Tree of Life is here mentioned as having leaves as well as fruits: "And the leaves of the tree are for the healing of the nations." These leaves are the scientific truths which God is now giving us—those beautiful truths of analogy which open to us the Holy Word, and clearly show us the origin and nature of our evils, and how to put them away and be healed. There were no healing leaves mentioned upon the first Tree of Life, for there was then nobody sick. All had health and life; their minds were open to truths from the Lord by intuitive influx, and the fruit of the Tree was all that they needed.

We have now taken a summary view of the five distinct features of the church, or of the five peculiarly marked states of humanity, in the spiritual history of our race, as definitely recorded in the Word of Almighty God. Let us now glance, for a moment, at the remarkable order of the succession of these states of the church in the fall and rise of humanity.

In the first, the Adamic state of the church, before the fall, we have the innocent, artless, infantile character of the race. The people were simple, open, sincere, affectionate, and true. They knew and felt no wrong. The will and the understanding were united. The will principle, as in children, ruled. And the will being right, they felt right; and therefore they saw and acted right. Love or charity was the first and dominant element in this church; they did right because they *felt* it to be right.

But in the second state of the church, the Noatic, the will was depraved, and therefore its impulses were wrong. It could not go right without instruction from God. They had to have an ark or doctrines. The will and the understanding were separated. *Truth*, or faith, therefore, and not love, was the first and dominant element in this state of the church : they did right because they *saw* it to be right ; and their wills had to submit to the dictates of the Truth of their faith ; they had to enter the ark and obey the doctrines.

But in the third, or Jewish state of the church, the will was not only depraved, but the understanding was darkened, so that they could neither see nor feel right. Therefore, neither love nor truth, neither charity nor faith, was, with them, the first and dominant element, but works or use. They did right simply because they were commanded, and were afraid to do otherwise. Here we have a trine in the states of the church. In the first, charity ruled ; in the second, faith ruled, and in the third, works ruled. The Lord led the Adamic church by charity, the Noatic church by faith, and the Jewish church by works.

And when works proved inefficient, and man lost the love of obedience, the Lord assumed our nature and established a church wherein truth led to goodness. Faith was the first or leading element of the Christian church, with charity as its life. Thus the Lord elevated the church from the plane of works to that of faith or truth as its guarding principle, still retaining the works and charity. This put the Christian church on a level with the Noatic.

But the province of the New Jerusalem is to bring the church up to the plane of the Adamic, when love will be the predominant element, retaining faith and works.

Thus the steps up the mountain are the same as the

steps down :—the Adamic church, of charity ; the Noatic, of faith ; and the Jewish, of works : and then, commencing at the bottom, we have the Jewish church of works ; the Christian, of faith ; and the New Jerusalem, of charity. Thus we see that charity, faith, and works are the three great elements of the church, embracing the Love, Wisdom, and Power of God ; and that no church can exist without them.

When love or charity rules, the church is in the highest or celestial state ; when truth or faith rules, it is in the spiritual state ; and when use or works rules, it is in the natural state. But there can be no church without works. For works are the basis and continent of the other elements. If Love rules, man sees the truth and does his duties from love of goodness. If Faith rules, it works by love and purifies the heart, by the love of truth. If Works of righteousness, or the keeping of the commandments in the reverence and fear of God, rules, it has the letter of the Law, which brings to view the light of natural truth, and inspires a love of use.

Now, in the New Jerusalem state, the church is to possess all its elements in their true order. All that there ever has been of the true church on earth, will be therein embodied. For nothing of the church has ever been lost. The Adamic church still exists, in its purity, in the celestial heavens ; the Noatic, in the spiritual heavens ; and the Jewish, in the natural heavens. The real fact is, that the church of God has never fallen. It has been the people that have fallen away from the church ; goodness, truth, and use cannot fall. They are divine and eternal principles. Thus it is an appearance only, that the church becomes depraved and falls. For the depravity is not the church. When, therefore, we look at the church, in its divided elements, we can see that there has been only one church on the earth. This church has existed under various states and dispensations, developing, in man, its various qualities and uses. Only that which was good, true, and useful, in the people, has been the church. Their falses and evils have been something else.

The church commenced with the creation of man. And, by means of it, humanity has been developed, by Divine influence, from its infancy to its manhood. Thus, the Adamic state was the church in its infancy; the Noatic state, the church in its childhood; the Jewish state, the church in its youth; the Christian state, the church in its early manhood; and the New Jerusalem state, the church in its age and maturity. In this state the seals of the Holy Word are loosed, and the Book is opened to the minds of men, and their minds are opened to the Word; and men learn, from God, the laws of the spiritual world, and of their own souls. Herein all the prophecies of the Word are fulfilled, and the canons of Scripture point no further.

This is then the full and crowning state of the church. Herein humanity is to be restored to the primeval order of the race, with this difference: then it was as an innocent, inexperienced, confiding child, loving goodness supremely, knowing no sin, and seeing intuitively, by the Lord's Wisdom, in the clear light of analogy, the higher laws of creation and providence: but now, it is to be as an educated man, knowing good from evil, loving supremely the good, and despising the evil; and seeing rationally and scientifically, by the same Divine Wisdom, in the same light of analogy, the same higher laws of creation and providence; and then loving and walking in those laws.

And now we see that there will be no more fall of man. For men fell from the want of experience, and of a knowledge of evil. Now the appalling consequences of evil are before the eyes of all, and are bitterly experienced by every individual. And all its dreadful qualities are depicted in the Holy Word, in the most striking colors. And, knowing the consequences, the world of mankind, when restored to millennial order, will no more fall into sin. Glorious and happy day, when all shall know the Lord, from the least to the greatest, when every knee shall bow, and every tongue shall confess that Jesus Christ is Lord to the glory of God the Father.

CHAPTER XXI.

THE few ideas which we shall advance upon the subject which has agitated the Christian world more than all others, will be drawn from the truths and facts which God has given us all in common, both in His Word and in His works. From them, and the history and experience which men of observation have had, of human nature, we may learn much about heaven and hell. Indeed, men, in this world, see and know a great deal more about heaven and hell than they may suppose they do. Few pass through this life, without having much bitter experience in things pertaining to hell; or without seeing many things that may give them rational lessons of heaven.

But, in order properly to investigate the subject before us, we must have just views of the nature and character of the Divine Being, as expressed in Chapter II. We must see something of the heavenly quality and light of His mind; and we must make that truth the touchstone, by which to decide every doctrine of the Holy Word. For the Lord is the truth of the Word, and the light of its doctrines. We must see that God is love, goodness,

mercy, wisdom, truth, purity, virtue, and every possible excellence, in full infinitude ; and that His sphere is heaven :
that He is the very light, and life, and peace, and joy,
and happiness of heaven ; and that everything opposite in
character to His sphere and qualities, is hell. Now,
heaven, with men, is a state of happiness, peace, and joy,
resulting from the true love and possession of these divine
qualities. And hell is a state of misery and unhappiness,
springing from the perversion and want of these qualities,
and from the love and indulgence of their opposites, the
origin of which is expressed in Chapter III. Therefore,
with the history of human nature before us, and the light
of the Holy Word, we may learn a great deal about
heaven and hell. And the knowledge we thus gain may
be depended upon ; for it will be founded in facts, and
drawn from rational and scientific deductions. All investigations, philosophically made, in the light of divine
truth, lead the mind to rest its conclusions upon eternal
verities. There is nothing uncertain and wavering in
the divine mind ; and all principles, whether good or evil,
when rationally seen, in the light of the divine mind, are
seen as they are. We may therefore gain a much better
knowledge of what heaven and hell really are, in themselves, from a rational knowledge of the elements and influences which constitute them, than we could from a
personal observation of them without that knowledge ;
for, in the latter instance, we should see only the appearance of things, without a knowledge either of the things
themselves, or of the causes from which they presented
such an appearance.

Besides, appearances there as well as here must depend,
in a great measure, upon the spiritual states of the observers. Hell would therefore appear much less revolting

a'nd forbidding to some minds than to others; and heaven, much less inviting and pleasant. Man's true ground, therefore, for a knowledge of heaven and hell, whether he be a resident of this world or of the other, is a clear understanding of spiritual things, drawn from the Holy Word of the Most High God. He must understand the real qualities of good and evil minds, and the laws and impulses by which their movements are propelled or restrained. Without this knowledge of the principles and elements of human souls, and of their operations, we should understand as little of the real nature and meaning of the scenery of the spiritual world, were we disembodied and in it, as the ignorant Hindoo does of the motions of the heavenly bodies.

A knowledge of the Lord, therefore, and of His Holy Word, is essentially necessary to a proper understanding of heaven and hell, or of any scenery in the spiritual world. Because it is by the light of the Holy Word, in the understandings of men, that spiritual things are seen and understood; and furthermore, because the light of that Word is the only true light of the spiritual world, which presents things as they really are. The light of the spiritual world is truth. But that truth strikes the eye of each mind according to the quality and sphere of the understanding. To minds therefore who do not understand the true doctrines and light of the Holy Word, things in the spiritual world are not seen as they really are in themselves, but only as they *appear* to be, from the states of those who see them. No one, therefore, but a good person, who sees the light of the Holy Word, and who understands it and loves it, could give us any true account of the scenery and things in the spiritual world, or of heaven and hell, were he to come from thence, and openly converse with us ; because he would have no true knowledge himself of what he had seen.

Everything in the spiritual world appears according to the quality of the eye which sees, and the character of the light which reflects it. And the light of the spiritual world is of all shades from truth to falsity. The light of heaven is truth, and the light of hell is falsity. Are we asked how we know these things ? We answer, because the spiritual world is a world of mind ; the eyes which see in that world are the understandings of men ; and the proper light for the understanding is truth ; and understandings are of all characters and qualities—some seeing in false light and some in true. And though falsity is darkness to the true understanding, yet it is as light to the perverted mind. But lest this answer should not satisfy the inquirer, we say further, that this is the law of mental seeing, even of persons in this world. If we present the truth to a mind who views the subject in a false light and loves that false light, we cannot make him see the truth. It is as darkness to him. It requires much clear argument and practical illustration to convince a man, confirmed in error from false education and evil loves, that his views are false. Such a mind, with overwhelming testimony, even while in an inquiring state, could see the truth but dimly, at first, and could only gain a clear view by yielding to its teachings, in opposition to his evil loves, and pursuing a new course of life.

Thus our chief dependence for a knowledge of heaven and hell is the Word of God, and a rational view, by its light, of the character of our Heavenly Father and of human nature in its lights and shades. And from the truths and facts which we have before us, on this subject, we may rationally inquire into what must be the nature and character of heaven and hell in the next life.

The first questions that naturally arise, on the subject, are, where is the spiritual world? and, how does it differ from this? The spiritual world is a world of mind; and therefore wherever there is a human mind, there is the spiritual world, whether that mind be in a body of flesh or not. The spiritual world can be no more separated from the material world, than cause can be separated from effect. Nor could one world exist without the other any more than cause could exist without effect, or effect without a cause. Wherever there is matter there is life of some quality; and that life is spiritual substance, and is a part of the spiritual world. But spiritual substances, like material, are of infinite varieties and organizations. There are the spiritual brain, eye, ear, heart, lungs, hand, foot; each of a different quality and organization, and all filled with life from the Lord, which is a higher quality of substance still. And the spiritual world is not only the cause of the material, but it is ever with it, organizing and moulding all its forms.

In the phrase *spiritual world* are embraced all spiritual substances, of every quality, infinite and finite, good and true, evil and false. Everything good and true, in that world, constitutes heaven; and everything evil and false constitutes hell. Where, then, shall we look for the spiritual world? Shall we look into open space for it? What is there there? The largest telescopes show us nothing but material bodies. Where is heaven? On one of the stars? Some have located it in the realms of space, beyond the planetary systems, nobody knows where. And where is hell? Some have located it in the sun, some in the earth, and some in space unknown. But such speculations are all drawn from the wild imaginations of the natural mind, for the want of the spiritual light of the Word. For we need not go out of ourselves, and the community in which we live, to find the spiritual world, and heaven and hell. Our bodies are in the natural world, and our souls in the spiritual. But our external minds are so much in the love of the world, and are so natural, that our natural bodies serve as a screen to prevent our spiritual bodies and senses from being open to the world to which they belong.

While, therefore, we are in the natural body, and in the love of self and the world, it is much better that the spiritual world should be shut from our view. For, in such a state of mind, we should not understand it, if we saw it. It would appear to us according to our states of mind, and not as it is in itself. We should have false views of it, and should express those views to others, and thus evil, instead of good, would be the result of the intromission.

Now, heaven and hell are not places, but states of mind. "The kingdom of God cometh not with observation:" is not "Lo here! or, lo there! for, behold, the kingdom of God is within you." And the apostle James says, "The tongue is an unruly member, and it setteth on fire the course of nature, and it sets it on fire of hell." Thus the tongue, by slander, may make a natural man angry, and thus set him on fire of hell. So we are taught that hell, as well as heaven, is within the human heart, even while the man may be living in this world. Indeed, heaven is in the souls of all good persons, whether they live in this world or the other. And hell is in the souls of all bad ones. The fires of hell are anger, hatred, revenge and malice ; and they sometimes burn with great rage against their victims. Heaven also has its fires, but they are the glowing affections of love, friendship, mercy and kindness.

The society of those who have heaven within them, constitutes heaven as a community. And that society extends, in its relations, to the souls of the good, in both worlds. And so the community of hell extends to all, in both worlds, whose ruling love is the love of evil and self.

When, therefore, a person puts off the material body, he finds himself, at once, in the spiritual world, without going anywhere. He was there *before ;* but his body prevented his being sensible of it. And as the light of that world now strikes the eye of his understanding, he decides what his heart loves most, rejecting the things adhering to him which are not in accordance with his ruling love, and choosing the society most like his own heart, whether it be of heaven or of hell. This examination, through which he passes, by the light of truth, thus operating upon his own mind, is the judgment. As he puts off the natural body and comes into spiritual light, he sees the things of the spiritual world according to his state. And if his ruling love is the love of evil, he sees things not as they really are, but only as they appear to him to be. His state falsifies the light, and evil looks to him as good ; and he chooses to retain his evils, and to have the society of the bad. And the same man falsified the truth while he was in this world. The truth undertook to show him the evil of stealing, lying, adultery and covetousness ; but he did not see the evil, as it was. The results of these vices looked good to him, and he sought them. And putting off the body did not change the affections of the soul. His only sure way of salvation was to change his ruling love, while in this world by resisting temptations and living a godly life, till his soul loved good and loathed evil.

But when the person whose ruling love is the love of good puts off the material body, and the light of the spiritual world strikes the eye of his understanding, he sees it as truth, and it shows him the things of the spiritual world as they are; he sees his remaining evils as bad, and loathes and rejects them; and he goes with his like. And this he had been practising in this world; and his spiritual eye was prepared for the light.

The punishment which the wicked receive is none of God's inflicting. He could not put evil into the human heart; and evil in the heart is the hell, and the cause of all the suffering. It is a hell of man's own making and choosing. But we are still asked how we know that the spiritual world is here in our midst, while we live in this world? We answer, the Holy Word teaches it, our reason declares it, and all we know of spiritual things confirms it. What is God but a spirit? and where is He not? And yet, where He is, there must be the spiritual world. And what are angels but spirits? And yet they are declared to be with us. And where angels are, there must be the spiritual world. What makes the trees grow, the animals feel, and men think and love, but life from God? And what is life but spiritual substance? Then wherever life is, there is the spiritual world.

Is not heaven here, then? Are not God and our guardian angels in heaven? And yet they are with us. And is not hell here? Are not evil spirits with men? Do we not behold sad pictures of their evil operations, upon the hearts of men, all around us? and do we not feel their deceptive influence on our own hearts? And yet, evil spirits are all in hell. But are hell and heaven together then? No. For there is a "*great gulf*" between them. Not a gulf as to space, but as to quality. Similarity of views and feelings brings souls together; dissimilarity separates them. Those the most like God are, apparently, the nearest to Him : those the most unlike Him are the farthest from Him. And yet he is omnipresent. It is the quality of the heart that makes the distinction.

But how can men, in this world, have something of heaven and hell in the same mind, and have their angels and evil spirits around them, and still heaven and hell not be together? The spiritual world is entirely above the measurements and reckonings which we give to time and space. A person who is being regenerated has something of both heaven and hell in him. But there is a great gulf between them. The heaven is forming in the internal mind, and the angels are guarding it; while hell still adheres to the external mind, and the devils are tempting it. But there is a great gulf between these angels and devils, and between the internal mind and external mind. They are unlike, and in warfare, and the two minds can come together, only as the evils are removed.

Heaven and hell have each their various societies in the spiritual world; those coming together, in each kingdom, according to their states, desires, and habits. And they have their distinct governments. Heaven is governed by love, and hell by fear. We know this from the way human nature is governed in this world. The good here are governed by love—the love of the law, love of order, love of virtue, the love of the neighbor. But the bad are governed by fear—fear of the law, fear of punishment. We know it also from the teachings of the Holy Word; for it speaks of the kingdom of God and the king-

13

dom of Satan; of the kingdom of heaven and the kingdom of hell. And it assures us that God reigneth over all—the evil and the good: that is, He holds the hells in check by fear, and the heavens He leads by love.

The commandments of the Word are the laws for the government of heaven and of hell, in both this world and the other. No human beings could exist without some light from the Word, received either by tradition, or otherwise, giving them some ideas of right and wrong, in some degree of light; for the human understanding must have it, or man must cease to be. And were a tribe of our race to become so low, on earth, as to lose all truth, of every degree, they would become extinct. It is true that the men of evil hearts, both in this world and the other, pervert the truths of the Word, when applied to their own evils; but they see their use, as applied to the evils of others, for the preservation of order and safety. Therefore, the hells of either world are governed and made tolerable, by the divine laws of truth and duty; but with this difference,—the heart here is masked; and men sin under the hope of escaping the evil of punishment by deception. But there the mask is thrown off, and the guilt of the transgressor is seen at once; and the punishment is rigidly inflicted. This is a necessity; because, without it, existence itself, in the hells, would be intolerable.

Societies of free, rational beings, with nothing true and good but what is given them, must necessarily need a law, from their Creator, to govern their conduct. And for this good reason, laws have been given. And when those laws are broken, either in this world or the other, men, and not God, inflict the outward punishment; while there is still the unhappiness of the soul within, resulting from the wicked state of the heart. All this light may be seen from the teachings of the Holy Word, and a knowledge of human nature.

Now, suppose all the people of the earth to be, in one moment, disembodied. They find themselves right where they are, but in the spiritual world, with spiritual bodies: their dispositions unchanged; God the same kind Father, but no more seen by them, on their entrance there, than He is here. Now, what will they do? Their eyes are spiritual, and the light of that world—the divine truth—strikes their understandings forcibly. They can read each other's thoughts and feelings. They will soon know what hearts are congenial and what are not. And they will separate into societies according to their states; and establish laws and rules of conduct for the good of the community. And those laws, after a few experiments, will all be the laws of God: for they will find that they cannot safely live under any other. The good societies will want no other: and the bad, will find that they cannot endure life under any other. Thus, when evil persons come together, in the spiritual world, each in the love of self and the love of dominion, they do, as bad men of intelligence would do in this world, if obliged to live in a community by themselves. Put, for instance, 10,000 bad men and women, of nearly equal abilities, on a solitary island which readily produces enough for all their physical wants; and let them hold the island, in common, as their home, and which they cannot leave. Notwithstanding the blessings of their home, it will be all bedlam with them, at once, until they have established a government and rigidly enforced t'·· laws. Men of corrupt hearts, and wise only in serpei wisdom, where they have no chance to take undue advantage without suffering the consequence, will establish and maintain wholesome laws, from selfish policy's sake.

Such is the government of hell; for human nature is the same, under the same circumstances, whether it be in this world or the other. And though their hearts may burn with anger, jealousy and malice toward each other, yet they will soon be tired of indulging their revenge, by wicked acts, from the sufferings of the consequences; for all the penalties of transgression are there promptly inflicted; and spiritual bodies are very sensitive. But against men in the flesh, in leading them astray, by temptations and deceptions, they are united, and do not punish each other for these acts. It is only for evils done to one another, that they inflict punishment.

Such is the character of heaven and hell. Heaven, a community of good men, filled with good principles; and hell, a collection of bad men, filled with bad principles. God is equally good to all, giving to the heavens everything they enjoy; and mercifully withholding the hells, through the fear of the law, from falling into more direful sufferings and destructive torments; so that they are not in what they themselves call misery, if they obey the laws. Yet the states of their selfish and revengeful hearts, when compared with those filled with love, gentleness, mercy and peace, are as hell to heaven, as darkness to light, as misery to happiness. And the Lord is now clearly opening the way by which we may escape the miseries of the one, and enjoy the happiness of the other. "If ye would enter into life keep the commandments," and seek the love of God and the neighbor: for "God is love. And he that loveth is born of God, and knoweth God. He that loveth not, knoweth not God, for God is love."

CHAPTER XXII.

"Ye must be born again."—JOHN III, 7.

"YE must be born again." Thus saith the Lord to
man. But what does He mean? I hear it said, that He
means that we must be regenerated. Very true; but
what is that? It is to give ourselves up to God, by faith,
and thus be born of the Spirit. That is true; but what is
that? It is to be made His children, by conversion,
adoption and sanctification. All true: but what is that?
It is to believe in the Lord, repent of our sins and be for-
given. All these answers are true; but a dense mystery
still hangs over the subject, because they all fail to tell
what these very things are in themselves. They do not
give any distinct idea of what the new birth really is,
or regeneration, or conversion, or faith, or justification,
or pardon, or adoption, or sanctification, or repentance;
and therefore, though the answers are all true, as far as
they go, yet they are all incomplete, need explanation,
and therefore fail to give the light needed; and consequently, often, by a wrong view of terms, they involve
the subject in much darkness.

But through the spiritual light of the Word, the mystery that commonly beclouds all these terms disappears,

and a clear, harmonizing light beams through them all, blending its rays in perfect symmetry and beauty. For, in that light, they all exhibit a plain, practical process of purification and development, pointing out rationally the true way of life, and convincing us that we must walk in it, or never experience the new birth.

Now, the new birth is a subject which, at times, has greatly agitated the human family. If we cast our eyes back, but five years, at the history of New York, we find it agitated throughout its length and breadth, upon this vital subject. Persons of all ranks and conditions were assembling on week days, in crowds, at prayer meetings, with anxious hopes of being, thereby, born again. And thousands, per week, were reported in the common newspapers, to be converted to God, and born of the Spirit. But much mystery overshadowed the entire scene; and many of its supposed converts now look back with wonder and ask what it all meant. And the spiritual light of the Word only can answer them. The occasion needed light. It needed knowledge commensurate with its zeal. It is good for men to feel that they are sinners, and to believe that they must be born again, or be lost to heaven; and to pray that they may be regenerated. But, to really obtain the blessing, they must perceive something of what the things which they need are, in themselves; and also of the process they must pass through, in order to obtain them. It is not a work in the dark.

Now, the new birth is a matter of the highest possible moment to man. It is the great object of our existence. And it may well engage the attention of every human being when the great Jehovah says, "*Ye must be born again.*" For what God says to us is, above all price, valuable. But what does He mean by "ye," when He says, "Ye must be born again"? He means the mind. The text has no reference whatever to the body, in either birth. *Ye* means the spiritual part, not the tabernacle we live in.

The first birth of the mind is natural. It is the external mind that is then born. It is born into a knowledge of natural things; and it learns them from without. All its affections and thoughts are exercised in this natural world, and upon natural relations and things. It has no love for anything higher. The only avenues to knowledge, for this external mind, are the five senses. And it is through them, as a means, that the natural mind is born or formed. This birth of the mind is necessary, before we can have any higher knowledge. "First that which is natural, and afterward that which is spiritual." There must be a natural vessel, as a receptacle of the spirit—a natural basis for the spiritual to rest upon. No matter how virtuous and correct the first birth of the mind may be, a new birth is, nevertheless, necessary, because we are designed for a higher mode of life. We must have thoughts and feelings for things higher than natural, earthly things; and the mind must be born into them.

Had man never fallen, the new birth would have been still necessary. The Bible commences by giving an account of the new birth of man, before he had fallen. God had brought mankind into existence, and they had grown up to years of understanding, simple, good and happy, natural people; the external mind was born only into natural knowledge. The first chapter of Genesis is a history of man's new birth into spiritual things. But in our fallen state, the natural mind is selfish and depraved; which makes it necessary to be born again, in order to enjoy true happiness, even here.

The first birth of the mind is natural; being born into
a knowledge of natural things. The second birth is spiritual; being born into a knowledge of spiritual things—
things of the soul, of God, of truth, of goodness, of heaven,
of happiness; and, by this new birth, are engendered and
brought forth thoughts and affections for these higher
things. And when this new birth is well advanced, these
spiritual thoughts and affections for heavenly things will
have the ascendency over the natural mind; and will
completely modify, change, govern, and infill with heavenly love and truth, all the natural feelings and thoughts;
so that the whole mind will be new and heavenly.

But what is this new birth, in itself; and how is it
accomplished? Let us examine into it. There is a birth
of the material body. That is first born an infant's body;
afterward, a child's; next, a youth's; and finally, a man's.
During this process, there is *gradually* born into existence the external or natural mind. But here we are
asked, why we speak of birth as a gradual work? We
answer, because birth is a creation; and all creations are
gradual. Everything that is made is born into existence;
and gradually born. Is the mind of the man born when
the body of the infant is brought into being? What is
birth? We must understand terms, or we cannot profit
by study. Birth is the production of something. Now,
whether that something be one hour, or a hundred years
in being produced, it is, nevertheless, a birth. The arrow,
in Virgil, is called the son of the bow; this is because the
bow gives birth to it when it is shot. This is a very
quick birth. The tree gives birth to the apple; but it is
the whole season about it. Washington is called the
father of his country; which means that he gave birth to
our freedom from foreign oppression; but he was seven

years about it. A man at threescore and ten, gives birth to a diary of his life ; but he was seventy years in doing it. He dies at a hundred years of age and goes to heaven, and this mode of life has given birth to an angel ; but it was a whole century about it. The sun has been giving birth to light ever since it was placed in the heavens ; but that birth is not yet completed. The orator gives birth to his oration, the author to his book, and the artist to his picture. All birth is progressive. Every development of body or mind is birth.

A few months give birth to the body of an infant ; twenty years more, to the body of a man. But, to the birth of a human mind, there is no end. It is capable of eternal development. But, to have that development orderly, heavenly and happy, it must be born again. The first birth of the human mind, at this age of the world, is, in its tendencies, natural, selfish, licentious, deceitful and cruel. It is a birth into the love of self and the world. It needs no argument to prove this. Any person, with an eye half open to his own heart, and to the community around him, knows it. And he, to whom these bad adjectives do not apply, has tasted the sweets of the new birth.

We said that the first birth of the mind is natural, selfish, licentious, deceitful and cruel. These tendencies it inherits ; and if it be not born again, it will go on developing, and confirming itself in all these evils forever.

The second birth is spiritual, benevolent, chaste, truthful and kind. Both of these births are progressive. They commence from germs, and are regularly born. How little does the infant of a day old know ! And how long it takes to develop and give birth to the natural mind, in the strength and energy of its faculties.

Now, the natural mind, as we said above, is formed
13*

by means of things from without, through the use of the senses. There is no mind when the body of the infant comes into the world. There is only the germ of a mind. But the infant begins to hear, see, feel, smell and taste things from without. And through these operations, thoughts and feelings begin to be conceived and born into action. Thus the natural mind begins to be born forth into actual life. And every new thing that the mind learns, loves and acts upon, gives a further birth and development to that mind. But as this natural mind is born through the means of things from without, by the use and gratification of the senses, this birth must of course be sensual and selfish, because it comes through the means of what the senses love ; and also because it inherits morbid and depraved tendencies from parents. Therefore, the natural mind is born supremely into the love of self and the world. All its knowledge is of things of the world : and all its affections are for or against worldly things.

This is now the first birth of all minds into this world. Such minds, therefore, will certainly quarrel for supremacy, in power and property, because each loves himself above all others. A society of such minds, from their very nature, cannot make a heaven. They must necessarily make a hell. Therefore, the Lord mercifully says to us, " Ye must be born again."

Now the second birth is a birth from things within, or from the Lord ; and not through the senses from without, except by analogy or correspondence. It is an entirely new mind : a spiritual mind—a mind that looks upward to God, and not downward to nature. When it contemplates nature, it looks through it, up to nature's God. It is a mind that dwells upon goodness and truth, virtue, righteousness, and peace. This mind is formed within the natural mind; and is called, in Scripture, the internal or spiritual man; while the other mind is called, at the same time, the external or natural man.

Now, this spiritual mind is as gradually conceived and born as was the natural mind. First, the natural mind is progressively born and developed to years of understanding, with all its affections and proclivities natural and worldly. True, while it has been taught religious things, and how to distinguish between natural right and wrong, the Lord has prepared within it some good ground, as the basis of a higher life; but the natural mind neither knows nor cares much about these internal preparations for a spiritual mind and life, until its more matured, rational faculties become seriously exercised, by the light of divine truth. But when man, by that truth, becomes convinced that the natural, selfish, deceitful states of the mind of mankind are the real cause of all the crime, sin and suffering of our race, he becomes seriously alarmed at the sad picture. And as he yields up his mind, in humble and solicitous contemplation, he becomes rationally and feelingly certain that, without some change in the hearts and minds of men, there can never be any true peace or happiness for the race. With these stubborn facts before him, he falls into a state of serious trouble, sorrow and solicitude; and he prayerfully desires, from his inmost soul, something better and more hopeful, for mankind. And here, in this humble and penitent condition, he conceives a desire for goodness and truth of heart, in himself and all others; and he resolves, daily, to do all that the Lord commands, and to shun every vice as sin. And now as he follows out this resolution, in dependence upon the Lord, he begins to feel, in the con-science-ground of his soul, the warming influence of love for the truth.

Here is the conception and commencement of the spiritual mind. The truth has passed from the understanding into the good ground, which the Lord had prepared in the heart; and here, in the spiritual region of the mind, goodness and truth have met together; and, from their embrace, a new mind is beginning to be formed, of which the Lord is king. This new mind is spiritual, pure and heavenly. It is conceived of God, or of goodness and truth, and it is yet to be born of God.

But how is it to be born? This is the important point to be well understood. Here is the germ of the spiritual mind within the very centre of the natural mind. The natural mind, with all its selfishness and depravity, surrounds it. But how is the spiritual mind to be born? Or what is the spiritual birth which this man is yet to experience? At an outward glance, it is simply this: the spiritual mind has yet to be born out into the natural mind, and, through that, manifest itself to the world. It must so completely infill, or fill out, the whole natural mind, that the natural mind will feel, think and act, under the power and influence of the spiritual mind. And the whole natural mind has to be thus renovated, changed, and cleansed, as the spiritual mind is born into it. But this can take place, so that the spiritual mind can get this perfect possession and control of the natural mind, only as the natural mind sees, repents of, and gives up its selfishness and depravity. And this is a long and laborious work, every step of which will require, of the natural mind, faith in the Lord, resistance of temptation, and obedience to the commandments, through prayer for aid from Almighty God. This process is the washing of regeneration, or the cleansing from sin. And as the natural mind is cleansed, the spiritual is born within it. This is the Christian soldier's warfare against the kingdom of Satan. The commencement of this battle is the commencement of the new birth. This commencement is conversion. And just so far as the natural mind yields to the spiritual mind and gives up its selfishness, in obedience to God's commandments, so far there is a new birth. Now, just so far as there is a new birth, so far there is remission of sins or removal of evils. So that, at conversion, there is a new birth,. to a very small extent; and there is, also, remission of sins, or cleansing from evils, to the same extent.

But the natural mind will often get angry, and deceive, and commit other sins, after the new birth has commenced. And, so long as it does this, its sins are not all remitted or removed; nor is the person fully born again. For " he that is born of God," the apostle says, " doth not commit sin; for the seed abideth in him, and he cannot sin, because .he is born of God." The idea here is, that when a person is really born of God, when he has given up all his sins, and the love of them, and has come to the sabbath of rest, he has no desire to sin; because he gives himself constantly to God, in obedience.

The new birth, then, springs from the creation of the elements of a new mind; of new and heavenly materials, within the natural mind; and then, through the gradual cleansing of the natural mind from everything evil and false, the two minds become as one—one in will, one in thought, and one in action. When this work is all accomplished, and our sins, or evil and selfish inclinations, are all removed, and the two minds are in harmony, the new birth is so far advanced that we can enter the heavenly society. But this will, by no means, be the end of that spiritual birth. When the natural mind becomes cleansed from all its sins, so that it acts as one with the spiritual mind, and the man enters heaven, his spiritual birth—his new creation—has only become fairly commenced. It has now but reached the glorious period in its progress, when it can be clearly and rapidly developed into more full and perfect states forever.

Now do we clearly see the philosophy of this new birth, and the perfectly harmonious relation which this doctrine bears toward all the other doctrines of the Word, and their complete oneness of beauty and symmetry, of law and order? Do we see the exact coincidence between the spiritual conception and birth of the Lord up to his glorification, and those of man up to his regeneration; so far as the finite can coincide with the infinite? Do we see the perfect protection and action of the freedom of man, and the distinct preservation of his individual identity, throughout the whole process; so that when he comes into the regenerate state, he can freely and fully enjoy it, to his soul's delight? Do we behold the complete correspondence between the assumed, external mind of the Lord, in the flesh, to be glorified, and the depraved, external mind of the man to be regenerated? Do we perceive the beautiful similitude between the glorification of the one, and the regeneration of the other? How the two external minds were, alike, free in the work? and how they both yielded to the influence of the same Divine Spirit within, and were gradually cleansed, and brought into perfect unity and harmony with the internal, or higher elements of their being? Do we see, in both instances, the seed of the woman, or truth from goodness, bruising the serpent's head; and thus doing the great work which is to be carried on till the human race is restored to heavenly order? Do we thus see how the Lord is to go on conquering and to conquer, until every evil be subdued; and still, in all things, the perfect freedom of man be preserved? Do we see, philosophically, how the Lord gained this great power over the evils of that humanity, by first assuming our nature, and thus coming into contact with those evils, where He could meet them, and all the hosts of hell, on their own ground, and in their own kingdom; and there effectually conquer them, by reaching the rational faculty of man; and, by operating upon his judgment by the truth, incline him, in perfect freedom, to see his evils and to fight against them, in the power of the spirit of truth, in dependence upon the Lord? Do we here see the great work of the atonement, which the Lord commenced in Himself, reconciling the assumed nature to the divine; and then, continuing the work among men? "God in Christ reconciling the world unto Himself?"

Whose heart, that feels the truth of this picture, does not glow with love and gratitude to that merciful Father who thus saves the world in freedom by coming, like a wise schoolmaster, down into our midst; and here teaching us, practically, how to solve the problem of human nature—how to work out, understandingly, every apparently dark and intricate question of our spiritual being; always presenting, with the theory, under every rule of life, a bright example, accurately worked out by His own wisdom, in a nature like ours; and clearly laid down and recorded, in the great chart of divinity and humanity—the Holy Word of Jehovah?

Do we, in this clear system of harmonious divinity, perceive the fogs of mystery rising and passing away from every doctrine, and behold the pure light of the holy city —the Lamb of God—the spiritual truth—beaming, in blending beauty, through every part? Do we see, in it all, the heavenly embrace of science and religion, of nature and revelation, of charity and faith, of love and obedience? Then, indeed, do we behold, opening up to our souls, the true way of eternal life, in a manner so plain, and in a light so clear, that we cannot mistake it. And having this light, are we fully aware of the responsibility under which it lays us?

God, in these latter days, is truly beginning to make, more fully, His "ways known upon earth, His saving health among all nations." The two great antagonistic principles of humanity—good and evil, in their truth and falsity—are now standing forth, in a more conspicuous contrast than at any former age of the world's history. The reason of this is, because a more spiritual and interior light, from the Holy Word, is penetrating the mists of external appearances; and right and wrong are beginning to be more clearly seen, standing face to face, in decided opposition. And as this spiritual light brings out more and more clearly to view the diversified features and the distinct qualities of the human heart, in its various selfish and benevolent states; wars and contests, mental and physical, of every character, will rage hotter and hotter. For the purer the light, the stronger will error oppose it; the higher the good, the more violent the evil will be against it; for the greater the contrast, the more bitter the opposition; because the devil, or love of evil, is ever tenacious of his dominion, and never gives up till he knows he is vanquished.

But the prince of darkness must yield his sceptre to the King of kings and Lord of lords. His reign on earth is limited. His days of dominion are numbered : for the time is promised when there shall be one Lord, one faith, one baptism ; and when all shall know the Lord, from the least to the greatest.

But, to accomplish this, we must be born again. "That which is born of the flesh is flesh, and that which is born of the Spirit is spirit." "Except a man be born of water and of the Spirit, he cannot enter into the kingdom of God." To be born of water is the first birth. It is to have the natural mind born of, and developed by, natural truth, to which water corresponds. To be born of the Spirit is the second birth. It is to have the spiritual mind born of, and developed by, spiritual truth.

But since the natural mind has become depraved by the fall, it has falsified and adulterated its natural truths, so that, in the second birth, the natural truths have to be purified from the falses, and made clean vessels, for the reception of spiritual truths. The new birth, therefore, creates the internal mind and purifies the external; so that the two minds are in union ; the external, bearing God's image, and the internal, His likeness; and both possessing His spirit and life. To obtain this birth, is the first and highest object of our existence. The means are amply provided. But it can come only through the free and willing exercise of our own hearts and minds, in obedience to the divine laws. "If ye would enter into life, keep the commandments." "Not every one that saith unto Me, Lord, Lord, shall enter into the kingdom of heaven ; but he that doeth the will of My Father who is in heaven."

THE END.